T0304903

Opening the Gates of Hell

Also by Mark Hodkinson

No One Round Here Reads Tolstoy: Memoirs of a Working-Class Reader
The Longest Winter
The Last Mad Surge of Youth
The Overcoat Men
That Summer Feeling
Believe in the Sign

www.markhodkinson.com

Opening the Gates of Hell

The untold story of Herbert Kenny,
the man who discovered Belsen

Mark Hodkinson

First published in Great Britain in 2024 by Radar,
an imprint of Octopus Publishing Group Ltd
Carmelite House
50 Victoria Embankment
London EC4Y 0DZ
www.octopusbooks.co.uk

An Hachette UK Company
www.hachette.co.uk

ISBN (Hardback) 978-1-78840-484-6
ISBN (Trade Paperback) 978-1-78840-485-3

A CIP catalogue record for this book is available from the British Library.

Printed and bound in Great Britain.

1 3 5 7 9 10 8 6 4 2

This FSC® label means that materials used for the product have been responsibly sourced.

Disclaimer: Some of the dialogue in this book has been
imagined for the purpose of storytelling.

'I think what is British about me is my feelings and awareness of others and their situations. We don't interfere. If we are heartbroken, we don't scream in your face with tears . . . we go home and cry on our own.'

Michael Caine, actor

'Heroes are not giant statues framed against a red sky. They are people who say: this is my community, and it's my responsibility to make it better.'

Tom McCall, former governor of Oregon

'I hope people can realise how far mankind can sink if they are not careful. Why is there so much hatred? It's something that I just don't understand. We don't choose our life, but we can choose whether we hate others.'

Corporal Ian Forsyth, wireless operator with the 15th/19th
King's Royal Hussars, among those who followed
Herbert Kenny into Belsen. Died 2021, aged 97

'We are not responsible for the past, but we are responsible for what we choose to remember and what we choose to forget.'

Kim Ati Wagner, Professor of Global and Imperial History,
Queen Mary University of London

'A hero is an ordinary individual who finds the strength to persevere and endure in spite of overwhelming obstacles.'

Christopher Reeve, actor, famous for playing Superman.

Contents

CONTENTS

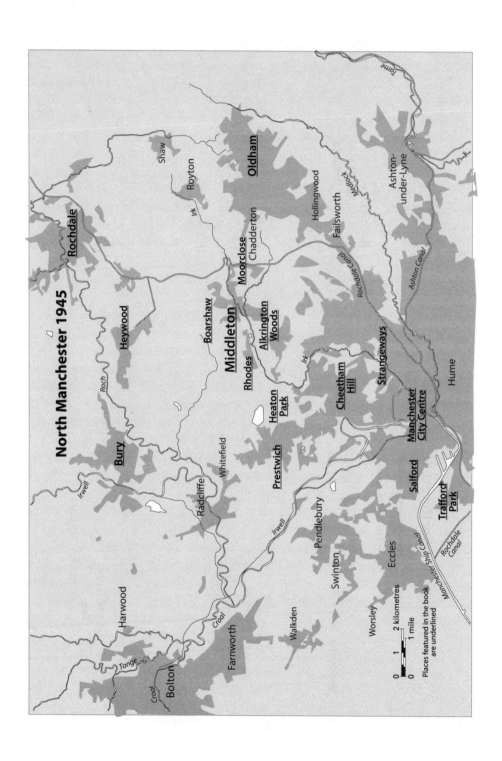

North Manchester 1945

Rochdale
Shaw
Royton
Oldham
Ashton-under-Lyne
Tame
Hollingwood
Failsworth
Medlock
Heywood
Boarshaw
Moorclose
Chadderton
Ashton Canal
Rochdale Canal
Middleton
Alkrington Woods
Ik
Rhodes
Strangeways
Cheetham Hill
Hume
Bury
Whitefield
Heaton Park
Prestwich
Manchester City Centre
Salford
Radcliffe
Irwell
Roch
Ik
Trafford Park
Harwood
Pendlebury
Eccles
Rochdale Canal
Tonge
Croal
Farnworth
Swinton
Worsley
Walkden
Bolton
Croal
Manchester Ship Canal

0   1   2 kilometres
0   1 mile

Places featured in the book
are underlined

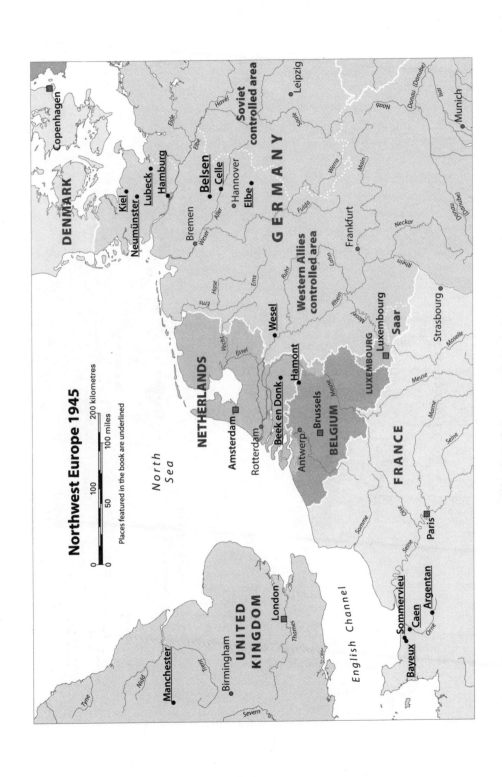

Northwest Europe 1945

0   50   100   200 kilometres
0   100 miles

Places featured in the book are underlined

North Sea

English Channel

UNITED KINGDOM
Manchester
Birmingham
London
Thames
Tyne
Nidd
Trent
Severn

DENMARK
Copenhagen
Kiel
Neumünster
Lübeck
Hamburg

NETHERLANDS
Amsterdam
Rotterdam
Beek en Donk
Hamont
Wesel
IJssel
Vecht
Ems

Bremen
Weser
Aller
Belsen
Celle
Hannover
Elbe
Elbe
Havel
Saale
Leipzig

GERMANY

Soviet controlled area
Western Allies controlled area

Werra
Fulda
Lahn
Main
Frankfurt
Neckar
Rhein
Ruhr
Hase

BELGIUM
Antwerp
Brussels
Meuse

LUXEMBOURG
Luxembourg
Mosel
Saar
Strasbourg
Moselle

FRANCE
Paris
Seine
Oise
Marne
Meuse
Somme
Seine

Bayeux
Sommervieu
Caen
Argentan
Orne

Munich
Isar
Donau (Danube)
Donau
Naab

Preface

———

The *Middleton, Moston and Blackley Guardian* in north Manchester reported back on a tiny patch of the world and the people within it. The office was a small, single-storey building on a side street in Middleton town centre. Rattling typewriters made the tables shake. Telephone directories and bound copies of the paper were piled high on the floor. A row of dented green metal filing cabinets ran along one wall containing press cuttings and photographs. Translucent panels were set into the roof, so we at least had an idea of the time of day. Most of the staff had a pen in one hand and a cigarette in the other, hence the windowless office (we never called it a 'newsroom') was constantly swathed in smoke.

I was lucky to have entered local journalism when it was still a relatively buoyant industry. The paper was thick each week with adverts from estate agents, car dealers, supermarkets and furniture shops. The editor used to say, 'They pay our wages, laddie' – a perfectly acceptable way of speaking to young people in the 1980s. A decade or so later these businesses would defect to the internet, where news was available instantly and without a charge. Before this coup de grâce, we had been well-staffed and even had an unofficial rest day every Thursday when the paper was 'put to bed' (that is, printed). While the editor was out overseeing this, we spent our time drinking tea and chatting. Or 'working up stories', as it was also known.

The only mandatory task on Thursdays was to ensure that material in 'the tray' was typed up ready for the next edition. 'The tray' – a wire basket atop a pile of copy paper – was a receptacle for dispatches handed in by readers. These were pieces of paper torn from notepads, sometimes infused with the smell of chip fat and featuring a replica of the Olympic Games symbol stamped in brown rings from the bottom of tea and coffee mugs. They were mostly readers' letters; notices of births, marriages and deaths; church meetings; amateur football match reports and bulletins from old folks' clubs, as they were then known: Hollin Golden Threads, Langley Autumn Club, etc. Over the course of the day, we each took turns at working through the contents of this tray. They had no real editorial worth but served a mutual obligation of a local newspaper. They also helped to sell copies.

One Thursday in May 1985, Tony, a senior reporter – middle-aged, unusually tall and with a perpetual cough – was reading *The Times*. He had spread it out across the desk, rising from his chair sporadically to flick ash from a ciggie (his term) into a dish positioned at the paper's edge. Tall Tony was always keen to snag us into discussions about national or international issues 'There's more to life than a councillor pointing at bloody potholes in the road,' he'd say. This particular day, *The Times* was running stories marking the 40th anniversary of the surrender of Nazi Germany to the Allies and the ending of World War Two. A G7 Economic Summit had been held in Bonn, West Germany, after which President Ronald Reagan and Chancellor Helmut Kohl had called at the site of the former Belsen concentration camp. A few weeks earlier, Chancellor Kohl had visited the site to mark the 40th year of its liberation, which predated the end of the war by three weeks. In a speech delivered at the time, he had accepted Germany's 'historical responsibility for the crimes of the Nazi tyranny', adding, 'This is reflected not least in never-ending shame. We shall not let anything to do with this be falsified or made light of.'

Unknown to Tony, or any of us reporters, details of a remarkable link to this global story lay a few yards from where we were sitting. A large manila envelope sat in the tray with 'Mr Kenny' written on the front in black marker pen. I opened it. A typed article of several pages' length was inside, held firm by a Bulldog clip. At the top, in the considered, florid longhand of what I presumed to be an older person, it read in capitals: 'THE ENTRY OF THE FIRST BRITISH SOLDIER INTO BELSEN'. The opening paragraph cited the speech made by Chancellor Kohl, quoting him verbatim: 'The first British soldier to enter the Belsen Concentration Camp will never forget what he saw and the feeling of horror he had and the horror of man's inhumanity to man.' I quickly realised that, although relayed in the third person, the article in the envelope was written by the very soldier to whom Kohl had referred. The piece continued: 'This British soldier was a corporal dispatch rider of the

35th Coy RASC [Royal Army Service Corps] attached to the spearhead advance of the Eighth Army. His name, Herbert Kenny.' Thereafter, in curt, workaday prose over 13 pages, Herbert recounted the journey to Belsen and his arrival at the site where he 'debarred the gate that closed the road to intruders and rode into the camp.' He wrote of the mass open graves and 'people walking around with a glazed look in their eyes, so terribly thin they looked like skeletons'.

I fixed the pages back under the clip and walked through to the area at the front of the building. Mavis was sitting at the front desk – 'reception' would be too grand a description. I asked who had left the envelope. She said it was 'an oldish fella, in his sixties' and that he'd 'scuttled off as quickly as he'd come in'. Herbert's phone number and address were written on the back of the envelope. I rang him and we arranged to meet the next day. Our phone conversation was matter-of-fact; I might have been arranging an interview with a Golden Wedding couple or a worker presented with a carriage clock after 30 years at the same factory.

Herbert lived alone in a neat council maisonette. The remembered detail of his experience at Belsen was acute; the story 'wrote itself'. I presumed it would be front-page news in the next edition. I was wrong. The editor liked to scheme the paper early to avoid what was viewed as unnecessary stress close to publication day; he was in his late fifties and could spy retirement. Accordingly, the prominence and positioning of stories bore scant correlation to their newsworthiness. My piece ran with the headline, 'The Man Who Found Belsen' with the subheading: 'Horror That Still

Lingers After 40 Years'. The article was 'buried' within the paper; it was a page-lead but placed close to the middle, serving as an unexpected and jarring prelude to the classified section comprising smudgy black and white photographs of houses, cars, caravans, newly-weds and missing dogs.

Back then, national newspapers and agencies combed local papers for stories to lift; the sugared term for this practice was 'cross-fertilisation'. The muted placement of Herbert's story may have served as camouflage, or the subject matter might have been viewed as distressing. Whatever the reason, my report was not picked up by other media outlets. The story has tapped me on the shoulder ever since. Across several house moves, I lost the cutting of the article, so it has felt as gauzy as a fading dream. Did it happen? Did I really spend an hour or two with the man who found Belsen? I was compelled to check. The office of the *Middleton Guardian* has long closed, the building now occupied by an estate agency. When I asked a journalist pal about those previously treasured bound copies of the paper, I was told they had been 'chucked in a skip, probably'. And the photographs and cuttings that formed a faithful chronicle of the town and its people? 'I think they've gone as well.'

Eventually I found the relevant issue in the British Library, the pages dust-dry and turned from white to ochre. Herbert was pictured on page 13 of the edition of Friday, 10 May 1985, smart and proud in his army uniform, coat collar turned up. I smiled as I recalled him pulling the photograph from a drawer, joking that he was a 'quite a handsome chap back then'. After the library visit, I did an internet search to see if, between then and now, he had been acknowledged for the key part he played in the relief of Belsen. The most definitive website, The Liberators of Belsen, had a roll call of those involved. High-ranking army officers, chaplains, medics, journalists and photographers were mentioned as being among the first into the camp, followed by a lengthy list of the others. In total, 1,241 soldiers and ancillary staff were named. Herbert Kenny was not among them.

Until 1985 Herbert had remained silent about his experience at Belsen. The 40th anniversary of VE Day had clearly acted as a jemmy on the slab stone of memory, and he was finally ready to set free those seared images of death, cruelty and suffering. Neither his family, the army or the medical profession had any awareness of his post-war, post-Belsen mental torment. There had been no succour, no counselling, no regimental reunions. The 'cures' he sought had been of his own devising – long walks, hard graft, regular exercise, even moving to another country. He had kept his secret of self for 40 years. He had been alone, always.

Herbert's formal education had been meagre, the same as most from poor backgrounds in the 1920s, when class sizes were large and teaching was done by rote ('chalk and talk'), limited primarily to The Three Rs of reading, writing and arithmetic. Despite this, he was a seeker of knowledge and had trusted that the process of setting down a memoir – he later expanded the initial piece with pages of handwritten notes – would act as time had done: moving him further away from those repugnant memories. After finishing the original article, I imagine him dithering, pacing his flat, putting the kettle on, staring from the window: what should

I do with it now? The *Middleton Guardian* was the nearest and most obvious outlet.

The material within that manila envelope had not been a 'pitch' designed to self-aggrandise or attract the media; Herbert knew nothing of that world. He had bashed it out, a man in the later years of life (he was 72 in 1985) jabbing an 'I was here' flag into the ground and recognising the singularity of his life experience. The Holocaust, at the time, appeared to be fading to black and had become, outside of academia, socially and culturally verboten, cauterised from collective memory as if people, by engaging with it, were afraid of becoming mired in the horridness, or somehow complicit. Later, films such as *Schindler's List* (1993) and *Life is Beautiful* (1997) would bring it back before the public, succeeded by a glut of books, documentaries and dramas. These had the effect of reducing the sense of proscription and morbidity, the impact on the individual seemingly diminished by belonging to a community of viewers, listeners and readers. Herbert could not have anticipated this, and must have felt a strong obligation to share his warning from history.

I have written thousands of stories in the course of my career, in newspapers and books. This one has stuck fast. I am its custodian. When we met on that overcast day in May 1985, it was as if I had made a pact: I would finish the job he had started when making those notes. I am from the same stock as Herbert Kenny – working-class, from north Manchester, of Irish origin on my mother's side. I know these people well. They are streetwise and have learned 'this, that and the other' in pubs and working men's clubs, on building sites, factory floors and lorry depots. Typically, they have each been conditioned – by family, workmates, teachers, friends – to accede or conceal their feelings, talent, ambition and, even, their life stories. Otherwise, they know what's coming: who do you think *you* are? Herbert was familiar with this diktat and very much the same as everyone else – an Ordinary Joe, a John Smith, a Tommy, a member of the hoi polloi that formed the substantial majority of the British Army, any of whom might have found themselves at the gates of Belsen on that day. Herbert, in revealing his story, had to renounce this ingrained reticence, diffidence and modesty: it did not come easy. He died in May 2001, aged 88. But who was he? How did he arrive at Belsen? What did he see and how did he feel? How did he cope afterwards, this ordinary man placed in an extraordinary, life-changing situation? How many other Herbert Kennys walk among us?

Until I contacted them, the Kenny family had not contemplated the notion of 'legacy', either for themselves or Herbert. His papers – that original article and the notes – appeared to have been passed among them indiscriminately; I suspected they had hardly been read. Those who agreed to be interviewed were unfamiliar with the process and spoke prosaically: he was a 'nice man', he 'didn't give much away'. Did they ask him about the war, about Belsen? 'Not really'. Their sort (regular, decent, down to earth) doesn't reflect or acclaim, they get on with it; the footprint of their lives is quickly washed away. Still, I expected them to assist in this commemoration of Herbert: why not? A handful were enthusiastic; others were unresponsive or guarded. I found myself reiterating the importance of Herbert's role in this major piece of world history, the necessity that he become known and be remembered.

His surviving daughters, June and Freda, both in their mid-eighties (two others, Edith and Linda, have died), declined to be interviewed or meet me, despite many requests. On an assignment of this scale, it was vital, naturally, that I sought clarification of their standpoint. I pondered whether they no longer wished to be associated with the Holocaust, that it had smeared their lives enough – Herbert made subsequent visits to the *Middleton Guardian* after I had left the paper, and the story was revisited on prominent VE Day anniversaries. Another more serious concern was whether they knew or suspected Herbert's story might be untrue or that he had exaggerated the role he had played. He might have been in the vicinity of the camp, for example, but not the first to enter. A family member acting as an interlocutor confirmed that the information I had was understood to be accurate; I received no word back on the sensitivity or otherwise of the Holocaust as a subject matter.

Eventually, I learned of a possible explanation, which I reveal later within these pages. I doubt most will consider it compelling enough for non-cooperation, but within families and friendship circles we each have our own sensibilities and sensitivities. While June posts frequently and warmly on social media about her father, she would clearly rather not play any part in my wider framing of his story, though she sent me a gracious letter where she answered a few of my questions – Freda did the same via her daughter, Chris. The rebuff from the sisters was unexpected, but I have to respect their feelings. Herbert was, to them, first and foremost, a father, and it is their choice how they wish to curate his memory. Thankfully, others provided invaluable artefacts, photographs and information, agreeing to lengthy interviews. On my part, after meeting Herbert and in view of his regular pursuit of publicity for his story, I feel he would have approved.

The sentence was characteristically phlegmatic: 'I debarred the gate that closed the road to intruders and rode into the camp, the first British soldier to do so.' Herbert's wartime memories are written in the type of notebook that is often left around the house to scribble down shopping lists or reminders of upcoming birthdays. The Big Value Jotter has a scarlet front cover and the familiar 'S' of the Silvine branding. A Spar price sticker is still on the back: 19p. Since he wrote the notes, this period of history – World War Two, the Holocaust – has been atomised and scrutinised. Whole libraries are given over to its study. A focus of such intensity has sought absolutes from tumult: who did what and when and why? Consequently, descendants of soldiers, along with historians and authors, have made various claims as to the identity of the first Allied soldier to enter Belsen, none of them categorically verifiable.

The liberation occurred when swathes of northern mainland Europe were in pandemonium. The Allies were advancing on a multitude of fronts and the Wehrmacht (the regular German army) was in retreat, with clusters of soldiers in mutiny. According to one historian, Lower Saxony, where Belsen was based, had become 'akin to the Wild West'. The few Allied officers forewarned of

Belsen's existence at short notice had expected to find a conventional prisoner-of-war camp on a scale considerably smaller than the one they encountered. In the circumstances – and also accounting for the soldiers' state of disorientation on making such an abhorrent discovery – no one had the time or inclination to record the roles undertaken by specific personnel, much less pose for photographs.

When I interviewed Herbert I had been a reporter for four years and had covered a wealth of stories. The paper's circulation area bordered Manchester city centre and included several 'newsy' districts. I had sat in on court cases and inquests. I had visited crime and accident scenes. I had written features on felons, magicians, boxers, naturists, traffic wardens, octogenarian swimmers, actors, musicians and drug addicts: all manner of life. I had learned to discern. I could quickly evaluate the strength or otherwise of stories. I could read people, spot their agenda. I had been trained to probe them – gently, politely, firmly – for information. In short, irrespective of my relative youth, I judged myself to be what older reporters called 'hard-nosed'.

In spite of the public perception, very few people lie to journalists, especially those working for local newspapers. Even so, on a story of such substance, as I sat with Herbert I did a mental check of obvious signs of duplicity. His speech pattern and tone of voice were consistent. He kept eye contact but not excessively so. He didn't fidget. He didn't bring his hands to his mouth. The detail was sharp, the memories sure. I left without a trace of suspicion that he might have fabricated the story. I recall distinctly – because I pressed him – that he didn't say he was *among* the first soldiers or *one* of the first to enter Belsen. He said he *was* the first. On taking possession of his notes, I checked for inaccuracies and discrepancies. The dates and the places tallied; this would have been extremely difficult to falsify in a pre-internet age. I consulted army records of 35 Coy RASC and they affirmed the locations of Herbert's unit, including that it had been at Belsen in mid-April 1945.

Herbert's notes are included here almost verbatim, with a little tidying up or excising to avoid repetition. They are interspersed among the pages and, where helpful, I have provided an explanation or broader context. I have mirrored Herbert's use of the word 'Belsen' to denote the camp. Over recent years it has been referred to increasingly as Bergen-Belsen to differentiate it from both the city in Norway (Bergen) and the town close to where the camp was based (Belsen); it feels an unnecessary convolution. The notes reveal the man. Until his arrival at the camp, they are candid and earnest and restrained, but the sentences shudder as he attempts to relate the abomination before him; most words fail, of course, in such a crucible of extremity. He reacts as most of us would in that same situation. He is bewildered, his innate decency and fairmindedness affronted and exhausted; he rages. At such times it is striking that he writes in the third person, as if putting a barrier between himself and all he sees, hears and smells.

I have incorporated a few anecdotes drawn from dimly remembered vignettes passed on by Herbert to either myself when we met, or others: we chatted for a good while after the end of the formal interview. Down the years, he did sometimes speak of the war, if not Belsen itself. I have occasionally used poetic licence to better walk in his shoes, to imagine how he might have felt or what was said at a given time, or better describe a scene or situation. Where there felt to be omissions or vagueness in Herbert's recollections, I have formed a composite, drawing on episodes or insights of family, friends, workmates or, in the case of his army life, soldiers who underwent similar experiences; nothing of import has been concocted.

I am now, obviously, much older than when I sat down with Herbert at a table in his maisonette, and of an age where I am better able to tell such an important story. In truth, it has been a challenge to render a man as anonymous as Herbert Kenny, where source material has been limited. As someone new to this field of history I was impressed by the level of expertise and forensic nature of much of the existing general research. I have tried to match this assiduity but without ever losing sight of Herbert, this Everyman who could easily have been a member of our own family, one of us. The task has been overwhelming at times. I have figuratively visited Belsen most days for almost a whole year. This is naught to that endured by Herbert, his fellow liberators and, most pointedly, those poor souls interned in the camp. In the end, through the thicket of time, I believe I have found Herbert: he passes through these pages.

By virtue of being born in 1912, Herbert's life was heavily bruised by two world wars. His father died in the first, when Herbert was six years old, and in the second he endured the hostilities of combat compounded by the psychological impact of Belsen. Phrases such as 'Lest we forget' and indexes of the dead on war memorials have become the wallpaper of our lives. The youngest soldiers to enter Belsen were 21, or thereabouts. If still alive, they will now be approaching their 100th birthdays. In a few years they will all have died. We may pay heed when we see poppies affixed to lapels in November close to Remembrance Sunday, but otherwise we *do* forget; we're too busy living. Those of us born after 1945 have had great fortune. Our corner of the world has remained in relative peace. We have not been persecuted for our race or religion. Bombs have not fallen from the sky. None of us has been forced to join the Armed Forces. Herbert and his kind didn't proselytise or seek gratitude. 'Lest we forget' is an entreaty for us not to make the same mistakes again. The freedom for which they fought came without caveats and included the freedom to forget, to move on. Christina Rossetti expressed this gift in her poem, 'Song':

> When I am dead, my dearest,
> Sing no sad songs for me;
> Plant thou no roses at my head,
> Nor shady cypress tree:
> Be the green grass above me
> With showers and dewdrops wet:
> And if thou wilt, remember,
> And if thou wilt, forget.

I have carried this story for many years, as Herbert did. I have written it because I owe it to him and others, the unknown and unsung, who, across many areas of life, have been burdened indiscriminately by great adversity and grief. They do really walk among us. And they inspire us with their grace, humility and strength. While this is a tale of systematic malevolence, it is also about the resilience of the human spirit and a celebration of hope: there is more good than bad in the world, however it may sometimes seem.

Mark Hodkinson

Chapter One

An Arndale Centre with a few houses around it

———

Place names in Britain are often remarkably specific. Of them all, Middleton (literally: middle town) is among the most utilitarian, which is probably why there are almost 50 instances, some as a single word, others with a suffix, such as Middleton Baggot (Shropshire), Middleton St George (Durham) and Middleton on the Wolds (North Yorkshire). The Middleton in south-east Lancashire – though some prefer to log its location as Greater Manchester – is roughly equidistant to Manchester, Oldham, Prestwich, Heywood and Rochdale, and is by far the largest Middleton, with 47,000 inhabitants.

This Middleton lies in a flat valley of the River Irk. The fast-flowing river and its tributaries became a source of power in the Industrial Revolution for cotton mills that bunched throughout the town, brick monoliths looming tall and wide above streets of terraced houses built for the workers. By 1900, across its nine square miles, Middleton had 22 cotton mills with more than 500,000 spindles twisting fibres around the clock, with staff on

12-hour shifts. They were infernal places. They were cramped. The thud-thudding machines were noisy. The air was clogged with cotton dust that coated lungs, often leading to a condition called byssinosis, also known as brown lung disease. A sweltering temperature of up to 30°C had to be maintained to save thread from breaking. Workers were fined for misdemeanours such as staring out of a window. Accidents were prevalent, occurring mainly in the last few hours of a shift when operatives were exhausted; it was not uncommon to lose fingers and limbs or suffer gruesome deaths trapped in machinery.

Life expectancy in Middleton during the Industrial Revolution was only 21 years; it was 38 in the more rural Westmorland. By the age of 13, in growth terms, boys from Middleton were a full year behind the national average. The textile-printing industry also thrived, the Irk providing energy to drive machinery. As the cloth passed through various stages, the abundance of water was used in dying and tanning. For almost 200 years the town was busy and grimy, smoke belching from chimneys, streams bubbling black with toxins, the houses small and overcrowded. Middleton had been shaped and sullied by industrialisation but, in most directions, open rolling hills were visible, promising a pleasant wander and respite from the toil. This adjacent splendour was thought to have inspired the description of Middleton as having 'a clean face and a dirty neck'.

The British cotton industry peaked in 1912, the year Herbert Kenny was born, but then began an inexorable decline. The outbreak of World War One meant cotton could no longer be exported and many countries set up their own factories. The huge market of India, which accounted for 60 per cent of Britain's exported cotton, was lost when Mahatma Gandhi called for a boycott of British goods in 1929 as part of the campaign to free India from colonial rule. Between the wars, the industry shed 345,000 workers and 800 mills closed. By 1958, for the first time, Britain imported more cotton goods than it exported. Lower overheads in other countries – paltry wages and squalid conditions reminiscent of those during the Industrial Revolution – meant Britain could not compete. By the early 1970s, mills were closing in Lancashire at a rate of one per week. Round-the-clock working became a four-day week, to three, two, one, gone.

The vacated mills were used as warehouses for carpets and wallpaper, curtains and bedding, while engineering firms moved into others to assemble machines for export to countries carrying out textile manufacture; the irony was not lost on the staff. Many mills were given over to the 'rag trade' where machinists, overlockers, cutters and pressers were set to work making items for brands such as C&A, Littlewoods and Marks & Spencer. The tobacco company, Gallaher, moved into Rex Mill in Middleton Junction – mills usually had short names to fit snugly on their chimneys. The workplace was known locally as 'Senior Service', named after one of Gallaher's main brands of untipped cigarettes. Sarson's Vinegar ('purity – strength – flavour') took over a former Co-op mill in Mills Hill Road to brew and bottle vinegar on site. Three other long-established companies in the town were Robert McBride Ltd, a supplier of cleaning products; the Bernstein Group, a kitchen manufacturing firm; and CPA (Calico Printing Association), where Herbert and other members of his family would work at various times.

Throughout the 1970s and '80s Middleton fell into a torpor with high unemployment and related social problems of increased crime, alcoholism and drug use. Conditions in mills had been poor but they formed communities of all ages with a high percentage of women; about two-thirds of all millworkers were female. Most had their own social clubs and sports teams but these disbanded when the mills closed. Government support was minimal compared to sums tendered to areas where other industries had closed down, particularly coal and steel. The media barely acknowledged the plight of textile workers, nor the towns where they lived. Instead, state-of-the-nation television documentaries and newspaper features were billed with poignant pithead imagery or switched-off, shelled-out blast furnaces. By the end of 1982, the year of the Falklands War, the unemployment rate in Middleton exceeded 17 per cent, higher than at any time since the 1930s.

Afterwards, the jobs available were mainly as casual workers at trading estates and retail parks, often sited where mills had once stood, though several would remain empty for years (and still do), boarded up and claimed by nature, the walls dabbed by sprigs of bellflower and arching stalks of buddleia. The deprivation and level of hardship was confirmed in press releases sent to the *Middleton Guardian* by various agencies. 'High Death Rate Shock' was one of my first front-page leads, in April 1983. The article was based on a report by the local health authority revealing that the area had 'one of the highest annual death rates in the whole of the industrialised world'. The risk of death for those under the age of 65 was 50 per cent above the national average; instances of lung cancer were almost twice as high. The causes were itemised: substandard housing, poor diet, pollution, unemployment and stress. Elsewhere in Manchester there were dashes of progressive living – refurbished buildings, a more youthful population, delicatessens, wine bars, antique emporiums, book shops and so on, but these were absent to the north of the city. Students arriving in Manchester didn't stray to Collyhurst, Moston, Blackley or Middleton. Moreover, even after three years of study in the city, most had not heard of these districts, let alone visited them.

Middleton had a few pockets of affluence with large, splendid homes on streets with suitably countrified names – Meadow Road, Woodlands Way, Parkside – but, as in much of north Manchester, it comprised mostly rundown neighbourhoods. As journalists covering this patch, we were routinely sent to conduct interviews at homes that the editor warned might be 'a bit scruffy'. We'd be greeted by barking dogs and led to a living room with a threadbare carpet, wallpaper hanging from the wall, knocked-over beer cans on a coffee table and, occasionally, down among the debris, a baby crawling towards an always-on television.

On my first week at the paper I was sent to Middleton Police Station and introduced to the officer who 'looked after the press'; they didn't have a designated press officer at the time. He smoked and was oblivious to the ash falling to the floor as he scoured the incidents log. 'Are you new?' he asked, without looking up. 'Yes, I started this week.' He smirked. 'Do you know about round here?' Before I could answer, he said: 'There's more crooks per square mile than anywhere else in England.' He then cough-laughed and it sounded similar to pins shaken in a bottle. On subsequent visits, he issued more of these homilies, usually prefaced with a rhetorical question. 'Why don't they admit it? Most coloureds have got a chip on their shoulder.' Another time, he set upon a discourse about a new sartorial trend he had noted: people wearing sportswear as casual clothing. 'All these fucking weasels are going out on the rob dressed like Daley Thompson,' he said.

Middleton had several council estates of varying sizes. Langley, the largest, was an 'overspill estate' set above the town on an expansive strip of land. Built in the early 1950s, it almost doubled Middleton's population, with 17,000 people living in 4,800 dwellings. The estate housed Mancunians who had either been bombed out during the war or whose homes had been demolished under slum clearance policies. Although Middleton was only six miles from the centre of Manchester, it had its own identity and infrastructure, which meant the union with incomers was uneasy.

Langleys were frequent visitors to the office. Most weeks we were summoned to the front desk for a 'Langley damp story' – usually a young, agitated mum blurting out details, breaking off to soothe a runny-nosed toddler in a push trolley. We'd send a photographer to her house in Ambleside Close or similar; streets were named after towns and villages in the Lake District. In the next edition, the mum would be pictured, pointing to a rash of mould above a cot: 'Damp Fears of Langley Mum'. The other staples were typical of most estates: occasional murders, fights, robberies, car crashes, acts of vandalism, and, in between, acts of generosity and kindness. Charity raffles and concerts were commonplace, held at one of the estate's many pubs and clubs – the Moonraker, the Mallard, Woodside Working Men's Club, Langley Labour Club among them. 'They're not a bad lot up there,' Chris, the paper's sports editor, would say. 'They'll knock out your teeth and nick your supper outside the Langley Friery [chip shop] but, the day after, they'll have a whip-round to buy you a pair of dentures!'

An old lady called in once to complain that the grass verges hadn't been cut *on* Langley (they always said 'on', rather than 'in') and could we write a story about it. Now, this minute. She was wearing National Health glasses with a lens covered by a plaster. 'I'm a Catholic, I vote Labour, I shop at the Co-op and I support Manchester United . . .' she said, establishing her credentials as quickly as possible. She couldn't hang about, she said, because she was on her way to the *hospikul* where she was hoping to get a *bokkul* of medicine for the gyp she was having with her belly. Her profile matched that of many people in Middleton, with the additional aspect of a large number being of Irish heritage, especially in Langley. Before she left to see the doc*toh* – this was how they spoke in north Manches*toh* – there was one final gust: 'Let's have it right, Sunny Jim,' she said. 'They can't cut the grass on Langley but they can spend a fortune on Rochdale. I've heard you can eat your dinner off the street in Rochdale, it's that clean.' This was to become a regular theme.

★

My career in journalism had begun 15 miles from Middleton, at the *Rossendale Free Press*, set among pie-and-peas Lancashire, with its rows of terraced houses stacked from sooted stone, a shoe factory on every street corner. After three months, I was offered a similar position as a trainee reporter at the *Middleton Guardian*, another title in the same newspaper group, but closer to my home in Rochdale. The editor at the *Free Press* wanted me to stay put. 'What's wrong with this place?' he asked with a broad sweep of his arm, indicating a Tuesday-afternoon-in-February Rawtenstall, as viewed from the windows of our first-floor office. It was raining. Two pigeons were peck-fighting over a pie crust on the opposite roof. The slates were grey; the sky was grey. He tried another line of persuasion. 'Middleton! It's just an Arndale Centre with a few houses around it.'

Indeed, for many years this was how Middleton was perceived; its shopping centre was a nose too big for a face, a candle too tall for a cake. As a young child I remember travelling there with my mum to sort out the rental of a new television set. The journey on the number 17 bus took us past the familiar – redbrick houses, privet fence front gardens, libraries, pubs, parks, shops, schools, and then we arrived at the flat and wide and dreary bus station at Middleton, with the Arndale Centre next to it, huge and unsightly. The colours were the first signifier of its otherness: shades of fawn running to cream and dull orange. The outer wall was covered in sections of tiles (cream, again) but otherwise it appeared to be wholly concrete and plastic.

How had it got there? From where had it landed? We told the story regularly in the paper. Back in the mid-1960s, land in the centre of Middleton had been made available at a knockdown price. Sam Chippindale, who traded as an estate agent above a butcher's shop in Otley, had teamed up with Arnold Hagenbach, a baker of Swiss ancestry with more than 40 outlets in Wakefield and Leeds, fêted for oven-warm bread and York ham. The pair made a portmanteau of their names (ARNold and ChippinDALE, aka the Arndale Property Trust) and embarked upon the 'Arndalisation' of Britain's town and city centres, predominantly in poorer areas of the north. Town planners and councillors embraced what was evangelised as modern and enlightened, and consented to these slabs of futurism being visited upon their patch. Shoppers could keep dry and warm, bathed in shiny bright light, imagining themselves to be in a *mall* – anything of American origin dazzled with social cachet. Councils eagerly dug up 200-year-old paving and cobble stones, CPO'ed (compulsory purchase order) dilapidated houses and shops, and levelled anything else in the way. They had been forewarned, though. 'There are people today amassing stupendous fortunes by systematically destroying our historic centres,' wrote James Lees-Milne, the architectural writer, in 1964.

And so it was built. Middleton's very own Arndale Centre, one of 23, was opened in March 1972 by Her Royal Highness, the Duchess of Kent. She dutifully cut the ribbon and most of Middleton turned out to see old retail favourites in a new setting: John Menzies, Freeman Hardy Willis, Woolworths, Boots, the Hen House (chickens on spits), Jon Migael (clothes on racks), Tench Sports, Central Records and Rumbelows – from where, a few years later, we would order our television. Thenceforth, the town became synonymous with its Arndale, considered, along with a sister development in Manchester costing £100 million, to be an emblem of an architectural style known as brutalism. Interestingly, Mr Hagenbach preferred rustic environs for his own delectation. He bought the 26-acre Burgh Island off the coast of Devon for the equivalent, in today's terms, of £2.5 million, with its art deco villa, ancient trees and fields undulating to the sea. The fresh air, over-warm bread and York ham worked a treat; he was 100 years old when he died in 2005.

I've returned to Middleton. The precinct has been rebranded 'Middleton Shopping Centre' and smartened up; it's still known locally as 'the Arndale'. In 2010 another major redevelopment saw the baths and civic hall flattened to make way for an enormous Tesco Extra with a proportionate car park, which means a visit to Middleton town centre feels similar to a walk around an airport drop-off zone but without the promise of a holiday on the other side of the huge, glass-fronted buildings. If he were describing and disparaging it today, the editor of the *Free Press* would have to modify his rendering of Middleton to, 'an Arndale Centre and a Tesco with a few houses around it'. I was last here 40 years ago when I was at the *Middleton Guardian*. Back then, if a story warranted it, the editor would make a note in the office diary: 'follow up' – the words ringed in felt-tip red. All these years on, I'm back here again, following up the story of Herbert Kenny, 'The Man Who Found Belsen'.

Herbert has been dead for almost 25 years but I'm trying to

imagine him flitting through these streets. Most of the time we get on with it: the errand, the plan, the day, the years. We barely notice the periphery. When we're out, we see other people but seldom think about them or, if we do, make quick assumptions. So, how was it for Herbert, returning to the everyday and the banal, week after week, month after month? As he browsed the shops here in Middleton, called at the greengrocer's, nodded to acquaintances, was the grief with him always as if painted black on his skin, or did it fluctuate as waves of nausea? Perhaps, for an hour or so, maybe a whole day, it slipped his memory and he was free, lost fully and happily to the routine of life.

He was a man who kept his counsel but in a place such as Middleton, where they gossip as naturally as they breathe, he was drawn into conversations with former workmates, friends, relatives. 'All going okay, Bert?' He mostly told them that he was fine, grand, mustn't complain. He was of an era where emotional suffering and sorrow was visualised as poisoned fumes, drawn into a box and the lid clasped shut. He was aware, too, of the soldier's promise. They shared an accord that they would keep it to themselves, the bloodshed and the grief. In fact, many saw the degree of concealment as a measure of their worth; it defined them. Herbert had spoken of his ordeal to his wife, Grace – though, even here, it pained him that he had flouted the soldier's oath of silence – but he wasn't going to seep his despair so easily, on an outing into Middleton to buy a couple of chops and a few bags of fruit. He was fine, grand, mustn't complain.

Herbert carried more than most ex-soldiers. War was inherently loathsome but, even at its most feral, it generally held to moral convention. There was a rationality, a justification, so that conflict became a means to an end, whether to secure land, protect a border or repel a sordid ideology. Herbert, as soldiers do, had endured the components of battle with a degree of acceptance – the shock, the noise, the mutilation and the death – because it had been comprehensible, ordered, and, at its most fundamental, soldier-on-soldier. This protocol of war had fractured grotesquely when he encountered Belsen in April 1945. Afterwards, he felt to have been in two wars, with different enemies. One was against the German army. The other, a battle with wholesale and sadistic evil.

Everyone either imprisoned at Belsen or responsible for its liberation had been left traumatised, changed for ever. They also felt stigmatised, discomfited that a mere tilt of circumstance had taken them to that place, that scene. Why us? Why me? In Herbert's case, this was exacerbated because of the exceptionality of being the first to push open the gates. He was alarmed and troubled by his *chosenness*: who wouldn't be? Over and over, he speculated whether it had been predestined, a call-out from the gods to play this special, cursed role.

As I walk through Middleton town centre, I see Herbert (in my mind's eye) passing by. He is wearing a fawn anorak, zipped up tight. He is thin, or *trim*, a term that implies a greater pride in appearance and a knowingness of oneself; he was devoted to keeping fit for most of his life. He has a certain poise, soft and swift in his shoes. He passes a man of a similar age who seems to want to chat. Herbert listens for a few seconds but issues a thumbs up and moves off. I ponder on whether Belsen made Herbert this way: restless, on the go, as if in the gunsight of the past but believing perpetual motion could skew its aim. At that very moment I contemplate another reason why it might have taken him 40 years before publicly sharing his story. Who would want to be the *Belsen man*? The more who knew about it, the more he was defined by it. And, most of all, he didn't want anyone's sympathy: what use was that?

I have lost Herbert. He has slipped across Middleton Gardens – more of a 'square' now it has been extensively flagged. He is walking away from the town centre, maybe heading for home. I change tack and think of the people I walk among (real, not imagined). Maybe some were soldiers who had served in the Falklands, Bosnia, Iraq, Afghanistan or elsewhere. Were they secretly despondent that they were seldom asked to speak of their experiences? Had we done them a disservice by being complicit in the concealment? It seemed unjust that they should go through it and not be able to talk about it: who made these rules?

I am in the YMCA charity shop, standing a couple of yards away from a man who smells as if he bathes in aftershave. His shirt is undone to the third button. A chunky gold chain hangs loose at his neck. The whole shop, about four of us, has already heard that he's just back from a *belting* holiday, him and a couple of mates. Been on a cruise, they have. He's now talking about his mother. She's got emphysema. More or less wheelchair bound, she is. Still got a cracking sense of humour. Can have a right laugh with her. As he talks, the lady assistant either nods or smiles in his direction, busying herself among the racks of clothes. The man draws breath. She steals the moment: 'How old is she now, your mum?'

'Eighty-three,' he says. 'She had me when she was 17.' He bids an extravagant, see-you-soon-my-love farewell. He closes the door with such force that boxes of jigsaws and ornaments almost fall from the shelves. The assistant peers through the window, making sure he's truly gone. 'Why won't no one tell him?' she asks the room. 'What, that he's got too much aftershave on?' asks a man wearing combat trousers and running shoes. 'No, that he's so bloody boring.' Welcome to Middleton.

Across the road I notice a few people puffing hard on cigarettes outside a pub. It's 11am on a Tuesday morning. I enter, expecting to find it empty, but it's packed, as if a cheerily hectic Saturday night has been set to repeat at all hours through the week. People are sitting, standing, wandering about, shouting to one another, whispering to one another. I make my way to the bar and realise that the pub is called the Harbord Harbord; it's printed on the beer mats. The barmaid is in her early twenties and has blue hair and a nose ring. I ask why the Harbord Harbord is called the Harbord Harbord. 'I don't know, I don't know,' she replies. She sees that I get the joke and smiles. 'Check the chart over there – it's all about him,' she says.

I should have realised: the busyness, a clientele of all ages, plates of food on the tables, real ale, tea and coffee refills, a small area set down as a 'library' – I'm in a Wetherspoon or 'Spoons as they are better known; it was a Kwik Save when I was last in town. I read the sign on the wall: 'Harbord Harbord, 1st Baron Suffield (26 January 1734–4 February 1810), was, between 1770 and 1786, a British landowner and politician who sat in the House of Commons. He was Middleton's last Lord of the Manor.' He's a fine old dandy too, sporting a lavish wig, red waistcoat and white stockings up to his knees. A man passes by carrying two pints of beer, dangling them from each hand as if they are marionettes. He sees me looking at the picture. 'He wouldn't last long around here these days,' he says, motioning with his head towards Harbord Harbord. 'How come?' I ask. 'He'd get filled in, looking like that,' he exclaims, incredulous that I haven't delineated the obvious link between dressing so flamboyantly and a sound beating. He sits down with his pals at the next table. They're good fun, joshing with each other and shouting over occasionally, asking whether I'm a red (Manchester United) or a blue (Manchester City). 'Do you know what we call this place?' asks one with pitted muck on his face. 'The Cardboard Hardboard!' Welcome to Middleton.

Herbert Kenny would have been ill at ease in the Harbord Harbord; he wasn't one for bonhomie and small talk. If he was flagged down by the postman or beckoned by a neighbour, he'd listen but invariably respond with a nod or a smile, rather than partake in tittle-tattle. He was far too polite to condescend or patronise, but, as he stood with them, making apposite facial gestures, his thoughts (to anyone who really knew him) were obvious: does it really matter? The same as many ex-soldiers, he had been left with an altered perspective. He had fastened a postcard to the corkboard in his kitchen with drawing pins: 'Don't sweat the small stuff'.

He had lived most of his adult life in Middleton and was familiar with the grumbling. 'Any day now, they'll be moaning that the rain's too wet,' he used to say. Several issues were habitual: the

Arndale Centre was a monstrosity; Langley was, in the vernacular, a 'shit hole'; Middleton Gardens needed 'digging up and putting back to how it was' and the *Bread Roll Christ* was a 'bloody eyesore' – this was a 20ft tall 'art installation' made from plastic bread rolls affixed to the back wall of the Arndale, flanked by 'corn dollies' assembled from scaffold poles. These were regular gripes but the one that most simmered and seethed was the governance of the town. Middleton had run its own affairs for almost a century until it became part of Rochdale Metropolitan Borough Council (RMBC) in 1974, under a national shake up of local government.

The subject was broached regularly with Herbert and he agreed that *old* Middleton had been 'grand', before adding, 'but you can't hold back progress'. On his regular walks he would see tantalising glimpses of the town's distinguished past, still visible though often abandoned to the elements or hewn into flats in garish 'refits'. Many of these buildings had been designed by the celebrated local-born architect, Edgar Wood. His first bestowal had been a shelter and drinking fountain installed in the town centre in 1887, when he was 27 years old. He proceeded to almost single-handedly shape Middleton, from pubs to churches, banks to offices, shops to houses. Other impressive buildings pre-dated Wood, including the Parish Church of St Leonard (1412), Hopwood Hall (1426), Tonge Hall (1584) and the Olde Boar's Head pub (1622). This was the Middleton, sturdy and traditional, to which many wanted to return – a time before the Arndale Centre and Langley had been 'dropped' on them, and the town wasn't run by *yonners* [a variant of yokel] from six miles up the road in Rochdale.

Herbert held to a personal creed of 'live and let live'. He'd been a welder and engineer in his working days, at various firms in Middleton, and had driven lorries and vans. He'd had workmates from Langley and didn't hold to the view that these incomers were crooks and wastrels. He wasn't a true Middletonian himself and shared a similar background to the *Langleys*. He'd grown up in Hulme, Cheetham and Lower Broughton, among similar poky streets from where the *Langleys* had been displaced. They had come to Middleton from Ancoats, Beswick, Collyhurst and Miles Platting, where the falling-down houses had been overcrowded, and owned by flinty private landlords.

During army service Herbert had often recognised a north Manchester accent among fellow soldiers – those *bokkuls* and *likkuls* – as they gathered around the billy cans and bains-marie at headquarters. Lawrence Frattaroli, from Miles Platting, had served with the medical corps. After the war he had moved with his young family to Calder Walk, Langley. His son Tom said: 'There was fresh air and grass at Langley, and the houses were brand new. In Miles Platting everything was black and covered in soot. We had a tin bath and five of us shared the same water because it took so long to heat up.' Tom was soon made aware of the stigma of living in Langley. He passed his Eleven Plus exam and attended Queen Elizabeth Grammar School, across town at Boarshaw. 'The teachers were open about it. In the first few weeks, if anyone couldn't grasp what they were being taught, they would say, "I can guess where you're from,"' he said. Herbert baulked at this kind of prejudice. 'There's plenty a good 'un, off Langley,' he'd say.

Chapter Two
A wretched mode of life

The names of the 284 men from Middleton who died in World War Two are inscribed on marble panels set into a curved wall at the town's Garden of Remembrance. In later life Herbert lived a few hundred yards away and passed it many times. Most of the deceased have English surnames but there is a smattering of Irish origin: Murphy, Power, Maguire, McCann and so on, reflecting the wider population of Middleton. The original Irish settlers had been invited by wealthy mill owners to join their workforce, and this number was augmented through the 20th century when second and third generation Irish migrated from the slums of inner-city Manchester; Herbert Kenny's family was part of this dispersion.

'Kenny' is an anglicisation of Ó Cionnaith, meaning 'descendant of Cionnaith', and is still prevalent in Ireland, chiefly in the west, in towns and cities such as Roscommon and Galway. The first Kennys came to England in the 1780s principally to work in the mills. The Great Famine of 1845–52 led to an influx of tens of thousands of Irish migrants into Lancashire who crossed the Irish Sea by steamship. The famine had been precipitated by potato blight. Easily and quickly grown, the potato had been a staple food for most of the population. Over a ten-year period, more than a million people died in Ireland, while a further two million, a quarter of the total population, fled to the United States, Canada, Australia and Britain.

Most migrants, seeking work, made their way to London or slums in the north-west clustered around mills, workshops and construction sites. Their arrival invariably coincided with outbreaks of epidemic typhus, referred to as Irish Fever, which was spread by body lice and thrived in congested areas. Few migrants spoke English and many were overwhelmed by the noisy, busy, smoky urbanised environment – a great contrast to rural life in Ireland. They struggled to find work and often turned to begging. *The Lancet*, the medical journal, described them as 'starving and fever-stricken' and claimed that 'they locate themselves in dog-kennels and cellars, and remain to glut the labour market and propagate a wretched mode of life.'

Migrants were blamed for rising criminality, violence, prostitution and alcoholism. An assumption took hold that the Irish, almost all of them Catholic, were morally deficient and prone to anger; this branding of the 'mad Irish' was an anecdotal, street-by-street creation reinforced by newspapers. Dr Thomas Clouston, an eminent psychiatrist of the times, claimed that cities had harmed the Irish, causing 'exhausted nervous vitality' that led to depression, schizophrenia and addiction. 'The Irish peasant, in his native country, has a marked immunity from these fatal forms of brain disorders,' he wrote, 'but when transplanted into centres of labour in Lancashire, he is apt to break down and acquire a form of mental disease.'

Many of the Irish in Middleton worked in nearby Rochdale and Oldham, walking to and from the mills along the towpath of the Rochdale Canal. They visited friends in the 'Irish Quarter' of Wardleworth, close to Rochdale town centre, where rumours had spread among the English of the alleged amorality of the Irish. They kept pigs, they had heard, with whom they played and slept. They were said to participate in 'clogging' where men stripped to the waist and kicked each other while wearing clogs. The first to kick his opponent unconscious was declared the winner and bets paid out accordingly. John McKenna, a man of Irish descent, committed a brutal murder that became part of local folklore for decades. McKenna, a 25-year-old plasterer, attacked his pregnant wife, Anna, while drunk, 'leaving her dead with a mass of fearful black bruises', stated the police report. He was found guilty and hanged in March 1877. Members of the press witnessed the hanging and it had a profound effect on an uncredited journalist from the *Rochdale Observer*: 'Certain classes are allowed to herd in cellar dwellings, amid the vilest and indecent surroundings. No effort is made to get this low class to take an interest in nobler and more purifying amusements than sitting in the beer house till they become dead drunk, fighting, dog racing, tossing, other forms of gambling, and ruinous vices. Until something is done for this class, which has no elevating power in itself, we must expect to have a plague spot in our community, a horde of savages to make society insecure and fill our gaols with criminals, to be maintained at great cost by the nation.'

Most members of the Kenny family tree, including Herbert's paternal ancestors, had gravitated to Lancashire after moving from Ireland. The census of 1891 revealed that 1,239 people with the Kenny surname (or Kenney – names were often misspelled on official forms) lived in the county, almost half the total number of Kennys in England. The first of Herbert's descendants to arrive from Ireland was his paternal great-grandfather, Thomas Kenny, born in Galway in 1825. He settled in York as an agricultural worker; for decades, the Irish, known as 'July barbers', had helped with the corn harvest on the Wolds of east Yorkshire. Many of these migrant workers remained in York and, by 1851, more than 2,500 listed themselves as 'Irish-born', living mainly in the squalid, insanitary alleys and yards in Walmgate, close to the River Foss in the city centre. Thomas Kenny lodged at a three-bedroomed house at 33 Walmgate in a typical arrangement, sharing with nine others who were also mainly agricultural workers, from Roscommon, Sligo and Galway.

While working at various farms, Thomas Kenny acquired a bent for tending horses. He moved with his wife, Mary (née Perry), to Manchester, where grooms were required to care for horses used in the cotton mills or to pull hansom cabs. Thomas and Mary had three children, Frederick, Minnie and Annie, and lived in Chorlton-upon-Medlock, a district now absorbed into the city centre of Manchester. Their dwelling in Cambridge Street was among approximately 200 back-to-back terraced houses pressed tight to mills between a railway line and the River Medlock. These properties were occupied almost wholly by Irish families who, as unskilled workers, received low pay and could barely cover the rent; the area was known as Little Ireland. Most worked at the huge Mackintosh & Co. mill, also on Cambridge Street, standing tall above the houses. The district was so overcrowded in the 19th century that up to 20 people from different families often lived together, sleeping in cellars. In 1845 Frederick Engels wrote in his book *The Condition of the Working Class in England*: 'A horde of ragged women and children swarm about here, as filthy as the swine that thrive upon the garbage heaps and in the puddles. The race that lives in those ruinous cottages or in dark, wet cellars, in measureless filth and stench, must really have reached the lowest stage of humanity.'

Thomas and Mary Kenny's son, Frederick Kenny (Herbert's grandfather), was born in 1865 and worked as an ironsmith before becoming a warehouseman. He married Amy Smethurst in 1884. She was one of 11 children born to Joseph and Elizabeth Smethurst, from Stockport and Bolton respectively. The marriage was typical of the urban working-class in Victorian times. Few left their neighbourhood and tended to marry people they had known since childhood or had met at work. Families effectively set up arranged marriages, with sisters regularly 'choosing' a suitable partner for their brothers. Amy was a 'fancy box maker' (handmade boxes to store hats, ribbons, jewellery, etc.) and had lived with her parents and siblings in Victoria Place, Chorlton-upon-Medlock. Frederick and Amy settled in Booth Street, Manchester, a mile or so from where they had both been raised.

The slums of Little Ireland were demolished in the late 1880s and most families relocated to Hulme, a short walk away. Herbert's father, Herbert Frederick Kenny, was born there in July 1884. After leaving school at 14, Herbert Sr worked as a carter for the Kewley family at their premises in Cawdor Street, Hulme; a carter sold produce placed on a trap (wooden trailer) pulled by a pony or donkey. Herbert Sr travelled through the city centre streets and nearby districts on market days, selling wares. He boarded with Robert Kewley, a man in his mid-sixties who had moved to Manchester from the Isle of Man and set up a family business with his two sons, James and Walter, and grand-daughter, Jessie. They all worked together and lived above the shop.

Herbert Sr married Eliza Ann Robinson at St John the Baptist Church, Hulme, in July 1908. Eliza was the daughter of Emma Flockton, a cotton worker who had married Thomas Robinson, a cabinet maker, of Caton Street, Hulme. Although precise details were never shared with the family, it was known that Eliza was illegitimate. A child born a bastard in the 19th and early 20th century carried acute social stigma. They were without full legal status and viewed as outcasts. The author Wilkie Collins fathered three illegitimate children and it was the theme of his novel *No Name*, published in 1862. The character Mr Pendril, a lawyer, expressed Collins's own feelings on the subject: 'It visits the sins of the parents on the children; it encourages vice by depriving fathers and mothers of the strongest of all motives for making the atonement of marriage; and it claims to produce these two abominable results in the names of morality and religion.' Eliza carried the ignominy all her life, aggravated by the fact that she believed she was the daughter of an extremely wealthy man.

Herbert Sr and Eliza's first son, Leslie, was born in October 1909, followed by Edna May in 1911 who died at 15 months old. Herbert Kenny was born on 10 July 1912 and baptised at Holy Trinity, an Anglican parish church in Stretford Road, Hulme; it was bombed during World War Two and demolished soon afterwards. A third son, Norman, was born in February 1914 and listed in the census of 1921 as an 'invalid'.

Chapter Three
1 OR killed 5 OR wounded

———

Herbert Kenny's childhood home was a two-up, two-down terraced house in Squire Street, Cheetham, a deprived area of Manchester two miles north of the city centre. Cobbled alleyways ran parallel to the houses, and snickets formed a lattice of streets. The houses were without bathrooms and had an outside toilet in the back yard. Cheetham, in the 1920s, was a township with its own town hall, assembly rooms, temperance hall and public baths. The availability of property at relatively cheap rent meant the area had seen several waves of immigration; in 1920 almost 80 per cent of homes in Britain were rented. The Irish had moved there in the mid-19th century, before Jews arrived in the 1880s, fleeing persecution and poverty in eastern Europe.

The shopping parade along Cheetham Hill Road comprised rows of stores with lavish window displays, their striped awnings stretched high across the pavement. Michael Marks and Thomas Spencer (Marks & Spencer) had opened the retail outlet, Penny Bazaar, at 20 Cheetham Hill Road in 1894; Marks lived above the shop for six years with his wife, Hannah, and their children. Another popular store, where the Kenny children were sent on errands, belonged to Marcus Falk, who crammed his double-fronted window with mirrors, casserole dishes, teapots, framed pictures, packets of cigarettes and pouches of tobacco; it was the first shop in Manchester to sell Yiddish newspapers. Herbert Sr, similar to most fathers of the period, played a marginal role in family life. Parenting was firmly demarcated with the father regarded as 'the breadwinner' and the mother, 'the homemaker'. The Kenny family came together as one every Sunday when it was a tradition to put on their best clothes and take a stroll to either Mandley Park in Broughton or nearby Crumpsall Park.

Herbert Sr left Kewleys to work as a lamplighter for the gas department of Manchester Corporation. He was based at the gas works in Water Street on the fringes of the city centre close to Salford, amid the wharfs of the River Irwell and railway sidings beneath Stephenson's Viaduct. He was issued with a bicycle and given his own 'round' of streets, where he extinguished lamps at daybreak and lit them at nightfall, using a pole with a wick at the end. He carried a heavy wooden ladder to place against the horizontal bars at the top of a lamppost when climbing up to replace a mantle or glass casing. The rigmarole of resting the ladder on the bicycle handlebars, threading an arm through the rungs to stabilise it while steering and keeping balance, took him a few weeks to master. Each lamplighter covered about ten miles each day and the job was held in esteem, with an associated romanticism. As he snuffed the gaslight each morning, he was viewed as the harbinger of a new dawn, akin to the shrill of birdsong. And in the evening, the ghostly silhouette cast from man, ladder and bicycle as dabs of light were conjured here and there, made the night-time navigable and less forbidding. Lamplighters were viewed in the same vein as park keepers or policemen – symbolic of reliability, trustworthiness and, by virtue of being outside at unusual hours, watchmen for the community.

When Herbert Sr met people on his round and back at the depot, talk turned increasingly to the rising tension between European countries: war felt to be looming. At the end of their evening shift, lamplighters would stop off for a pint or two at a pub before heading home. Herbert Sr was kept abreast of the news when he visited The Empress in Cheetham Hill Road, where newspapers were left on the bar and tables. A recurring topic of discussion in the pubs and on street corners was which country was on whose side at any particular point. By 1914 there were two distinct groupings – the Central Powers (Germany, Austria-Hungary, the Ottoman Empire and Bulgaria) and the Triple Entente (Britain, France and Russia), while Spain, the Netherlands, Switzerland, Norway, Sweden, Denmark and Albania had all declared themselves as neutral.

Herbert Sr had listened to the regulars in The Empress, some of whom, when it came to the possibility of war, were *forrit* and others, *agin it*. The *Manchester Guardian*, one of the papers left out in the pub, had branded any potential conflict as 'an act of supreme and gratuitous folly'. The delicate balance was finally upset when Germany invaded Belgium, invoking various pan-European treaties. King George V declared war on Tuesday, 4 August 1914. Most of the population were in favour, believing that Kaiser

Bill – the German emperor, Friedrich Wilhelm Viktor Albert – was set on the annexation of Europe, including Britain. Scenes of jubilation broke out, borne from a belief that the country was 'standing up for itself'. More than 10,000 people descended upon Buckingham Palace, cheering, waving flags and singing the National Anthem, a spectacle that was repeated in cities throughout the country as swarms gathered outside civic buildings.

At the outbreak of war, the British Army had only 120,000 soldiers, compared to the two million of the German army. Lord Kitchener, the Secretary of State for War, was told to quickly bolster the ranks. The government decided against conscription, preferring a policy of 'mass persuasion'. Millions of posters were printed, informing men that joining up was both a national duty and a sign of masculinity. The message was also carried in packets of cigarettes at a time when 60 per cent of men smoked. W.D. & H.O. Wills, the Bristol-based tobacco company, issued a 'recruiting' card in every packet with entreaties such as 'Line up boys! – enlist today' and 'More men and still more until the enemy is crushed'. The likelihood of a German invasion of Britain was stressed, and anyone unwilling to help resist this was portrayed as contemptible. Lord Kitchener realised more would enlist if they could serve alongside their friends, relatives and workmates; this was especially appealing to close-knit, traditional communities in the north of England. They became known as 'Pals Battalions'.

Herbert Sr witnessed the great fervour to serve King and country on the streets of Manchester. The cavernous Free Trade Hall in the city centre was requisitioned as a recruitment centre.

Queues formed hours before registration began; up to 1,500 men were processed every day. Streets were cordoned off near the Artillery Barracks in Hyde Road to quell crowds. As they waited, recruits were serenaded by a band playing patriotic songs. News photographers encouraged would-be soldiers to throw their hats into the air. The only stipulation on joining up was that men had to be aged 19 to 38, stand taller than 5ft 3ins and have a chest measurement no smaller than 34½ inches.

During the late summer of 1914, the phrase 'the war to end all wars' took hold, lifted from a series of pieces written by H. G. Wells. This was understood by the public to be a promise: a single, sure push for victory, though it may incur personal sacrifices and a loss of lives, would lead to peace for several generations. Many believed it would be a battle easily won and that army service amounted largely to an exciting overseas jaunt. Few had travelled more than a handful of miles from their birthplace and were eager to escape teeming, smog-clogged cities; in the early 1900s, 700,000 people lived within 30 square miles of the centre of Manchester. Recruits relished the prospect of guaranteed pay, fresh air, regular food, exercise and being among men of a similar age.

Women were targeted specifically with propaganda, their femininity defined by their capacity to make men behave 'responsibly' and join the army. One poster showed a man sitting in an armchair, his young daughter on his lap and son playing at his feet, with the caption: 'Daddy, what did You do in the Great War?' The White Feather Brigade comprised women who handed out feathers as a token of cowardice to shame men reluctant to enlist. Herbert Sr did not need to be persuaded. Although he had a strong impulse to remain at home with his three young children, especially after the death of Edna May, he was generous of spirit and saw the greater calling of helping the country secure long-term freedom for *all* its children. He signed up as a Lancashire Fusilier (2nd Battalion, 4th Division, Company WO329) in August 1914 and became Private 8820. He was 26 years old.

He reported to Wellington Barracks in nearby Bury where he was kitted out and did weeks of drill training – the military term for marching in formation, so that soldiers could be transported without getting mixed up with other troops. He was brought up to full fitness, given rifle instruction and undertook guard duties. In the autumn of 1914 he travelled with the battalion to bolster forces manning coastal defences in Humberside. Hull was a key port within flying and sailing distance of occupied Europe. The seaside towns of Scarborough, Hartlepool and Whitby were later attacked by the Imperial German Navy on 16 December 1914, killing 122 people and wounding 443.

Herbert Sr was based at the East Hull Barracks in Holderness Road, a mile or so inland from the Humber Estuary. The drills resumed, carried out at East Park, Hull's largest public park. 'Not the Lambwath' was a regular groan from soldiers based at the barracks. The Lambwath Drain was a narrow watercourse running 12 miles through scrubby fields that regularly became sodden, turning pathways into cloying mud. 'It's the sort of stuff you'll be mashing through to get at the Jerries,' they were told of the training excercise. As they followed its route, usually on a slow jog, they were told to make a mental note of the hamlets, to make the training exercise pass more quickly. Most could reel them off long after the war had ended: Benningholme, Fairholme, Skirlaugh, etc.

Herbert Sr's unit joined the frontline on 2 December 1914, drafted in to fill the depleted ranks of the 2nd Battalion of the Lancashire Fusiliers. He arrived in West Flanders, Belgium, a week after the First Battle of Ypres ended. There was a series of combat 'engagements' close to the city of Ypres, and at the second of these, in 1915, the Germans used weapons of mass killing for the first time on the Western Front – gas and flame throwers. Tens of thousands were wounded or killed from both sides and hostilities seldom waned, even outside the five time-periods later designated as formal battles.

A deadlock set in along the Western Front and Allied leaders wanted to open new fronts elsewhere in a bid to shorten the war and staunch the loss of lives. In April 1915 Herbert Sr's unit relocated to the Dardanelles, a narrow 60-mile-long strait linking the Mediterranean with the Black Sea that divided Europe from Asia and had been of strategic importance for centuries. The objective was to secure the waterway and attack Constantinople (now Istanbul), the capital of the Ottoman Empire. Herbert Sr was among troops who landed at Suvla Bay on the Aegean coast in August 1915, a failed last-ditch attempt to outflank the Ottomans further up the coast where the ANZACs (Australian and New Zealand Army Corps) held the line. His unit also took part in several unsuccessful efforts to capture Krithia, a village located on a plateau high above the Dardanelles. The 'Gallipoli Campaign', named after the main town on the peninsula, lasted almost a year before the Allies retreated. The fighting had been fierce, leading to the deaths of 56,000 Allied soldiers, and the wounding of 123,000.

Herbert Sr returned to the Western Front in January 1916. Between July and November, he fought in the Battle of the Somme, one of the deadliest conflicts ever known. Three million took part, of whom a million were either killed or wounded. He then moved with his unit to engage in the Battle of Arras where the British offensive secured a swathe of territory in the first few days, before stalemate ensued. During the five-week conflict, the British Army incurred 160,000 'casualties' – the military term for anyone killed, wounded or missing in action. Herbert Sr returned to Belgium in the summer of 1917 to participate in the Third Battle of Ypres, also known as the Battle of Passchendaele. The aim initially had been to push through to the port of Zeebrugge, where the Germans had established a U-Boat base, but after weeks of torrential rain and a failure to advance any meaningful distance, a ridge in the east of the city at Passchendaele became the new, more limited objective. Heavy shelling destroyed drainage systems and turned the battlefield into a quagmire. Many soldiers drowned. 'It was worse when the mud *didn't* suck you down. When it yielded under your feet, you knew that it was a body you were treading on,' wrote Charles Miles, a British soldier, in his diary. The capture of this small strip of land, described as 'the worst place on earth', came at a dreadful cost: more than 500,000 casualties from both sides. In his poem *Memorial Tablet (Great War)*, Siegfried Sassoon wrote:

I died in hell –
(They called it Passchendaele). My wound was slight,
And I was hobbling back; and then a shell
Burst slick upon the duck-boards: so I fell
Into the bottomless mud, and lost the light.

The war was still raging early in the summer of 1918. Russia had signed a peace treaty with the Central Powers (Germany, Austria-Hungary and Turkey), effectively surrendering a third of its population and territory, much of its industry and almost 90 per cent of its coal mines. Fifty divisions of the German army, each with between 12,000 and 25,000 soldiers, were now freed from the Eastern Front to bolster those fighting in the west. The Germans sought a speedy victory before the huge manpower and hardware resources of the United States could be deployed; more than 10,000 US marines were joining the Allies each week throughout 1918. The first German 'Spring Offensive' was launched against the British on the Somme in March, followed by another, the Battle of the Lys, in the British sector of Armentières (a small French town at its border with Belgium), a month later. The third Spring Offensive, the Battle of the Aisne, began in the French sector along Chemin des Dames, a ridge of land running through northern France. Herbert Sr fought in all these battles.

By June 1918 Herbert Sr would have believed that he was having a 'good' war: he was still alive. His unit had been in the vicinity, if not always active, in several ferocious battle zones, but he had remained free of serious injury. He was a signaller, a role that placed him in great danger. He was charged with the vital job of establishing and maintaining communications, chiefly operating radio equipment or sending telegrams to commanders from the frontline. Cables that he laid across battlefields often became severed by enemy shellfire. He had to stray into 'no-man's-land' to locate the two ends of the cable and – amid the chaos and storm of explosions, under a hail of bullets and shells – reattach them. As midsummer approached, he found himself based in the hamlet of Riez du Vinage, close to Béthune, a town in northern France where, a few weeks earlier, a German bombardment had killed almost 3,000 British soldiers and 100 civilians. The writer C S Lewis, was one of those wounded. He was 20 years old and serving with the Somerset Light Infantry. He later wrote in his autobiography, *Surprised by Joy*: 'The frights, the cold, the smell of high explosive, the horribly smashed men still moving like half-crushed beetles.'

On Monday, 16 June 1918, Herbert Sr was one of several in his unit ordered to 'hold the line'. The area had been deemed a 'quiet sector' – though it was never truly *quiet* – and preceding nights had been recorded in the battalion diary as 'situation unchanged'. The assignment of taking up position in a trench on a mild summer's night when the sky was open and milky dark was much less onerous than it had been in the oily, noisy blackness of Ypres in midwinter. The danger was still present, though, regardless of conditions. The next day, 17 June, a page in the battalion diary read: 'Heavy artillery active during the night, 1 OR killed 5 OR wounded'. An OR was an 'Other Rank', denoting a soldier who was not an officer. Herbert Sr was the OR who had been killed. He was buried at Lapugnoy, a small rural town 33 miles southwest of Lille, and posthumously awarded the 1914–15 Star Medal 'for service in specified theatres of war betwcen 5 August 1914 and 31 December 1915'. The war ended five months later, on 11 November 1918.

Chapter Four
You need running, lad

———

Herbert Kenny was two years old when his father went to war, and a month short of his seventh birthday when Herbert Sr was killed in France. In the intervening years they had seen each other only two or three times because, as a private, Herbert Sr was granted leave every 15 months or so, whereas officers were permitted three or four home visits per year. Even before the war, he had been a marginal figure in his children's lives. His job as a gaslighter had meant that he was out in the evenings and slept during the day, after the early rises. Herbert was left with no real memory of his father, though he often looked at the framed picture of him on the sideboard. Herbert Sr was photographed in army uniform, a hint of a smile below the customary thick moustache of the times. To young Herbert, he was simply another man, largely indistinct from others who passed by on the street or they saw at the shops. As Herbert grew older he began to see how much he resembled his father, everyone commented on it. 'You're like two peas in a bloody pod,' his relatives would say: those dark eyes somewhere between a chuckle and a quandary, the strong nose, the leanness, and an easy demeanour that suggested a trust in the world – they could be the same man.

Eliza Kenny, Herbert's mother, moved her young family from Cheetham to Lower Broughton, Salford, about a mile away, to live with her widowed elder sister, Ellen Lowe; it reduced living costs for them both. House moves had to be undertaken on the back of a horse-drawn cart. Eliza and her three boys arrived at 67 Duke Street, sitting among their piled-up, strapped-down artefacts and furniture, to live in another rat-run of tightly bunched terraced houses. Eliza was one of 200,000 war widows who each received a weekly allowance from the Ministry of Pensions, collectable from the nearest Post Office. She had to keep a clean house and show herself to be a devoted and virtuous mother because the amount received depended on the ruling of a Special Grants Committee which assessed her moral fibre. Malicious neighbourhood gossip made known to authorities could form the basis for a pension to be denied or revoked. Herbert Sr's rank as a private meant that Eliza received less than she would have done, had he been an officer.

Widows were warned that if they entered a relationship with another man, he would be expected to support her children. Eliza received a little extra for each of the three boys, classified on official forms as *orphans* – a word that quarrelled with her tongue every time she spoke it; she was perturbed by the pity and beggary it felt to purport. The family's impoverished state upset Eliza, particularly because she had been told that her father was a member of the Kilvert family, the owners of N. Kilvert & Sons Ltd, the lard manufacturers of Stretford, Manchester. Kilvert's, founded in 1821, was one of the first food brands established nationally in Britain, predating other famous companies such as Cadbury and Fox's Biscuits.

Mothers of illegitimate children habitually exaggerated the status of the father, or fictionalised them, as if to compensate for their absence. Nonetheless, Thomas Kilvert, the father of the company's founder, Nicholas Kilvert, had run butcher's shops in Salford and Chorlton, and lived at White Cross Bank, Salford. Eliza's mother, Emma Flockton, was brought up and worked in these areas, within a mile or so of the Kilvert factory complex, which was designed to resemble a walled village. Emma had been an operative in cotton mills but also spent time as a maid at the grand houses nearby, although later generations of the Kilvert family relocated to live in mansions in rural Cheshire. Sexual relations between masters of the house and servant girls were fairly common, often resulting in illegitimate children; a certain level of compliance from the girls was regarded as an extension of duty. Whether true or not, Eliza believed steadfastly that she was an unacknowledged descendant of the Kilvert family and held dear the belief all her life.

Eliza fell upon an idea to augment the family's income. The cellar of the house at Duke Street was turned into a dairy as they began making ice cream. The boys helped, firstly shopping for milk, sugar, eggs, cream and vanilla, before mixing the ingredients in outsize bowls and scooping it into the wooden ice cream maker. Eliza would press down the heavy lid as the boys summoned all their puff to budge the crank which, in turn, set the paddle (known as a 'dasher') in motion, stirring the ice cream. The making and selling of ice cream in Manchester was done mainly by Italian families who had settled in nearby Ancoats, an area known as Little Italy. The Kennys had a handcart and made a small profit, but it remained a homespun affair compared to the Italian traders such as the Pandolfos, the Boggianos, the Scappaticcis and the Silvoris who became well-known across the city, expanding to become retail dynasties.

When Herbert was a young teenager the Kenny family moved again, to Boarshaw, a district of Middleton. Although they had travelled only a few miles north-east from Lower Broughton, it was a more desirable neighbourhood. Soon afterwards, a house became available across town, at 31 Chapel Street, Rhodes, and they packed up their belongings once more. In the late 1920s Rhodes was bounded by countryside and in sight of the gentle inclines of the Pennines before they stretched onwards and grander into Rochdale, and then Yorkshire. The streets had an open vista and a wide variety of houses, the brickwork shining orange in the rain. Rhodes, gauged by outsiders, was a suburb or district of Middleton, but for centuries its residents had claimed village status. *The Imperial Gazetteer of England and Wales*, an early topographical census, listed it as such in 1870 but it later became a standard urbanised 'ribbon development' with streets and houses, pubs and business premises, huddled to Manchester Old Road (the A576), leading to Manchester in one direction and Middleton, the other. Nevertheless, for many years, Rhodes – especially when the Kennys lived there – had a strong sense of kinship and was largely self-sufficient with its own shops, chemists, community centre, youth club, post office, GP, police officer and designated midwife.

Herbert's first job, at 14 years old, was working at a local butcher's owned by Mr Eves – very few knew his first name. On Herbert's first day he was told: 'You're here to do the lugging.' He was thin and wiry and strong, and quickly grew to enjoy the work. Sides of beef almost as tall as himself were rugby tackled from the cart and pinned down to the block or carried through to the larder at the back of the shop. He got caught up constantly in the red and white ribbons hanging down at the front door to deter flies. He was frequently spotted eyeing up the knives, saws and cleavers. 'You'll get your hands on them in good time, kiddo, when I think we can trust you not to cut your fingers off,' he was told. In quiet periods he was asked to 'fettle the window', which meant repositioning sausages laid on the artificial grass or righting tipped-over figurines of plastic cows. At other times he was thrown a dishcloth and told to wipe down the wall tiles. Twice a week, he did the rounds on a bicycle, filling the basket up to the brim and dropping off cuts wrapped in kraft paper and muslin. Herbert was diligent and listened attentively to Mr Eves as he talked him through the various processes – make the fillets shapely; cut the chops squarely end-to-end, so no bugger gets the last off the rack and complains that it's skimpy; put aside the smallest morsels for stews and, always, the scraps and dabs go in the sausages.

At first Herbert had presumed he was being trained up; it seemed that way, but Mr Eves was difficult to read and regularly contradicted himself. He was grumpy, especially early in the day, but lit up shiny bright whenever a woman entered the shop, telling her how lovely she looked that fair morning and how, with 'that lovely black hair', she was a spit of Gloria Swanson. The following week, he'd have her down as Joan Crawford. Mr Eves finally informed Herbert that he wouldn't, in fact, be promoted from butcher boy to butcher's assistant. The manner in which he was told stayed with Herbert and he took it as a life-lesson. He related it to others as an exemplar of false promises and as a warning to be wary of the mealy-mouthed and circumspect. 'He sat me down and started off telling me how I was a good lad, keen and that, honest to goodness,' Herbert would say. 'And then he got round to talking about this nephew of his who was a bit of a daft ha'p'orth and, truth be told, didn't know his arse from his elbow but, you know, it was his sister's lad, like, so, well, he had no choice really – he had to take him on.' At the time of their chat, Herbert had not fully understood what he'd been told and asked Mr Eves: what about me? 'I'm laying you off, Bert. Can you drop off your spare apron at the shop tomorrow?'

Herbert began a friendship with the daughter of neighbours living across the road, at 26 Chapel Street. Grace Hardman, three years younger than him, lived with her parents, James and Edith. Herbert and Grace 'clicked' and began dating, tramping the lanes above Rhodes towards the village of Bowlee, passing farmland that would later be sold off to accommodate the M62 motorway and Langley estate. They were regulars at the two cinemas in Middleton town centre, the Empire in Corporation Street and the Palace in

Manchester Old Road. On hearing that the couple were heading to the Empire, James Hardman used to tease them with, 'Don't forget your brollies.' Before its refurbishment in 1915, the venue, formerly called Matthews Pavilion Theatre, had been better known as 'Owd Gaff'. Rain seeped through the roof and the temperature fluctuated between extremely cold or scorching, depending on whether the management had fired up the large iron stove in the middle of the auditorium; in winter, patrons arrived early to position themselves close to the stove and cheered when more coke was added. 'They've sorted it now,' Herbert would tell James. 'It's dry and plenty warm enough these days.'

James Hardman worked as a stenter operator at the Calico Printers Association (CPA) in Rhodes; a stenter was a machine that applied chemical treatments to fabric. James 'put in a word' for Herbert and, after leaving the butcher's shop, he was taken on. The CPA site was easy to spot because a 350ft high chimney was at its entrance, the tallest in Europe for several years and known locally as 'the Colossus of Rhodes', a title borrowed from the statue of Helios, one of the Seven Wonders of the Ancient World that had stood beside the Mandrákion harbour in Rhodes, Greece. Other nicknames for the giant flue were Big Bertha, Schwabe's Chimney (named after the company's founder) and John Ashton's Monument, honouring the builder from nearby Blackley who had overseen its construction from 1.5 million bricks, enough, it was said, to reach London (212 miles away) if they were laid end-to-end. The link to the other Rhodes was mined regularly for comic value, especially when it became an affordable holiday destination in the 1970s. Travel agents in the Arndale Centre would put up window displays advertising package holidays with the caveat, 'Not Our Rhodes!' written underneath.

Within weeks, several of the older staff at CPA had commended Herbert for being a 'little grafter'. He began as a labourer, scooping up cloth cut-offs from the floor and putting them in skips, before wheeling them out to the yard. He cleaned machinery, dismantling parts to gain access with a rag or a scrub of wire wool. His dexterity and independent nature were noted: he could be trusted to 'get on with the job' without either *buggering it up* or 'shouting for help every five minutes'. Many lads of Herbert's age had been lackeying for months, if not years, but he was soon asked if he wanted to be trained up as a fabric welder. He was taught how to use heat and pressure to fuse cloth pieces together. After a few months he progressed to become an oxyacetylene welder; there felt to be a greater purpose in handling a torch that spat fire to repair or disassemble machinery. He learned the basics during a week or so that his foreman called an *induction*: keep your goggles on or your mask pulled down at all times; make sure your hands – and everything else – are well away from the hot metal; focus on the tip of the flame, and don't have the acetylene gas above 15psi (pounds per square inch) or 'next time we see you, you'll be flying over Rhodes Chimney'.

An hour or so after starting work each day, the sweat made Herbert's clothes stick to his skin beneath the overalls. By 'scran time' a few hours later, a patch of damp was visible under each arm at the top of his welding apron. He revelled in the physicality of the job – manoeuvring gas cylinders on to the trolley, lifting metal plates across the table, and manipulating the gas tubing so that he wasn't 'fighting' with it when he pointed the torch. He had little interest in formal sports but imagined the job as a physical work-out. The heat and the exertion made him tired at the end of the day but he felt it to be a wholesome, healthy exhaustion. He was a jittery sort. His mother had often called him Jazzer Collins when he skittered around the home as a boy, trying to outrace his shoes. When he asked who Jazzer Collins was, she replied, 'I don't know, but I've heard he's a fidget-arse like you.' An older engineer at CPA, noting Herbert's restlessness, proffered a solution: 'You need running, lad. You're like a cooped-up greyhound in here. Get out and do something of a weekend.' It gave Herbert an idea.

He enlisted with the Royal Tank Corps of the Territorial Army (TA) on 31 January 1930, aged 17. He viewed it mainly as an additional way to keep fit but was well aware of what signing up may later entail; his mother, Eliza, had felt obliged to point this out, reflecting on what had happened to Herbert Sr. The life and death of his father had always seemed to be a *story*, and Herbert had not been able to make him feel real. He had tried to assemble him from the recollections of others, but it was difficult. His mother barely mentioned him; Herbert couldn't decide whether this was because she thought it improper to speak of the dead or she didn't want her sons pining for a man they could never meet. His Auntie Flo (Florence Annie Kenny, Herbert Sr's elder sister by three years) occasionally became maudlin, especially after a few glasses of sherry, and would tell Herbert that his father had been 'a brave lad' or 'had got unlucky' – referencing his death a few weeks before the war's end. These fragments of exposé dissolved as they left her lips and if he asked for more, she answered, 'What's done is done.'

As well as the photograph of Herbert Sr in army uniform, Eliza had kept a cutting from the *Manchester Evening News* dated 5 July 1918. Under the headline 'Fallen Fighters' were two pictures side by side, one of Herbert Sr and the other of a private called H Rollings (it didn't include his full first name) of Blanchard Street, Hulme. They had been killed within a fortnight of each other in France and were featured because they both lived within the paper's circulation area. As a boy, Herbert had quizzed his mother about the cutting, intrigued by Private Rollings. He couldn't understand why they were pictured together: 'Is that Dad's friend?' he asked. Rollings was clearly much younger than Herbert Sr and could have passed for a 14-year-old. Another of Herbert's questions was: 'Did Dad have another son who died?', meaning Private Rollings. 'No, he didn't, Bert. That's just a fella,' replied Eliza. On the Friday afternoon when Herbert signed the papers to join the TA, he knew so little of his father and the diconnection was such, that Herbert Sr's death stood neither as a warning nor a salute to a valour that he might wish to emulate. They each had the same name and the mutual resemblance was striking but fate had made them strangers.

The expansion of the Territorial Army through the 1930s had been strategic to provide the British Armed Forces with sufficient numbers should another war break out; the government did not want to have to quickly assemble another Kitchener's Army. A new condition of joining was that recruits had to agree to the 'general service obligation', consenting to combat deployment overseas if required. One of the first training camps Herbert attended was in South Wales – soldiers were posted a good distance away from their families because, before this policy, relatives had frequently turned up with food (pork pies and bottles of beer were staples) for their loved ones or to merely wave from the perimeter fence. Another factor was that the army no longer wanted Pals Battalions. Losses had been too concentrated in individual families and communities during World War One. Herbert relished the regular breaks from work, visiting new places two or three times a year on manoeuvres, usually in rural areas. He told Grace it was 'hard graft' but rhapsodised about the country air, the fields and trees, the dawn chorus, foxes scampering through the bracken, the mucking in, the laughs and the daft lads who 'struggled to tie their own shoelaces without their mams' help'.

Chapter Five
The Hun keep stirring it

Eliza Kenny doted on her sons, and family members presumed she had waited for her three boys to grow up before starting a new relationship. She befriended Clement Jackson, a master tailor 11 years her senior, who had spent his childhood years in Fielding Street, Middleton, with his parents, Joseph and Susannah, and three siblings. Eliza and Clement married in February 1931. Norman, Eliza's youngest son, was 17 at the time, while Herbert was 19. Leslie, the eldest, had married Bertha Evans five years earlier in February 1925 at the age of 16 – Eliza and Bertha's parents had to give their permission. The phrase 'he's very much his mother's son' was heard regularly in family circles as Herbert increasingly revealed traits similar to Eliza, chiefly a curious nature and sureness of self. Clement became close to Eliza's children and grandchildren and was well-liked, though he did not bond particularly with Herbert. 'He was very much a gentleman, was Grandad Jackson,' said Herbert Jr, Herbert's son. 'As a tailor you'd expect him to be well-dressed and he always was, with a collar and tie and a good suit. He had a car when not many people did, a lovely old Ford.'

Almost five years after his mother's marriage, Herbert and Grace were wed, on Saturday, 7 December 1935, at All Saints Church, Rhodes. He was 23 and she was 20. The following summer, their first daughter, June, was born, followed by Freda, in July 1938. The family moved to 66 Boardman Lane, Rhodes, about half a mile from Chapel Street, where both Herbert and Grace had lived with their respective parents before marriage. Herbert's disabled brother, Norman, died in February 1938, aged 24. The specific nature of his disability wasn't known, but Herbert told his children that Norman struggled to walk, and both he and Leslie, the other brother, carried him on their backs, even in adulthood.

Newspapers, tatty and stained with oil, were routinely left on the Formica tables in the works' canteen at CPA. Herbert would lay them flat, ironing out creases with one hand, holding a butty in the other. He tried to keep up with the news, but he had other preoccupations: two young daughters and another on the way (Edith), due in the autumn of 1939. He had first become a father at 24, comparatively late among his relatives, friends and work colleagues. He relished family life; it seemed to shield him from all that was going on in the world. 'What do you think, Bert?' asked workmates at every incremental nudge towards another war, specifically – as reported in those discarded newspapers – the rise of Adolf Hitler and Nazism, Germany's annexation of various territories and Britain's policy of appeasement. Everyone became aware of the growing preparedness across the country. Millions of gas masks were being assembled in Blackburn. Mock air raids had taken place in Birmingham involving 30,000 people. Paintings from the National Gallery had been taken to a slate mine in North Wales for safekeeping. Churches were holding 'pray for peace' services. When asked, Herbert invariably shook his head or issued a platitude. He wasn't being apathetic or evasive but was lost to the main focus of his life – kids, wife, job. He also tried to avoid wider discussions on politics and felt similarly about gossip; it was grit that could spike and ruin a day.

Herbert was enthusiastic about appliances and bought a Lissen Messenger radio for £6.19.6 (he kept the receipt in case it was faulty and had to be returned); his wage at the time was a little under £5 per week. 'It's got three valves and four nifty little buttons,' he enthused. In the evenings after the children were put to bed, Herbert and Grace listened to the new radio. The BBC, formed in 1922, had established its own news operation in 1934 but Herbert used to say he didn't want any 'mither' after work and preferred variety programmes such as *The Air-do Wells*. No one in Middleton spoke as they did on the radio, addressing each other as 'old boy' and 'dear chap', but these 'turns' were still considered funny, especially Herbert's favourite, Max Kester, with his oddball ditties – 'Pancake Tuesday is celebrated with song, dance and indigestion . . .' On Saturdays they listened to *In Town Tonight*, listed in the *Radio Times* as 'A topical supplement – 30 minutes of diversified entertainment'. Herbert enjoyed the insight he gleaned from this precursor of the chat show; it possibly marked the beginning of his desire to self-educate.

In September 1938, Herbert and Grace, along with millions of others, had heard the broadcast by Prime Minister Neville Chamberlain after he had signed the Munich Agreement, ceding an area on the Czechoslovakia–Germany border known as Sudetenland, to Hitler. The usual programmes were suspended to accommodate the special coverage, during which Chamberlain announced: 'My good friends, for the second time in our history, a British Prime Minister has returned from Germany bringing peace with honour. I believe it is peace for our time. We thank you from the bottom of our hearts. Go home and get a nice quiet sleep.' The phrase echoed Benjamin Disraeli, who had made the same claim in 1878 on returning from the Congress of Berlin, an agreement that initially brought peace to the Balkans but many felt was a precursor to World War One.

Leslie Hore-Belisha, the Secretary of State for War, announced plans in March 1939 to expand the TA from 130,000 to 340,000 men, and double the number of divisions. Workmates had teased Herbert that the TA was 'glorified Boy Scouting', but he responded: 'We might come in handy if the Hun keep stirring it.' Despite this acknowledgement, in early 1939 he wrote in his notes that being called into action was 'the last thing on my mind'. This may have reflected an absorption in the TA training exercises. He was disciplined, and focused almost exclusively on what he called the 'job in hand', whatever that might be at a given time. Soon afterwards he stated that he 'didn't know what would happen about a war', suggesting that he and other TA soldiers had started to anticipate conflict.

Herbert began to follow the news more closely and was drawn into conversations about events and episodes in Germany. These centred routinely on Adolf Hitler and whether he was 'a bloody nutcase', 'megalomaniac' or – with that 'stupid haircut and silly 'tache' – a 'comedy turn'. Herbert's workmates speculated on what would happen next: 'One of Hitler's own will see him off', 'the politicians will sort it out between themselves' or, most worrying, 'he'll stop at nothing.' Most of the middle-aged men at CPA had served in World War One. More than 200 of their pals from Rhodes had been killed in France, and their names listed alphabetically, Fred Alderson to William Yates, on a framed roll of honour pinned to the wall at All Saints Church. Each year, those men fortunate enough to have survived, stood by the war memorial in the church yard on Remembrance Sunday, staring hard at the sword, laurel leaves and roses (for Lancashire) chiselled into the stone obelisk. They had a broader view beyond workplace chatter and were surprisingly well-informed. Herbert sat down with them occasionally on the wooden benches by the staff lockers, sipping tea from a tartan flask. They would mention the Wall Street Crash, the Great Depression and how Germany's middle class felt it had missed out on the 'Golden Age of Weimar', many of them losing their savings during the hyperinflation of 1923 and turning to Nazism. 'Hitler's a figurehead, a bloody opportunist, but that doesn't make him any less dangerous,' they'd tell him. Others cautioned: 'He's a charismatic little bugger and you can go a long way with charisma. People are always looking for someone to follow.'

Herbert was aware that some of his colleagues viewed him as a quiet man, possibly shy, but he held to the maxim that he'd rather say 'nowt' than talk 'piffle'. He was more at ease with the old boys and had learned how to prise information or an opinion from them. He'd simply ask: 'How do you mean?' or 'I'm not sure I understand...' and a river of conversation became the sea. He was fascinated by the insight and context they provided on Germany and Hitler, but he still viewed it in basic terms. He explained it as such to the younger lads at work. Hitler was a bully in the pub, he said. Imagine him 'acting up' in the Carters Arms or the Waggon and Horses, telling everyone what to do, putting frighteners on them and, worse, saying he was going to come round to their house at closing time and put them out on the street. 'What would you do?' Herbert would ask. They shook their heads at first, taking it in, but then responded: 'I'd punch his lights out'. 'Well then,' said Herbert.

Factors that nurtured fascism in other European countries after World War One – high unemployment (three million people were without work in Britain during the 1930s) and poor living standards, especially in the north – had not led to a broad systematic pursuit of scapegoats. The Jewish Labour Council had warned of such a development in a pamphlet issued in 1935:

At present the country is in the grip of a crisis. Millions of men, unemployed or only partly employed, are contemplating the future with abject despair. When they are tramping the streets in search of work, most of them do not think of the basic social causes of their poverty and hopeless position. At such a time, Mosley seizes his opportunity to play upon the old racial and religious prejudices. 'The Jews are to blame!' he shouts. 'The foreigners are the cause of your misery.' And in their wretchedness and bitterness some of the victimised workers imagine that they see prosperity amongst the foreigners.

A sizeable minority had fallen in thrall to Oswald Mosley, founder and leader of the British Union of Fascists (BUF). By the mid-1930s, the BUF was reported to have 18 branches in Manchester and surrounding towns. A small group of his supporters, known as Blackshirts, gathered every Friday on a cobbled area near the Assheton Arms in Long Street, Middleton, carrying out drill exercises. Rallies had been staged in Queens Park, Harpurhey, four miles south of Middleton, and meetings held at Belle Vue Gardens in Gorton, and the Free Trade Hall. The same as most of the British people, Herbert was dumbfounded by the treatment of Jews by the Nazis which, during the mid-1930s, was worsening on an insidious basis. He'd read that they had been forced to carry identity cards stamped with a 'J', their children banned from state schools and the men ordered to take the name 'Israel', and the women, 'Sarah'. All his life, Herbert had instinctively supported the underdog and viewed Jews as such, feeling sorry that many had been displaced to live in ghettos around the world. In simplistic terms, he admired their pluck, how they worked hard and had a strong communal spirit.

Fascists paraded occasionally through Cheetham Hill and Strangeways, areas of Manchester with large Jewish populations, antagonising locals before meeting up at Walter's Café close to Victoria Station. Slogans such as 'Christians awake! Don't be slaughtered for Jewish finance' were daubed on walls in Fallowfield, and a BUF member was fined 20 shillings by city magistrates for chalking fascist slogans on a wall at Boggart Hole Clough in Blackley. The response, whether impromptu or via the various affiliations in Manchester – Young Communist League, the Challenge Club, the Youth Front Against War and Fascism – was to confront antisemitism at its source, whether hand-to-hand on the streets or by outnumbering and shouting down speakers at BUF rallies with chants of 'The rats, the rats, clear out the rats' and 'One, two, three, four, five, we want Mosley, dead or alive.'

Herbert held the same view as most of Britain's Gentile working class – that Mosley, his blackshirts and sympathisers were largely figures of fun. Most acknowledged Mosley's magnetism and skills of oratory but mocked him as a poor man's Adolf Hitler or Benito Mussolini, the fascist prime minister of Italy. Fascism, with its bombast and garish theatre, was widely viewed as a 'foreign' idea, distinctly un-British. One or two young men known to Herbert had 'their heads turned' by Mosley but they were dabbling in fascism, viewing it almost as mischievousness. They quickly re-evaluated their commitment to the cause after being chased down Cheetham Hill Road or taking a bashing at Belle Vue. Several years later, Herbert would see Mosley as a much more malevolent force when, after the war, he stated that 'Buchenwald and Belsen are completely unproved' and 'pictorial evidence proves nothing at all.' Herbert, justifiably, was incredulous and disgusted at such a distortion put forward by Mosley and other 'Holocaust deniers'.

Middleton was home to only a handful of Jews but the population of neighbouring Prestwich comprised one-fifth Jews which, with the Manchester districts of Crumpsall and Cheetham Hill, and Broughton in Salford, formed the second largest Jewish community in Britain, after London. Herbert was accustomed to seeing Jewish families at Heaton Park, the 600-acre expanse of greenery between Middleton and Prestwich. They shared picnic space and the children often played together, paddling at the edges of the boating lake. Herbert would queue for ice cream at the wooden kiosk and chat with the dads, him in his Sunday Best, them in their frock-coats, shtreimels (large round fur hats) and with Payot (long, curled sidelocks). One Sunday, Herbert struck up a conversation with a man who introduced himself as Gedaliah Korn. Herbert told him that he'd never heard of anyone called either Gedaliah or Korn before. 'Just call me Ged, everyone else does,' he said. 'And Korn is the nearest and simplest version of my real surname – the original has got a lot of S's and Z's in it, put it that way. It's a good job we left it behind in Lithuania!' They both laughed. On subsequent visits to the park, they often chatted. Herbert referred to him playfully as Mr Korn, and Ged reciprocated by calling him Mr Bert. Herbert thought it fascinating that, although they should dress so unalike and come from such different backgrounds, the Jew-boys (a term not used pejoratively at the time) had the same north Manchester accent as he did, and were 'as Mancunian as can be'. Another of his favourite adages was that 'it takes all sorts to make the world go round'.

Chapter Six

This country is at war with Germany

The slow-slow-quick march to hostilities was without the fervour and flag-waving that had engulfed the country at the outbreak of World War One, during which more than 880,000 British soldiers died on the battlefields or later from their injuries. On a single day in northern France – Saturday, 1 July 1916, the first day of the Battle of the Somme – 19,240 British soldiers were killed and 57,470 injured. In total, 12.5 per cent of all those who had served in World War One did not return home; Herbert's father was among the fallen, of course. While many army veterans working at CPA were reluctant to reveal details, Herbert had been chilled by their terse, abridged vocabulary of war. These salt-of-the-earth men, to whom understatement was worn as an overcoat, had described their experiences variously as horrendous, gut-wrenching and, most graphically, 'hell on earth'.

Newspapers described Germany's policy as 'expansionism', which Herbert and others took to mean that if Hitler and his armed forces were not resisted and repelled they would eventually invade and plunder Britain, inflicting a subservient way of life on the population. A poll revealed that 83 per cent of British people felt involvement in another conflict would be justified. The measured move to war was evident in Middleton as elsewhere. Trial blackouts were held over two nights in May and several more in August 1939, with an ARP (Air Raid Precaution) warden posted at the corner of Cross Street and another at Burton Street. Arthur Horridge, owner of Horridge's electrical store, allowed his premises in Wood Street to become the site of emergency telephones. Lords of Middleton did the same at their butcher's shop in Old Hall Street. The Women's Voluntary Service re-opened its headquarters within the gas showroom in Long Street. Middleton Corporation ordered 200,000 sandbags and began training schoolteachers to become ARP wardens. A water tank was installed at St Leonard's in case the parish church, dating back to 1412, caught fire in a bombing raid; police officers were called several times to reprimand children jumping in and out of the tank.

War was declared at 11.15am on Sunday, 3 September 1939. 'This country is at war with Germany,' announced Neville Chamberlain in a five-minute speech broadcast on the BBC Home Service. 'It is the evil things that we will be fighting against – brute force, bad faith, injustice, oppression and persecution,' he added. Two days earlier, Germany had invaded Poland, a country which, the same as Greece and Romania, Britain had pledged to support. The outbreak of war coincided with Wakes week in Middleton, when mills and factories shut down, and people boarded trains to holiday resorts such as

Blackpool, Morecambe and Fleetwood. Most came back early to enable children evacuated from industrial areas to take up their rooms at hotels and holiday camps by the seaside. The Rector of Middleton, Thomas Sherwood Jones, announced that 'Nowster', the name given to the bell at St Leonard's, would no longer toll between 9.50pm and 10pm each day, as it had for as long as anyone could remember; it would sound again only to warn of an invasion or the end of the war. The National Service (Armed Forces) Act was passed, making it compulsory for men aged 18 to 41 to join the forces. Herbert was prepared and fully expected to serve his country, but was thwarted.

Then came the call-up of all military forces. After a few weeks in various barracks, some of us were brought together, wondering what would be happening. Several names were shouted out, including mine. To our surprise we were told that we were going home because we were needed in civil employment. Mine was to do with metal. I was an oxyacetylene metal cutter, working on dismantling heavy machinery. This would be useful to the war effort. I, of course, wanted to have a go at these Nazi people. Perhaps I was selfish, not thinking that if I joined up I would be leaving behind my wife and three children. I was given a certificate saying I was required in civil employment.

More than five million men were exempt from military service, among them dockers and railway workers, teachers, police officers, doctors, bakers, clergymen, farmers and agricultural workers.

Mechanics and engineers such as Herbert were also excluded if their particular skills were considered more useful to the war effort than in the services. Herbert was of a small number of men of 'fighting age' from Rhodes who had not been enlisted. Posters began to appear on noticeboards in Middleton. 'England Expects' was written above a depiction of Britannia defiantly holding her trident and shield, bearing the Union Jack insignia. Another carried outlines of shadowy figures wearing spiked *Pickelhaube* helmets advancing towards bayonets: 'We beat 'em before, we'll beat 'em again.' The *Middleton Guardian* rallied townsfolk in a leader published six days after the declaration of war. The tone of authority and solemnity was such that it might have been carried in *The Times*:

'*Fortis in Arduis*' – 'courageous in adversity.' That is the motto on Middleton's coat of arms. There is a living force and gusty life in that motto which has made it peculiarly apt in these dark days. We have been living in the shadows, a world of half realities, and with the war has come a strange and paradoxical feeling that the worst has happened and we shall acquit ourselves in the trials before us in the spirit of the motto of this ancient town of ours.

We came back to work this week after the Wakes holidays in a strange and changing town. The boundaries have shrunk. We seem one family. The barriers are down and from now on there will be work for all to do. It will be done. There is unanimity of opinion we have never known before. There is an absence of hate against the German people that evidences an encouraging sanity of outlook.

We have lived while history was being made, and we have heard speeches made by the men we have elected to govern us that echo our own thoughts and put into words things which we know in our hearts and minds, but are too inarticulate to utter. One man is our enemy, and that man will go the way of all tyrants the world has ever known. He has a bill to settle. As the days go by we shall accommodate ourselves to changed conditions. Already we carry our gas masks as naturally as we put on trousers on rising from bed. We have declined to be rushed. We have shopped normally, and the shopkeepers have not been besieged.

A discipline has been self-imposed more effective than any governmental decree could secure. Keep a good heart, we are going to win through! Of course we shall; life would not be worth living, a world under the Nazi heel, degraded and enslaved. We have little to lose. Our very lives are not ours, but England's. And this old and pleasant land of ours is worth more than we could ever pay. It is not perfect, God knows. There is poverty and grime, misery and unemployment. But they are problems we are solving and will yet solve, and are only a small part of the picture. We all think of England in a different way. Our own bit is Middleton. It is England in miniature. Our men fought at Flodden [the Battle of Flodden in 1513 when the English were victorious against the Scottish and French], they died for liberty at Peterloo. Our roots are in the England of Old Bess [nickname of Queen Elizabeth I].

Herbert, at 27, began to feel conspicuous as he undertook his routine walks around Rhodes and Middleton. The area comprised mainly unskilled workers who had been eligible almost en masse to serve their country. This meant that men of a similar age to Herbert were either at training camps or, when back home, usually seen in uniform. He was chastened making his way through quiet streets, letting on to old folks or women, second-guessing what they might be thinking: why aren't you away, getting ready to fight the Germans? He wasn't a 'shit house', a phrase he had heard used to describe a local man who had erroneously claimed to have had a 'dicky back' in an attempt to avoid enlisting; a few weeks earlier he had played for Rhodes Villa FC. Herbert was compelled to tell them the reason he was still walking these wartime streets, but prided himself on his integrity and guarded his privacy: *what's it got to do with you?*

Unusually, he found himself thinking about his father. As an adult, and especially since having children himself, Herbert had become increasingly aware of all that they had not shared, the small joys – a walk together, fishing at Rhodes lodges, a cup of tea in a café – and then the big events: his marriage to Grace, the birth of his children. He was conflicted. His emotions were further muddled with the birth, in October 1939, of Edith, their third child. He recognised that caring for two toddlers and a new baby was an onerous task for Grace to shoulder on her own. Over several weeks he had a strong pull to take advantage of his reserved occupation status and remain with his young family. But, he told himself, plenty of others had children, especially his Catholic workmates who traditionally had large families, and they'd gone off to prepare for war. Much the same as his father, he was convinced that 'one last smack on the snout of Jerry' and he'd be back home enjoying peace for the rest of his days. And wasn't it a different war to the one in which his father had fought? On the radio it was rendered constantly as being *strategic*, distinct from the crude annihilation of World War One, where a bullet or shell seemed to be primed for every soldier. He redoubled his efforts to enlist.

I could not rest, so I kept trying to volunteer, to no avail. Soon, all men came to the reporting system on what kind of work you did. I went to report, though I didn't need to. I told them I was a truck driver. Later, I was called up. My wife never really forgave me for doing that.

Herbert began basic training at Victoria Barracks in Beverley, East Riding, located on a hillside on the outskirts of town and known for its microclimate of almost continual wind and rain. He rode the 85 miles from Middleton on his newly acquired motorcycle, taking a short detour to visit Selby Abbey; he'd read about its Benedictine origins in a magazine article. The journey was fraught with the huge kitbag on his back; he'd slipped his arms through the handles and 'worn' it as he might a rucksack, mindful to stay balanced. When he arrived at the barracks, construction work was underway for a large camp of huts in an adjoining field to accommodate extra soldiers.

He was already acquainted with the composition of army life through his time in the TA. On parade, he made sure his kit was in pristine condition with the brasses glinting, boots polished, webbing perfectly Blancoed (Blanco was a compound used to clean, colour and waterproof), and bayonet shining. He had learned the etiquette of interaction with higher ranks: play it straight, no back chat, don't seek to ingratiate. Before leaving for Beverley, Grace had asked Herbert what he was looking forward to the most. He told her it was 'a good night's sleep'; the children had gone through the usual round of illnesses that had seen them awake and crying through the night. He didn't get his wish. In fact, it was a feature he mentioned often when asked about army life: the noise men made while sleeping. They snored, they croaked, they gagged, they wheezed and some ground their teeth so much that he expected they would spit them out as broken mints in the morning. Others chunnered, shouted or screamed. There was always a regular 'midnight choir' of farting, followed by cheers as to the vigour or tuning. If still awake, Herbert soon learned to duck under the covers whenever he heard movement from one of the bunks; the 'piss-pot strollers' didn't always find the latrine in the dead of night.

He was also familiar with parade ground culture and saw it played out in the first few days of arriving at Beverley. The sergeant, a thickset Scotsman, picked out his scapegoat – a tall, thin lad from Barnsley, or, in the corporal's words, 'a lanky streak of piss'. He was mocked for his accent – 'Ow do', 'reet' and 'nah then' – and ordered to speak the King's English or 'shut the fuck up'. Herbert understood that this bullying served as a warning to the rest of the platoon and was believed to be to everyone's benefit: the weak would become stronger through humiliation, broken down to be reassembled by the routine and communality of army life, therefore strengthening the whole group.

Officers quickly noted Herbert's aptitude with a gun. He had handled them at the TA's rifle range based in the drill hall at Middleton. 'I love the shooting but can't abide the smell,' Herbert used to complain when he returned home from the hall. He was referring to the nearby Tonge Dye Works. Fumes belched out of its tall chimney, dispersing chemicals and toxins, painting trees and hedges at the back of the hall a terracotta colour, as if they were rusting; for the rest of his life Herbert would associate guns with a 'chemically' smell. He was asked at Beverley to show others how to use the Short Magazine Lee–Enfield (S-M-L-E, or 'Smelly' for short), a bolt-action, magazine-fed repeater rifle. Another tip that Herbert was able to share with them was the mnemonic BRASS: Breathe, Relax, Aim, Squeeze (the trigger) and Squeeze the trigger again, for follow-through.

Most had no experience of guns and were timorous around them, closing their eyes when they pulled the trigger and wincing as the bullet left the barrel. Herbert noticed a few rubbing their shoulders afterwards, griping that the recoil had more force than they had expected. He offered encouragement: 'You'll soon get the hang of it, lad.' He'd walk along the line of soldiers and repeat the same mantra every few yards: 'Grab the stock firmly but hold the gun comfortably. Position your fingertip gently on the trigger. Squeeze it without jarring the gun by applying slow, steady pressure until it fires. Remember, if you jerk the trigger, you'll miss your target.' He was at his most exultant, exhibiting a learned skill allied to his bent for engineering. 'How come you get to do this?' asked one of the soldiers. 'Probably because I'm older than most of you lot and I've got a rough idea what I'm doing!'

One of the young recruits had been given the nickname Yokey because, coming from Norfolk and speaking with a strong accent, he was reasoned to be a yokel. He lived on a farm in a hamlet called Bittering, a place name that always made Herbert smile when he later retold the story. He was expecting Yokey to be competent with a gun but he invariably missed the target. 'Doesn't your dad have you shooting rats and mice on the farm?' asked Herbert. Yokey said that he did. 'And do you hit them or keep missing them like you're doing here?' 'I hit them every time,' he answered. 'Well, that's a mystery,' said Herbert. After the session, Yokey told Herbert that his father had advised him to deliberately conceal his gunmanship. Herbert was baffled. 'If they find out I can shoot,' he explained, 'they'll make me a sniper and snipers always get killed in battle.' The revelation stuck with Herbert; it was the first time he had encountered subterfuge in the army and it made him ponder on whether, in contrast, he was too willing, too trusting.

While at the barracks another of Herbert's talents was noted:

Then one day while doing our physical training I was ahead of the others, younger men than me. I had since the age of 12 been interested and, in fact, kept myself fit and knew quite a lot on physical training. So that day I was chosen to help train those men who were way behind in that line and bring them up to standard, joining the others. I really enjoyed my job.

The Scottish sergeant had warmed to Herbert, though he would pull rank by calling him 'Sonny' or 'Sherbert'. One afternoon, Herbert had set the platoon off on a five-lap run of the parade ground in their gym kits. 'Look at them fucking hot-heads,' said the sergeant. Herbert asked what he meant. 'Those lemons at the front. They'll be whacked out in no time, breathing through their arses. No discipline. They'd be useless in battle.' He then pointed to the stragglers at the back: 'Lazy bastards. Wouldn't want them by my side trying to heave our way through mud and shit with Jerry at our heels.' He fell quiet for a few seconds before starting up again: 'But, Sherbert, those we most have to watch out for are those sneaky, conniving bastards who have tucked themselves in the middle of the pack, coasting, hiding, just doing enough. They're the fuckers who'll put a bullet in your back and piss off into the woods, given half a chance.' Herbert wasn't sure if it was a joke – the sergeant had formed a rationale to vilify every single soldier. Herbert pointed this out. 'So what? I hate them all,' the sergeant responded. 'I hate the Germans. I hate war. I hate Glasgow Celtic Football Club. And I want to go home as soon as fucking possible.' Later, in retelling the tale, Herbert couldn't recall the sergeant's name but said that, while he was the most cynical man he had ever met, he was also one of the funniest. 'The army's like that,' he would say. 'All sorts of rum buggers thrown together.'

Chapter Seven
Packing and unpacking a kitbag

———

Unlike those who had served in World War One, most men of Herbert's generation did not 'go off' to war, at least not for the first three years of its duration. Instead, they were taught skills and their fitness maintained in readiness for strategic deployment. The 1914–18 war had been a struggle of attrition and artillery, set within established battlefields where soldiers fought in trenches using the industrial might of machine guns, field guns, grenades, shells and poisonous gas. Winston Churchill, who became prime minister in May 1940, told Parliament: 'In the last war, millions of men fought by hurling enormous masses of steel at one another. "Men and shells" was the cry and prodigious slaughter was the consequence. In this war nothing of this kind has yet happened. It is a conflict of strategy, of organisation, of technical apparatus, of science, mechanics and morale.' He was citing advances in communications and weaponry. Armed forces would engage in 'theatres of war' – the Germans devised the term *Blitzkrieg* ('Lightning War') to describe high-speed mechanised warfare in a particular area – and civilians in their own countries were also deemed legitimate targets, through aerial bombing. 'The whole of the warring nations are engaged, not only soldiers but the entire population: men, women and children,' said Churchill. 'The fronts are everywhere. The trenches are dug in the towns and streets. Every village is fortified. Every road is barred. The frontline runs through the factories. The workmen are soldiers with different weapons but the same courage.'

The declaration of war had minimal impact in the first eight months, a period known as 'the phoney war'. The French dubbed it a *drôle de guerre* (funny war), and the Germans, *Sitzkrieg* (sitting war). This ended on 10 May 1940 with Germany's invasion of France and the Low Countries – Belgium, the Netherlands and Luxembourg – which pushed the British Expeditionary Force (BEF, the British Army's fully trained soldiers), along with French and Belgian troops, back to the French port of Dunkirk. A huge rescue mission known as 'Operation Dynamo' began on 26 May, organised by the Royal Navy, to bring soldiers back to Britain. Shallow coastal waters meant that warships were limited to picking up soldiers from the East Mole, a narrow 1,400-yard breakwater made of concrete and wood at Dunkirk Port. The British Admiralty appealed to owners of small boats to help with the evacuation and more than 800 vessels transported troops across the English Channel. These were known as 'little ships' and, eight days after the operation had begun, the last of nearly 340,000 soldiers arrived home. Although the British Army had been in retreat, the episode was perceived as a triumph for morale because very few were killed and the rallying call to ship owners was viewed as a summons to the wider population; it forged the 'Dunkirk Spirit'.

On a Sunday outing to Heaton Park, Herbert saw Mr Korn with his family. He noticed that there were more Jewish people than usual. Herbert had an idea why this was the case but asked all the same. 'It's getting bad over there, Bert. These are the lucky buggers who've managed to get out. Laski is doing his best to get more over.' Herbert asked who Laski was and was told that he was Nathan Laski, the president of Manchester's Jewish Representative Council. 'He's Polack. Bit of a stubborn bugger, fancies himself, but at least he's pulling his finger out and having a go,' explained Mr Korn. At the start of the war more than 70,000 Jews had been accepted into Britain and they had confirmed the incremental nature of their persecution under the Nazis. On 9 and 10 November 1938, pogroms had been carried out across Germany, Austria and the Sudetenland that led to the murder of almost 100 Jews, the destruction of 267 synagogues, and 30,000 arrested and taken to concentration camps. It became known as *Kristallnacht* and the 'Night of Broken Glass' because streets had been left deep in shards of glass after the violence, vandalism and looting; many considered it to be the authentic beginning of the Holocaust.

On leave from spells at training camps, Herbert was astounded to find members of the British Union of Fascists (BUF) literally at his front door: had they no shame? The BUF was canvassing in Rhodes for a forthcoming parliamentary by-election. The standing MP for Middleton and Prestwich, Nairne Stewart Sandeman, a

Conservative, had died after suffering a fractured skull when knocked down by a car. The major parties had made a pact that a successor to a deceased MP would stand unopposed during wartime, but the BUF put forward Frederick Haslam, a 43-year-old design engineer with a distinguished record in World War One; this was highlighted to appeal to the patriotic instincts of voters. Across the country, membership of the BUF was said to have risen to 50,000. Oswald Mosley visited Middleton in May 1940 where he was due to speak in support of Haslam from a flatbed lorry parked in Market Street. Before Mosley's arrival, anti-fascist slogans had been daubed on factory walls. He had barely started when he was pelted with bricks and had to scurry into the Middleton Corporation Electric Showroom; several people later appeared in court charged with affray.

Ernest Gates, the Conservative candidate, received 32,036 votes, compared to Haslam's 418. The 97.4 per cent majority remains the highest of any contested British parliamentary by-election. Unlike other sectors of Europe, Britain had retreated to traditionalism during the volatility of the 1930s. The winning candidate, Ernest *Everard* Gates, was archetypically Establishment. His father was managing director of Saltaire Mill in West Riding and the family owned a country house with a croquet lawn. He had been waved off to Cambridge University in a Bentley bought for him by his father and, at 22, had inherited Old Buckenham Hall in Norfolk. Meanwhile, Frederick Haslam, the defeated BUF candidate, was arrested and interned in the Isle of Man. The government had introduced Defence Regulation 18B which allowed British citizens to be imprisoned without charge, trial or right of judicial appeal, if the Home Secretary believed their liberty was 'not in the national interest'. Herbert was pleased. He told neighbours that only 'a wrong 'un' or 'someone not right in the head' would knock on doors with such a message, considering all that was going on in the world.

In the summer of 1940, the Luftwaffe (the German air force) had five times as many aeroplanes and pilots as the RAF. In preparation for a ground invasion, Germany attempted to gain air superiority in the 'Battle of Britain' which lasted from 10 July to 31 October 1940. Thousands of skirmishes took place over the English Channel and southern England, during which 2,500 German aircrew and 544 RAF Fighter Command pilots were killed. The victory for Britain was due largely to the Dowding radar system, devised by the RAF a few months before the war, which gave pilots advanced warning to intercept raids. Afterwards, Churchill paraphrased the St Crispin's Day Speech given by the king in Shakespeare's *Henry V*: 'Never, in the field of human conflict, was so much owed by so many to so few.'

Manchester was an obvious target for air strikes, especially the industrial hub of Trafford Park where more than 70,000 people were employed, close to the vital transport links of the Bridgewater Canal and Manchester Ship Canal. The most devastating bombing occurred on two consecutive nights in December 1940 when almost 700 people were killed and 2,000 injured. Two of the city's most historic buildings were damaged, the Free Trade Hall and

Manchester Cathedral, and parts of the city centre was reduced to rubble, closing off main thoroughfares including Deansgate and Oxford Street. When the sirens stopped each night, families from Middleton would congregate at street corners, looking across to the city skyline a few miles away where fires were burning.

Herbert spent much of his time packing and unpacking a kitbag, either heading to or returning from one of the hundreds of army camps, from the Scottish Highlands to Cornwall. On home visits, he said a few times that 'everything has changed but nothing has changed'. The 'everything' was the regular blackouts, sirens wailing, scurrying footsteps as people raced to shelters. And then the waiting, the anxiety, the fear. Come the morning, if there hadn't been any bombs dropped, it felt as if the night before had been a dream. The 'nothing' was cars travelling down Manchester Old Road, dogs barking, the flow of the River Irk, trees bare or flushed green to reflect the season, and people nodding or stopping to chat: life going on as ever before.

Families had quickly become accustomed to sleeping in their cellar or Anderson shelter – a curved structure made from corrugated steel panels dug into the ground and covered with sandbags and soil; by March 1940, 600 had been delivered to homes in Middleton, with 300 more on the way. The town was outside the Manchester evacuation area, so its 3,500 children remained at home with their parents. They still attended school, though the day was sometimes interrupted by air raids when they were led to trenches installed on the school field or nearby land.

These were open 'slit' trenches, offering no protection from a direct hit but shielding them from flying debris. A similar trench was dug for civilians at Market Place in the town centre, but letters appeared in the *Middleton Guardian* questioning its effectiveness. After several weeks of debate, the consensus was that the country was new to war and 'everyone was doing their best'. Geoff Wellens of the long-standing Middleton family of undertakers was taken as a baby to an unusual location for safety. The family lived above their business premises at 54 Long Street and when sirens sounded, they decamped to the cellar and slept on coffin racks.

Middleton was not a target particularly but because it was surrounded by farmland and countryside to the east and north, German pilots would double-back and bank over the region after dropping bombs on Manchester or Liverpool; this meant they frequently released excess shells over the town. One landed on Manchester Old Road, close to North Manchester Golf Club, fracturing a main water pipe and bursting the banks of Rhodes lodges. Seven bombs were dropped on houses in Middleton Junction but none exploded; locals named the area 'Holy City' to mark its good fortune. The pilots had probably been targeting the nearby A.V. Roe & Company, the aircraft manufacturer in Chadderton, Oldham, where Lancaster Bombers were assembled.

One night, residents in Hebers, Middleton, heard the sound of a V-1 flying bomb, known as a doodlebug and an early example of a cruise missile. They ran for cover but it sailed overhead and continued its journey to Lees, Oldham, where it hit a row of terraced houses, killing 27 people. Another time, a German fighter swooped down over Slattocks on the Middleton–Rochdale border and aimed machine-gun fire at a farmer ploughing a field. A similar attack was carried out on a couple of five-year-olds while they were on their lunch break from Parkfield Junior School, Middleton in 1942. 'I went to play with my friend Rita McCleary at some land known to us as "Sand Hills" on spare ground,' said Jean Faulkner (née Biltcliffe). 'We heard a loud noise, looked up and saw a plane swooping down on us with German crosses [*Balkenkreuz*, an adapted version of the Iron Cross] on it. We dived into the hole we had dug and the plane started to fire at us before gathering height and zooming off.' [1]

The most serious wartime incident in Middleton was an attack in March 1941 on an RAF base about a mile from Rhodes, at Bowlee on the border with Heywood. The base was a storage and maintenance depot for barrage balloons. These huge inflatables were used as a deterrent to stop pilots flying low over intended targets. Planes could become caught up in cables that tethered the balloons to the ground, so, to avoid them, they flew at a higher altitude, putting themselves at risk from larger calibre anti-aircraft gunfire. The daylight raid was carried out by a pilot belonging to the elite Luftwaffe aircrew called 'Experten'. He released nine 50 Kilo HE (high explosive) bombs and about a dozen IBs (incendiaries) from his Junkers Ju 88 combat aircraft, killing an airman and airwoman, and seriously injuring four others.

The precision of the attack at Bowlee unnerved locals: how had the Germans become aware of such a relatively small RAF station on fields 'in the middle of nowhere'? The Home Front propaganda posters fastened to walls in local pubs took on a greater poignancy: 'Loose talk can cost lives' and 'Furtive Fritz is always listening; be careful of what you say'. The *Middleton Guardian* began reporting in code, knowing that locals would decipher it easily, while hoping to confound 'agents of the enemy'. Rhodes became known as 'North Western Village'. A typical article read: 'On Sunday the people of a certain North Western Village spent a very disturbed night. There was a sequence of "alerts" which lasted until nearly dawn. Then, shortly after three o'clock, a whining scream could be heard followed by an enormous explosion.' A bomb had been dropped near a footpath, causing a crater of about 18 feet in diameter. The paper sent out a reporter to gauge the reaction of residents. The piece read: 'A tenant who escaped with broken house windows, jokingly told our representative, "Tell them we can take it."'

Herbert was ambivalent about the prevailing spirit of 'life must go on'. He'd note the forthcoming events publicised around town. In one particular week this amounted to a Grand All-Star Concert at the Queen's Park Hippodrome in Turkey Lane, Harpurhey; dance sessions at Middleton Baths (Old Time on Thursdays, 7.30pm until 11pm); Frank Randle starring in *Mother Goose* at the Empire, Oldham; film shows at the Palace Cinema (*Summer on the Farm* and *Workers and the War Front*, courtesy of the Ministry of Information) and, at Grotton Lido in Saddleworth ('the local pleasure beach'), an appearance by the Barton Hall Works Band. On Christmas Eve of 1941, the Glen Gray Band appeared at the Baths Ballroom in Middleton with more than a thousand in attendance. They broke out into samba rhythms which, according to the *Middleton Guardian*, led to an outbreak of 'a new dance called the "Conga"'. Herbert would exclaim, 'Don't they know there's a bloody war on?' before conceding that, 'I suppose acting on as normal is the best way to show 'em we won't be beat.'

Although he didn't attend himself, Herbert was pleased that 'at least some folks are trying to work out what's going on'. Meetings were held regularly in public halls in Middleton. Mabel Tylecote spoke at St Gabriel's Schoolroom in Tonge on 'Labour's Programme' and was joined by another Labour activist, George Cornes, to cover the same subject at the New Jerusalem Church, Rhodes. Joseph Belina, billed as a 'Czech Trade Union Leader', spoke on 'Trade Unionism Under Nazi Rule' at the Co-Operative Hall in Long Street.

Hundreds of men in Middleton joined the Local Defence Volunteers (LDV), known colloquially as Look, Duck and Vanish. At the order of Winston Churchill, the name was changed to the Home Guard. More than 1.5 million signed up across the country. These were either too young or too old to serve in the regular services, or they worked in a reserved occupation. They were charged with enforcing curfew and blackout laws, and were to act as a defence force if the country was invaded.

The Home Guard in Middleton was affiliated to the Lancashire Fusiliers and known officially as the 65th (Middleton) Battalion. They were each given a khaki uniform, a pair of binoculars and a 'practice' rifle made of wood. One of their first jobs was to paint markers on kerbs and trees, so that people could find their way home in the blackout. Within weeks, a strong community spirit was forged as they met up for training in church halls, parks and school fields. As a show of solidarity and reassurance, they marched regularly through the town. A special camp was held at Ashworth Valley in the west Pennine hills above Rochdale and Bury. Many had not been out in the countryside since childhood and made new friends as they gathered around crackling campfires, boiling stew in huge pans. They were photographed by the *Heywood Advertiser*. Thomas Varley, from Alkrington, Middleton, summed up how many were feeling: 'I've met some good lads here and enjoyed myself. It might seem an odd thing to say when we've got a war on, but we're better prepared for it in good spirits rather than moping.' Herbert, similar to many full-time soldiers, was often condescending about them. He arrived home peeved one evening. 'I've just been stopped and asked to show my papers by Albert Fletcher, that trumped-up little sod from Boarshaw. He thinks he's a general, now they've put him in uniform, given him a broomstick and told him to pretend it's a gun. He's not a full shilling, that lad. He's of more use to Hitler, than he is our lot,' he said.

Chapter Eight

All hell broke loose on that gun

The streets in Middleton were packed. The coffin, draped in a Union Jack, passed by, carried on a gun carriage. Herbert was among those standing on the pavement, head bowed. He was pleased that his leave had coincided with the funeral of Harry Lee. Harry, 23 years old, was the first soldier from Middleton to die in World War Two. He had been serving with the Royal Artillery, taking part in a training exercise with a dozen others in May 1941. Much the same as Herbert and the new recruits at Beverley, they had been learning how to handle guns in a restricted space. The weapons were supposed to be unloaded but one contained a bullet which was fired and hit Harry in the neck, killing him instantly. Herbert didn't know him personally but was aware that he was one of four brothers serving in the army. They had all been members of the Church Lads Brigade at St Michael's, Middleton. While on leave, Herbert was pleased to be able to help Grace around the house and with the children; she was seven months pregnant. She gave birth to their first son in July 1941.

OPENING THE GATES OF HELL

He was given the same name as his father and grandfather: Herbert.

The death and funeral of Harry Lee served to further unite the town. Scores more volunteered to join the Home Guard. Scrap metal and wastepaper was donated to the salvage appeal, items to be recycled for the war effort. The Mayor's Spitfire Fund was a huge success with almost £350,000 invested in government savings bonds to purchase weaponry. Whist drives were held twice a week at the Rhodes Church School with whip-rounds 'to provide cigarettes and other needed comforts for the lads of our village now serving in His Majesty's Forces'. Food rationing had begun in January 1940, and clothing in June 1941. The public was encouraged to make or repair clothes, grow food and rear livestock. The Ministry of Agriculture took out adverts in newspapers with details of 'What to do . . . to get 15lbs extra meat in a year.' People were advised to breed and slaughter rabbits in their back yard or garden for 'nourishing and tasty food over and above the normal meat ration'. The Bury Area Butchers' Buying Committee, which included butchers from Middleton, advised that it could still supply meat but 'owing to the shortage of beef, customers are respectfully asked to take lamb and mutton. Beef is required for our Fighting Services.' An appeal for volunteers to staff a British Restaurant at the school room at Providence United Reformed Church was vastly over-subscribed; more than 2,000 of these community restaurants had opened to cater for those who had been bombed out or found themselves without enough food.

★

In his civilian workplace Herbert had felt largely inconspicuous. He was recognised as a grafter, with his speed and standard of work noted, but he blended in among the fawn coats and boiler suits, lost amid the grunting of machinery, the drilling and banging, the popping and sizzling of welding torches. As a soldier, he had expected to feel similarly but found himself increasingly praised and singled out, asked to share his expertise with others.

He began to receive offers, in person or by letter, to help train recruits in gunmanship or PE.

> I received quite a number of letters from different units and took up some of the offers. I did just that, but one of my officers was upset and said I was a fool for going and would be sorry I went. I later remembered his words.

Herbert, keen to learn new skills, undertook training in driving light and heavy vehicles at Somme Barracks, Sheffield, before being offered a place on another course.

> I was at a loose end for a few days, then an officer asked if I would be interested in motorcycle riding. I had one at home. I said yes! So away I was, on a dispatch riding course, quite a tough one at that, some very rough riding was involved. I passed first-class.

The training for dispatch riders (DRs, sometimes known as 'Don Roberts') began on the parade ground at the barracks. The first session was dedicated to 'Know Your Machine'. Most already owned or had ridden motorcycles but the officer still ran through the basics. Afterwards, he handed each of them a regimen, listed alphabetically, and ordered them to 'remember it, because your life might depend on it one day'. Herbert was conscientious and put it in the back pocket of his trousers. He'd retrieve it from there frequently, mainly for reassurance that he had everything covered: air filters, battery, brakes and brake pads, carburettor (keep clean), chain (check and lubricate), coolant, drive chain, fuel hose, grease bearings, oil, spark plugs, tyre pressure.

Traffic cones were placed on the tarmac and they had to manoeuvre around them, slowly at first but then picking up speed. The officer carried a clipboard and was constantly taking notes. He'd break off to shout, 'It's all going in here, lads,' pointing to his scribblings. After a couple of hours, he made them gather around him. He told them he'd written down three columns, each comprising a list of names: he'd made a similar analysis as the Scottish sergeant had done when observing the runners. 'Right, do you want to know what each of you are?' he asked. They chorused a loud, 'Yes, Sir'. He proceeded to reveal the *Steadie Eddies* ('so bloody slow, the war would be over by the time they'd got there . . .'), the *Jitterbugs* ('they'd be off the road and in a ditch in five minutes') and the *Spot-Ons* ('lads who might possibly turn out to be half-decent dispatch riders'). Herbert was a *spot-on* and, with five or six others, was told the course would continue 'over there, in the muck' – the instructor pointed in the rough direction of the Peak District.

Over the next month, Herbert regularly set out over rough moorland, forming a crocodile line with other riders behind the instructor as he picked out paths strewn with boulders and fallen branches, dipping down to fords deep in murky water. 'Nice and inclement' was the instructor's cry as he appeared to choose days when they seemed to be submerged in rainclouds, the wind zipping across bracken. They were trailed by a Bedford QL truck, though it was unable to traverse the steeper slopes which meant they sometimes had to push their damaged or stalled motorcycle a mile or so, and load it on to the vehicle. 'Careful at all times, no one wants a truck stop,' shouted the instructor, acknowledging the immense effort required to push a motorcycle through a squelchy bog.

Next, I took a map reading course. I enjoyed that, too. It involved European map reading. I passed that first-class. I had plenty of time on my hands again. I was there for three months, then to a transport unit, that was the 35th Coy, R.A.S.C. [the Royal Army Service Corps, responsible for keeping the army supplied with provisions – food, water, fuel etc.]. I did a lot of vehicle work there, then given a motorbike of my own. We went out on lots of training in different areas. This went on until we moved south in early 1944, down into Kent, continuing our work for what might come later.

Herbert passed his army medical and was declared to be A1 and FFI – fit for active service and free from infection; this would contrast markedly to his status of health after the war. On the day of his medical, Herbert had learned that Grace was pregnant again with their fifth child. Linda would be born in October 1944 while he was away at war. By now, Herbert was familiar with the fastidiousness of army procedure. He slept in a hut containing 20 two-tier bunks. At reveille they had to fold their blankets and lay their kit out on the bed for inspection. Everything had to be spotless. They were ordered to scrub the floor and walls. If a speck of dust was found, even beneath the beds, they were yelled at to clean it, *this minute.* They were drilled from 6am until 8am and told to move everywhere 'at the double' – twice as quickly as they would normally walk. They were marched to the parade ground, the cookhouse, the shower block (where the water was invariably ice-cold) and to the camp barber where most received a 'number one', the clippers set to cut hair down to stubble. Dentists were kept busy at training camps. In peace time, people visited a dentist only when they had toothache, but the army was keen to ensure that soldiers were fit and well to remain on active service. They were ordered to brush their teeth daily. Any teeth with decay were extracted, sometimes without anaesthetic because the busy dentists could only spend a few minutes with each soldier.

While training, Herbert had found himself billeted at hotels, village halls, schools and private country houses; the army had a shortage of accommodation and, unlike the US Army, preferred not to establish 'tented cities' which might become targets for German air raids. Herbert was informed that, as a DR, he would be expected to hand-deliver messages that couldn't be transmitted by field telephone. He would also act as a pathfinder, riding ahead of the main unit. He was kitted out with a Colt 45 automatic pistol, breeches, a crash helmet, jerkin (sleeveless jacket), mackintosh coat, riding boots, gloves and goggles. He was given a booklet entitled 'France' which gave brief details about the country and the language, including how troops should behave when interacting with the civilian population; Herbert read it but considered most of it to be common sense. Finally, DRs were presented with 'commando equipment'. These were items designed to be hidden about their bodies to help escape if taken prisoner – a silk map that folded into a tiny square, several tiny compasses to sew into a uniform lining and a three-inch file. They were ready.

The leaders of the Allied Forces had accepted that an offensive strike had to be mounted to defeat Germany and liberate Europe. Operation Overlord began in the early hours of Tuesday, 6 June 1944, D-Day, when, under the cover of darkness, 18,000 paratroopers were dropped into Normandy from more than 1,200 aircraft. The largest ever naval bombardment saw the Allies use more than 5,000 ships and landing craft to deliver 156,000 troops on five Normandy beaches, code-named Utah, Omaha, Gold, Juno and Sword. They met fierce German resistance. More than 4,000 Allied soldiers were killed on D-Day and more than 5,000 wounded. The First Infantry of the US Army met particularly intense resistance across the six-mile stretch of Omaha beach, suffering 2,400 casualties.

The plan, after gaining control of 50 miles of beachfront, was to proceed through Normandy to the city of Caen, nine miles inland, and begin an incremental liberation of France. On the afternoon of 6 June, Winston Churchill sent a telegram to Joseph Stalin, leader of the Soviet Union, whose Red Army was pushing on from the east of France: 'Everything has started well. The mines, obstacles and land batteries have been largely overcome. The air landings were very successful and on a large scale. Infantry landings are proceeding rapidly and many tanks and self-propelled guns are already ashore.' He told Parliament that the operation was proceeding 'in a thoroughly satisfactory manner'.

> After hard work in special training, my part in the invasion of Normandy against the Nazi troops began three days after the first wave of liberation armies, navies, air forces, of ours and our Allies. We were not allowed to go on the D-Day mission because we were a different force of men. We were the supply force to the troops who had gone ahead to the landings. Everything was organised so that the supply could follow up in order to keep the first fighting men fed with ration of food and all essentials.

On Friday, 9 June 1944, Herbert boarded a Liberty ship to sail to Normandy. These huge vessels could carry almost 9,000 tons of cargo, the same weight as 300 railway trucks. They had been mass-produced quickly of low-cost construction with large sections welded together rather than riveted. A few hours before boarding, he was issued with a gas mask, hand grenades, two days' worth of food rations and a map of specific grid references.

> Previous to our going aboard, all our vehicles and equipment – in fact, everything we needed for our landing and establishment in Normandy – were taken aboard. This all went into one hold and

we went aboard into another hold, where there were hammocks for us to rest (when we could rest). There was not much space but we sorted ourselves out. We were well seasoned soldiers, so we did not look for comfort. There was grub in the way of quick-heating canned food, and tea, sugar, dried milk, to make a decent brew. This was the kind of food and drink that all the troops had, to help us carry on after our landings.

Dwight David 'Ike' Eisenhower, the Supreme Commander of the Allied Expeditionary Force, had earlier issued an Order of the Day to troops:

Soldiers, sailors and airmen of the Allied Expeditionary Force! You are about to embark upon the Great Crusade, toward which we have striven these many months. The eyes of the world are upon you. The hopes and prayers of liberty-loving people everywhere march with you. In company with our brave allies and brothers-in-arms on other fronts, you will bring about the destruction of the German war machine, the elimination of Nazi tyranny over the oppressed peoples of Europe, and security for ourselves in a free world.'

Commanding Officers (COs) of the British Army passed on a 'Message to the Troops' set out by Field Marshal Bernard Law Montgomery, the Commander in Chief of the Allied Ground Forces: 'If things go as planned, and every man does his job to the best of his ability, Germany will be out of the war by October or

November – and Japan six months later.' Soldiers around Herbert had barely boarded the ship when they began questioning the communiqué delivered from up on high. 'Did you notice those five words at the start – *if* things go as planned', said one. 'Things never go to plan, not in a war.' Another asked what Monty's role was, whether he'd been first on the beach when they reached Normandy. 'He'll be back in Blighty doing what he does', came the reply. 'And what's that?' 'Twiddling his moustache and polishing his big conk.' Herbert felt it disrespectful but found himself smiling; he knew he'd remember these conversations for the rest of his life.

Then to the sea. This was early morning. We were on our way to action one way or another. I think we were all a bit nervous but raring to go. We knew our enemy was on the other side and had to be dealt with, if we were lucky and with the grace of God. Once in the Channel, we were heading west and slightly south towards Normandy. The wind got up, a strong one at that, together with rain. The boat was rocking wildly at times. A lot of the lads were turning green and leaning over the side heaving. Some of the blokes lay on their hammocks staring at the cross beams – this upset their stomachs. Oh, what a mess. Luckily, me and a few more were okay. We were issued with tinned food and soup. The soup came in a tin where you pulled a short cord which ignited some of the tin, thus warming it up.

The gale had blown us off course. There we were, suddenly stuck on a sandbank. It seemed that the captain was a very old seaman and would not take advice from the second in command, who was a younger man with full knowledge. Someone told me the captain was an American, long retired, who'd volunteered to do the job. So there we were on a sandbank, suddenly hearing a loud crack. The deck opened up from starboard to port. Oh hell, we thought. This would happen to us: stuck on a sandbank and Jerry screaming down, guns blazing, diving away at us. Do not, for a moment, think that because men had gone ahead to make the landings, that it was easy for us. We, like the troops upfront, were under fire from the enemy aircraft and big guns. We were as prone to be hit and killed as our mates up forward. We lost some of our boys on the journey. There were pom-poms [QF 2-pounders, 40mm auto-cannon anti-aircraft guns, named after the sound they made when fired] on board and some of the crew manned them.

We were under attack for a while. Suddenly, one gun stopped. I went to take a look and both men manning it were laid out. I called to one of my mates, 'Come on, let's have a go.' A gunner came over from the hull and said, 'Do you know how to handle this?' I said, 'No'. 'Right,' he said. 'I'll show you.' He quickly did, showing us how to reload, and away we went, just as Jerry decided to have a go. We waited. Luckily, we lined up as one came in. I held on for a little while. He was rattling our screen. I pressed and all hell broke loose on that gun; it really needed some holding on to. A few planes flew right into our shots, dipping into the sea. First one down, we were dancing with pleasure. One down, hoping for another. Some of the other gunmen were lucky, too. We could not leave the ship while under fire, though. Suddenly, some of our fighters came along and chased Jerry away, and gave us cover. We waited a while with no more trouble. We decided to get off somehow. Over the side went the landing craft – huge rafts big enough to take our vehicles and other equipment. We lowered some boats. The rafts were used for our Bedford wagons to get them ashore.

I and some others went with the vehicles on the rafts. They were chained and made secure, except for one. Someone had been neglectful, so we lost a vehicle fully loaded. The sea was very rough and we were in trouble with not another ship in sight. We were being carried right off course. At last, we made it. The wrong beach but there was nowhere else we could land. It was a small beach [close to the village of Arromanches] which, to our surprise, seemed quiet.

Chapter Nine
One by one, the planes came in

As the landing soldiers made their way through the waves, water swelling up to their chests, they had expected to hear the rapid rattle of an MG machine gun, followed by its booming after-blast, or the pop-pop-ack of a Schmeisser – they had been briefed on their enemy's likely weapons. Herbert was incredulous that there was no machine-gun fire sweeping the beaches, though there was sporadic shelling. He had to resist the urge to duck for cover, knowing this would leave him under water, unable to see or breathe. The motorcycles were unloaded from a container and passed to the DRs as they neared the beach. Herbert focused on keeping the BSA (Birmingham Small Arms) M20 above the waves which were now at his knees. He held it side-on in front of him as if it were a shield, using all his strength, aided by the small amount of buoyancy provided by the water. He found himself talking to the machine: it's me and you now, girl.

Whenever he had gone off-road in England, he had been impressed by the BSA. The flywheels were bigger than on an earlier version and its lower compression ratio made it 'zippy'; the rider could pull away quickly in any gear. On the open road, with its 496cc four-stroke engine, it was sturdy, although Herbert and the other DRs were concerned that its weight might hinder manoeuvrability – the joke was that BSA stood for Big, Slow and Awkward. As he had expected, it took a great effort to push it through the watery sludge at the sea's edge but, fired by adrenalin, he heaved it until the tyres found purchase on the flatter, firmer sand and he was able to skip on to the seat and pull away.

> I found an opening that would take us off the beach, under the cover of some trees. I came to a sandy pathway wide enough for our vehicles. We made our way without hindrance for about half a mile and came to some countryside, small fields surrounded by trees. This was ideal for cover but we were still not sure what might lie ahead for us. We took it easy and moved as quietly as possible. We made camp in a field out of view of the roadway and assembled all the vehicles, leaving some men in charge of the camp as we went on a reconnaissance to see what was ahead. We saw a sign which said 'Sommervieu'. We took this to mean it was a holiday village or perhaps the name of a normal town; either way, a place where we should be heading to.

Sommervieu was a hamlet two miles from the coast with a population of about 300 people.

We came to the village. How many houses, I don't remember. There was a main street, all houses with the odd street running off. As we approached, there were some shots fired our way, without any of our men being hit. We decided our plan was to stay low and up against the house walls, keeping covering-fire on both sides of the street. We each had hand grenades with us. Some of us got to the first side street and met no opposing fire. We realised the gunfire was coming from rifles and not automatics. This meant to us that the main body of the enemy had left just before we had arrived. Not being sure who and what type of person was firing at us, we threw our grenades through the upstairs and downstairs windows under our own covering fire. This did the trick. There was some screaming, a woman's scream. Only then did we know who was firing at us. We were sorry to learn afterwards that two or three women had gone down from our fire and grenade attack. The women had been left there by the Nazis to slow us up. Some of the younger women had been having relationships with the Germans [The French referred to this as *collaboration horizontale*. These women, after liberation, were sometimes publicly humiliated. Their heads were shaved, their bodies daubed with swastikas and they were paraded through the streets.]

The French civilian population generally carried out their businesses as normal, some viewing it as a commercial opportunity, even in battle zones. The tabacs, shops selling tobacco products, did the most trade; cigarettes were a de facto currency during the war. Only minutes after an exchange of fire, soldiers in Herbert's unit 'gasping for a tab' would queue to buy cigarettes, patiently negotiating an on-the-spot exchange rate for the sterling in their pockets. Wounded soldiers were taken in by the French until medics arrived, usually following the trail of blood. After making camp, soldiers called at nearby farms in search of food to supplement rations; it was usually the first time either party had met a foreigner.

> Older women didn't put up any resistance and were glad to see us. The younger ones thought it was right to put up resistance because their men [German boyfriends] had asked them to do so. This was understandable but it would have been easier for them to come out into the open and there would have been no one hurt. And it should have been known that we, the British, were friends of France, not the real enemy, who had taken over their country. We were there to chase the enemy out, then go home to our own country.

The landing soldiers had faced comparatively limited opposition on the beaches around Arromanches, but still suffered losses and casualties; 652 Allied soldiers and 335 Germans were killed, most of them buried later at the Ryes War Cemetery in Bazenville. British soldiers left a permanent record of their brief stay at Sommervieu. They scribbled their names, girlfriends' and wives' names and favourite football clubs on a wall of a barn where they had bunked down. There was even a 'stag list' – army slang for the roster of men designated guard duty. Most were from the north-west of England. Two of them, signing themselves as J. Kendall and J. Bibby, both of Lancashire, recorded the date: 9 June 1944 – the day when, most likely, Herbert had also reached Sommervieu. The graffiti was uncovered when the barn was renovated in 2019.

Herbert spent four days at Sommervieu. The war diary of his unit, the RASC 8 Corps, revealed the regimented nature of a soldier's life.

6.30am – reveille

7.30am – breakfast

12.30pm – dinner

17.00pm – tea

20.00pm – guard mounting

21.00pm – lights out

While Herbert's unit moved on, the Royal Engineers 24th Airfield Construction Group remained to build a temporary aerodrome. In just over a week, two parallel airstrips were installed from compacted soil and a roll-down wire known as Square Mesh Track, or SMT. Herbert had seen the trucks arriving, loaded with heavy machinery, and was proud to be part of a team that had secured this small piece of land; it gave him heart for what lay ahead. His unit set off in the direction of Bayeux, a town four miles inland of about 10,000 people and the home of the famous Bayeux Tapestry.

★

Herbert took great care of his belongings. Back home at work, he was fastidious when handling the welding equipment. He didn't mind colleagues teasing him that he was 'by-the-book Bert'; he was secretly pleased. Although only days into active service, he had already formed a personal regime. Every night he wiped away mud and grit from his motorcycle with soapy water. He topped up the fuel. He polished the handlebars and the rest of the metalwork with dabs of Brasso. He had started to appreciate the robustness of the BSA. He'd been impressed that though it had received a 'good soaking' on the beach, it had fired up every time without a splutter. Most soldiers held an affection for the inanimate, often bestowing them with pet names – a rifle, a water bottle, an item of clothing – but a DR and his motorcycle was a special bond.

> We made for Bayeux, but with caution. Me and a couple of others rode ahead on our bikes. All went well. We thought ourselves lucky when we went in. The enemy had left some hours earlier.

The Germans, realising they would be considerably outnumbered, had left Bayeux soon after news reached them of the D-Day landings. The French Resistance had made this known to the Allies to avoid an unnecessary bombing campaign. Bayeux was strategically positioned, with thousands of soldiers and vehicles able to pass through to combat zones. The medieval streets were too narrow for most military vehicles, so engineers built a road around the centre. The Bayeux Tapestry was kept in an underground shelter at the Hôtel du Doyen, where it was unfurled every few weeks to check its state of conservation.

All was quiet. Maps were checked and we made our way towards Caen, which was some distance away [18 miles] but with a lot of open ground before it. There wasn't much cover there, if any [Caen and the area to its south were flatter and more open than the 'bocage' country in western Normandy, a terrain of mixed woodland and pasture]. There was nothing in sight for miles except signs of fires in the distance, and, of course, plenty of noise – gunfire and all the ingredients that go with it. Caen was under fire from our boys but we were also under serious fire. Jerry was well dug in and had gone to ground. They were giving us a rough time. The return fire was doing a lot of damage to our boys, some badly wounded and dying. Transport in the form of ambulances or any other way was used to bring lads back. There was a lot of blood lost while that fight was going on. I guess a lot was lost on the other side, too, but they could not be shifted from Caen.

The RASC, to which Herbert was assigned, was a logistics corps, and said, in military parlance, to be responsible for 'everything bar the shooting' – weaponry and ammunition was provided by the Royal Army Ordnance Corps. The RASC supplied food, water, fuel, clothing, furniture and the stationery required for essential paperwork. The corps was also accountable for land, coastal and lake transport. Historians, placing the RASC in a modern context, described it as 'a huge portable Amazon depot'. Films made after the war would suggest it was a conflict won through strategy, firepower and personal bravery. While these were vital components, another critical factor was the more mundane and routine function carried out by the RASC and its equivalent in other Allied forces. Soldiers were unable to fight without being clothed, fed and sheltered, and couldn't move without vehicles and fuel.

Days went by. Our platoon was back a bit and we were not allowed to go forward to help. We were mad, really mad, to think our boys were suffering like that, and we could not help in the fight. We had to be moving back and forth, picking up supplies of food, drink, whatever would be needed, and messages had to go back to keep HQ in the picture. I did a lot of riding, taking convoys of vehicles to base to pick up supplies and bring them back to our camp, which was established in a corner of a field under camouflage. Although we were followed sometimes by fighter planes from the other side, we were lucky no one was hit. We were all able to get back to our platoon without any losses. Food and drink was sorted out for our boys. For a while the supplies were in two or four-men packs. The packs were boxes of wood. Inside were provisions of tinned food, hard tack – which was a thick biscuit substance, really hard, that needed to be soaked for hours in water, but they were mainly for eating in an emergency. If a man was in a position he could not get out of for a while, there were cigarettes, matches, tea, sugar, all in cubes and milk, but it made a good cuppa. There were boiled sweets, a kind of energy supply.

Dispatch Riders viewed themselves as 'a team within a team' and were seen as such by other soldiers. They formed a distinctive camaraderie because of the nature of their role, which could be lonely and dangerous. They travelled on roads and tracks that were often bombarded with artillery and mortar fire. They lived by their wits and skills, as both a rider and map reader; a wrong turn or overshot road could be fatal if they ran into enemy fire. One of their most hazardous tasks was to ride with a squadron of vehicles – cars, trucks, tanks and SMVs (Specialised Military Vehicles), stopping at crossroads to fasten divisional signs and arrows for others to follow. The crewmen in tanks were largely out of sight and protected by armoured steel, while the DRs, for a few hours or so, became SDs – sitting ducks. DRs operated under strict orders, as all soldiers did, but were perceived as having greater independence because they sometimes travelled alone. On a very basic level, they were envied for having a motorcycle and able to ride it on a daily basis, without being 'herded around' the same as most soldiers. They were so associated with their motorcycles that they were teased when they dismounted: 'Look here, chaps – a DR walking!'

One time, late at night, Herbert was chatting to a fellow rider who put forward another suggestion as to why 'being a DR wasn't so bad, all in all'. Herbert asked him to explain. 'Well, Bert, I know we'd never do it and we might even get a bullet in the back for it, but do you ever think, just now and again, that we could give the throttle a good twist and bugger off somewhere away from all this?' Herbert asked where he would 'bugger off' to. His colleague had already planned this imagined desertion. 'Up in the mountains or by the sea. Maybe shacked up with a buxom fräulein or mademoiselle who'd have you up all night, giving it billy-o until the bedsprings twanged and your ears were popping.' Herbert told him that he had a wife and four children at home, and another on the way, but conceded that it was a tempting proposal, although he 'should leave it as a pipedream for now'.

When a special floating dock was built and ships could bring more and better food supplies, we had bakers making fresh bread every day. We had some veg brought over, but not enough of the vitamin stuff like greens and tomatoes, which contain vitamin C. We were supplied with tablets, to pass on to keep everyone going with the extra vitamins required to stay healthy. Without the right vitamins and minerals, a person is open to disease because of low resistance. In time we were fairly well supplied with bread, and wherever camps could be set up, cooks made field fires and an oven. Cooked meals were supplied through hay boxes, to keep food warm in transit. Of course, there was some of our frontline fighting men who could not just come back to a camp and sit down to a meal. They had to be kept well fed in other ways. No one went short, once we were established.

It was hard going, fighting for Caen. A message was sent back to the UK that we could not move Jerry out. One Friday, after we, in our camp, had been raided by enemy fighter planes, machine-gunning us, late in the afternoon, we heard a droning sound growing louder all the time. Looking up, we saw literally hundreds of our planes coming in a 'V' formation. We cheered and cheered.

We knew this was going to ease the taking of the town. One by one, the planes came in and over the town, dropping their bombs, then up and away and back home. A few planes were knocked out of the sky but the majority were clear, leaving the town flat. That saved a hell of a lot of trouble.

If only it had come days before, a lot of our ground boys would have been saved. But that was how things go. The air-forces could not be everywhere at once. Our boys moved in to mop up. Just as we received a signal to move out to another place, it seemed the Americans somewhere west of us were in difficulties and our platoon was needed there. We were in need at various places after that, always on the move with an independent roving commission, so it seems. After helping out the American section, we got out the maps, worked out our code again, and moved north-west.

Chapter Ten
The familiarity of death

___

The battle for Caen lasted six weeks and led to almost 75 per cent of the city being destroyed. The German Panzergruppe West put up fierce resistance. Hundreds of Panzer tanks, 88mm anti-aircraft and anti-tank artillery guns, mortars and machine-gun nests were dug in around the city, in recognition of its strategic value. Caen spanned the Orne river and Caen Canal, two vital natural lines of defence in warfare, and its excellent road system was ideal for moving troops and weaponry onwards to other parts of France; the flatlands to the north of Caen were ideal for airfield construction. The mission cost the lives of almost 30,000 British and Canadian soldiers, and Allied bombing missions led to the death of 3,000 civilians, equal to the number of fatalities inflicted on the German army. Caen was finally liberated on 19 July 1944.

I, again with another DR at the head of the column, made for Argentan. This was a town about 20 miles south-west of Falaise in the piece of the country that was all farmland; often valleys and hills. A big section of the enemy was in there. It was named 'the Falaise Gap'. We were in big trouble. There were tanks, gun-carriers and plenty of armaments holding us back. Eventually, rocket-firing Typhoon planes [Hawker Typhoons, single-seat fighter-bombers] were sent in and cleared the lot. We went in afterwards on a check that the Typhoons had done their job. Everything was knocked out – men, guns, horses, cattle. What a mess.

The campaign to secure the Falaise Gap (also known as the Falaise Pocket) was the decisive engagement of the Battle of Normandy. The 'gap' was an area of land about 10 miles wide between the towns of Falaise and Argentan, through which German platoons were making a retreat. Bottlenecks formed as their path was blocked by burning wreckage and piles of dead bodies. They tried to escape through fields but they too became impassable as debris built up at gateways. More than 10,000 German soldiers were killed and 50,000 captured. Argentan, a town of approximately 7,000 people, was almost completely destroyed. Its train station had been blown up soon after D-Day and the B-17 and B-24 bombers of the US Eighth Air Force had bombed the town extensively on 6 and 7 June. Argentan was liberated on 20 August by the US Third Army, under the command of General George Patton. Beforehand, there had been eight days of violent engagement with the German 9th Panzer division and the 2nd SS Panzer Division Das Reich.

Scores of villages were razed during these hostilities. Corpses of soldiers, civilians and livestock were scattered across streets and fields. Abandoned equipment blocked roads. Pilots reported that they could smell rotting flesh while flying over the site. Dwight D. 'Ike' Eisenhower later wrote in his book, *Crusade in Europe*: 'The battlefield at Falaise was unquestionably one of the greatest "killing fields" of any of the war areas. Forty-eight hours after the closing of the gap I was conducted through it on foot, to encounter scenes that could be described only by Dante. It was literally possible to walk for hundreds of yards at a time, stepping on nothing but dead and decaying flesh.' Herbert had witnessed first-hand this carnage and destruction, but then rode into a scene of remarkable contrast.

We were at Argentan for about four days. While we were there, the people of the town gave a celebration party at the main hall for us as a welcome. All the people pooled in for food and wine, and it was a nice party with plenty of dancing. That was the only time we saw anything like that. We had to leave guards at the camp. Halfway through, there was a changeover of guard so the others could come along to the party. On the second day at Argentan, a big convoy of Yanks came trailing through, all singing and getting the booze down them. Two or three fell off the back of these trucks. We picked them up and sobered them up and later one of our trucks took them to their camp approx 20 miles further on.

When we left Argentan and travelled past the American camp, we were amazed how fast the evening was falling back. Remember, it was a June landing and quite a few weeks had passed. It must have been August easily but we had no time to think of the time of the year, just to keep going on. We did know one thing – we were clearing the enemy out gradually from France. Next, would be Belgium. The fighting was hard going and there were lots of bodies from each side lying around. But we had to go on and leave the fallen ones to be attended by those following us.

Herbert had become aware that DRs were at a marked disadvantage to other soldiers when caught in a hostile environment. The helmet had the effect of sealing a DR 'into his own world', and the sputter and vroom of the motorcycle engine drowned out the sound of artillery fire. During the occasional lull, he sometimes parked up, removed his helmet and turned off the engine. He could then better hear the distant popping and whistling of shells; the sense of danger increased ten-fold. He had discussed the matter with fellow DRs and they each took a stoical approach. 'If it's got your name on it, Bert, you're done for, whether you hear the thing coming or not,' said one. Another tendered: 'It's not as if you can jump into the nearest bush if you're on a motorbike, so you might as well hold on tight and hope it whistles over your head.'

We passed through and around villages and towns. Here and there, some lovely French countryside was still identifiable, but a great deal was churned up. Towns and villages had been hammered. This was war, real war. But it had to be: you cannot let a lot of gangsters dictate and terrorise other people into submission. They have to be stopped and this was what we were there for – to stop them.

German soldiers were seldom seen alive; this was a feature of World War Two where there were few instances of close, hand-to-hand combat. A would-be attacker would have to survive a gamut of artillery, mortars, machine guns and small arms to directly engage the enemy. A tacit agreement also existed that an outnumbered or surrounded force could surrender and become prisoners-of-war, negating the need for further hostilities. On the few occasions when enemy soldiers came within close proximity, the British said they could 'smell a German before they saw him'. Most Germans, especially officers, wore aftershave, particularly eau de cologne, at a time when British men considered this effete. Herbert, as a DR frequently riding upfront or flanking the main unit, might have been expected to stand a greater chance of seeing the live enemy, but when he did, it was usually a glimpse, sometimes imagined, as they darted among the trees or rubble. Streets and fields were strewn with spent shell cases, steel helmets, water bottles, empty ammunition boxes and webbing equipment. On journeys that Herbert made several times while stationed nearby, he used burnt-out wrecks of vehicles, discarded military hardware and even prostrate bodies of dead German soldiers as navigation aids; he had quickly become accustomed to the familiarity of death.

Still in France, we carried on and eventually came to a village. I did not know its name. I still recall the sight that met my eyes. The whole place was flat, just a pile of rubble, except, right in the middle, was a church, a church of old stone, very old. It was still standing, with hardly a scratch. Next to the church was a cemetery. The surrounding wall was slightly damaged, nothing that a few hours' work would not put right. We saw some freshly dug graves near the hedges, with rifle and helmet stuck on the top (Tommy helmets). We only stopped there long enough to check the place for casualties, but we found nothing further than the few rough graves of some of our British boys, then we left it behind. We had to go on, for our job was to keep up with the forward troops for their supplies, never far behind and still under shell fire. It's a nerve-racking business being under shell fire.

I cannot tell you the names of the towns or villages. No time to bother about things like that. It was just carry on and keep going all the time, sometimes slowly, other times quickly; it depended on how fast or slow Jerry was falling back. If I had the right maps, I feel I could find the places and names without much trouble. We had the general direction to follow and that is what we did, not stopping along anywhere, of course. We had left Normandy behind and, by this time, we were well into France. A few towns were hardly touched by heavy gunfire. We passed on through those. The people we saw were cheering and waving, but there was no stopping for us. There was a war to win. Not us alone, but a great combination of troops and supplies. Good communication and hard work did a lot towards keeping the Nazi hordes on the run. Not without casualities, of course. There were losses on either side.

A HQ was set up. This was a meeting point, a consolidation point. It was well under natural cover. We were planning a great build-up of heavy materiel, tanks, guns, troops, transport and everything that was needed for a stronger push. We were heading for Belgium and Holland. Some of our troops had been at it from the landings. Now, I thought, was the time for these boys to get some relief. A man cannot go on and on without tiredness, and these men were tired. I knew that, because I was tired, damn tired, and I managed at times to get a little bit more rest than those poor so-and-sos out there. It's a tiring business, this war game. Did I say game? Not really a game, but one hell of a fight. But we were fit, well-trained and maybe could stand it a bit longer than the man in the street. We were fighting now without a rest or special exercises to keep fit.

I was called to my Commanding Officer. He told me I had been chosen for a special job, a job that would need intelligence, common sense, good map reading and routing. He told me I would have to go back some miles and make good routes for the safe movement of soldiers and equipment to specific map references. I was to choose two of my mates who I had confidence in. I knew just the two. I was to give them certain work to do and they were to report back to me at the reference number I gave them. I would also be in contact with the Corps of Military Police, especially at their HQ, to arrange points of turn off and road surfaces for heavy and light transport, the tanks and guns for military personnel. This meant the police were to act as traffic direction officers of all transport moving to the main reference numbers that my two mates and myself, especially myself, had worked out.

I was my own boss with two men working with me. Our panniers were strapped to the rear of our bikes. We were loaded with what we would need, i.e., a small 'bivvy' [bivouac shelter], mess tins, tin plates, and mugs, tea, sugar and milk in small squares, similar in size and shape to Oxo cubes. Being in France, farmers helped us through a lot, an egg and some bread here and there. I would report to our HQ every now and then, also to the Police HQ to keep them in the picture, ready for the big push forward of all our traffic. I gave different routes for different vehicle weights and all went very well. I made a good job of it and helped out sometimes in controlling the traffic and, believe me, there was a lot of traffic. I got a good pat on the back for what I had done (Big Head). I felt I had done something really worthwhile on that job. The other two boys, two good lads, all helped as we shifted Jerry back a lot more. My map reading course I had taken back in England had paid off. This job lasted a couple of weeks or so.

The routine acceptance of death was illustrated in Herbert's low-key account of an incident in which eight men lost their lives.

There was one thing that went wrong, no fault of mine or my men. A sergeant driving a three-tonner loaded with men would not take an order from me to slow down, going down a steep road. Earlier I had stopped each truck in turn and asked the driver to keep in low

OPENING THE GATES OF HELL

gear all the way. I told them that the lives of those men in the back (about 30 of them) depended on the driver. I explained that speeding would be dangerous because, at the bottom, was a sharp right turn over a bridge, a narrow bridge. Allowing one vehicle at a time, I told them to take it steady and they'd be okay. They took notice of me and made the manoeuvre easily. But this 'big head' sergeant, whose stripes made him bigger than anyone else, after I advised him to go down slowly, he told me to FXXX OFF and who the hell did I think I was, telling him, a sergeant, how to do his job. I told him straight, there and then, that the stripes I had plus what was on my helmet RASCTC [Royal Army Service Corps Traffic Control] was far higher than his and I would see that he would have no stripes if anything went wrong. On his way he went. One of my men was halfway down and tried to make him go slower. The sergeant said 'get stuffed'. When he got to the bottom, about half a mile down, he realised my truth, but too late. He tried to take the bend, went through the stone parapet and down onto the railway line below, which was quite a drop. There were about 20 men with their equipment on board. Seven were dead, some were badly injured and others not too badly. The driver had broken his arm but his co-driver was dead. What a mess. Later on, the sergeant was stripped down to private.

I now had to deal with the situation. I called my halfway man back and stopped all the traffic. I went to a small village nearby and they all turned out to help; they were marvellous. We got the injured up the railway banking and away in ambulances. The dead were put in tarpaulin sheets and we toppled what was left of the vehicle down the railway embankment. But we were then surprised to hear a steam train coming along with Americans on board. What they were doing in that area, we didn't know. We stopped the train. The driver said they had found it a few miles back and decided to use it. I said they were in the wrong sector. 'Ah, hell. Not to worry,' he said. I asked what would have happened if we had been Nazis. He said he'd never thought of that. Typical Yank. I said, 'Are you going on?' He said, 'Sure, we got plenty what we need.' I asked him to make sure the track was okay. He walked away, came back and said everything was fine. Just as they were moving off, a big door slid open on a wagon. A soldier put his head through to see what was going on. I called to him that he should put his head back in. He said, 'Ah, nuts.' The door caught a bit of the canopy frame of our broken vehicle and slid closed before I could warn him again. He was dead. The door had crushed his neck (quite a day that was). We fastened cables to the wreck of our truck and pulled it up.

My CO told me I had done the right thing and it was a job well done. Finally, all the traffic was sorted out and assembled ready for another big push forward. This time we were to take parts of Belgium and Holland. The year was passing. Autumn was upon us and we were moving again, back to our old job as supply, which meant going back and forth building our own depots as we went on, while, at the same time, keeping our boys loaded with all the material they required in food and clothing, which was needed as it became colder. One big supply after another was coming across the Channel by air and sea. My mob was keeping over to the left, which finally brought us into Holland, about eight kilometres beyond Eindhoven, to Beek en Donk, a little place by a canal [the Wilhelmina canal], a short distance into the countryside.

We came across a house where the people gave us hospitality. Very nice, friendly people. There were some outbuildings where we made billets and there was tree cover for our vehicles. Us DRs were billeted in a part-glass, part-brick attachment to the main house and a few times we were invited in to sit by a big warm stove in their living quarters. The cold nights were coming on. They were burning wood and it was cosy. These people did not have much. The father of the family worked for the local council, trimming hedges in the surrounding country lanes. For their kindness, we helped them from our food rations – a bit of chocolate, some tea and sugar. We were repaid by them washing our clothes, darning our socks and so on. We had some fresh veg and it was really beautiful, straight from his big garden. We were there for some time.

Winter was approaching and we were told a lot of snow would be falling before long, especially between where we were and the river we would have to cross later, the Maas [also known as the Meuse, 575 miles in length]. I have just said winter was approaching. Well, it *was* winter. December, in fact. Christmas was around the corner. We had not realised it. We were so busy getting on with the job. We were up to our necks in a Liberation war, and somehow, we had to get on with it. It had to be won. There was one thing we were aware of, at least. Although we were losing some of our men, and, believe me, they were giving their lives for the liberation of others: God was with us all the way. I know that is the way I was feeling.

The frequent mentions of God by Herbert were not particularly statements of religious faith. He was not a churchgoer or especially interested in religion. Most soldiers, bounded by violence and death, sought solace in faith or superstition.

Now the snow was falling heavily. Everything was quiet. The snow seemed to be bringing our war to a halt. Our platoon managed to get some rest. Then we had to move from Holland and move slightly east into Belgium. Just over the Dutch/Belgian border was a small town called Hamont [now known as Hamont-Achel], which is where we met up with 'B.R.A.S.B.' [an acronym not widely used but thought to be: British Royal Army Service Barracks], our HQ. The idea was that we would be all together and billeted within reasonable distance of each other. About five miles to our east was the town of Helmond on the banks of the Zuid-Willemsvaart canal. This canal was huge and stretched for miles. After Hamont, we, the dispatch riders, were billeted at a big house down a country road leading out of town within easy reach of B.R.A.S.B. Our platoon formed a depot on the outskirts, organising supplies for troops ahead of us. This went along very smoothly.

There was a big push forwards. The heavy snow had slowed things down. All seemed still and quiet. Christmas had passed. January was here and we hoped the New Year would bring some results. We were on our way again. It had stopped snowing and was getting mushy, but it wasn't a full thaw. There was more snow and sleet to come, mostly sleet and it was damn cold. Riding my motorbike was a hard task.

The COs had been telling DRs for several months about the imminent arrival of a new make of motorcycle, a Matchless G3/L. Herbert had asked how it could possibly better the BSA, which had been a model of reliability. 'It's supposed to be less of a bone-shaker, apparently,' he was told. 'How's that?' asked Herbert. 'Something to do with the hydraulics.' A few days later, in response to Herbert's interest, the CO handed him an advert cut from an army briefing, headed: 'Ride TELEDRAULIC . . . and all roads are smooth!' The text read: 'TELEDRAULICS just gobble up those bumps and pot holes and make all roads feel smooth. In other words, they give superb road-holding and faultless steering.' The 'Teledraulics' was a suspension system incorporated into the front forks to provide a few inches of 'give', unlike the standard fixed 'girder' forks of the BSA.

I was a top-class DR. I could practically ride up the side of a house (as the saying goes). I knew my job and was glad to do it. The down part about it was that when other DRs couldn't face it, it was always me who had to carry out some of the most rotten jobs. It wasn't too bad crossing the River Maas but the rest of the journey close to the Rhine was a lot more difficult. It was 50 miles of hard pushing, through tough weather conditions. A halt was called. We came to a farmhouse and barn. The house was used by the CO and some others of our platoon. There was a small number of clerical men attached to us, for paperwork involving supply and rations. We DRs settled for a short time in the barn. There was hay and it was nice and dry. As we were always exposed to the weather, we were naturally wet and cold. We dried out the best we could. It surprised me how we got away without colds and flu. We, of course, were toughened soldiers. We spent a large time out of doors. We must have acquired our toughness from that.

The small team of DRs grumbled about the impending switch to a different motorcycle, partway through a war. Herbert was a few years older than the others and they turned to him as their 'spokesman'; they knew he was respected by the COs. 'Tell them, Bert – it's bloody dangerous. Who knows what might happen while we're all over the shop getting used to a new bike?' He'd heard similar gripes whenever there were changes at work, but they were invariably for the better and, moreover, he liked to embrace progress, or at least not bellyache about it.

Although DRs were weighed down with equipment, both on the motorcycle itself and strapped to their body, they soon found that the Matchless was noticeably a few pounds lighter, making it easier to ride, and push and pull through swampy terrain. The compact structure was similar to the BSA and it was later described in army circles as 'a supreme plodder with a very nearly bomb-proof engine'. The rear wheel was detachable and the front stand made it easier to fix a puncture or replace an inner tube. Most of all, the

DRs acclaimed the 'Teledraulics'. At first they said that the steering felt *wobbly* or *bendy* but they quickly became accustomed to the extra six inches of 'bounce' provided by the forks. 'It's like surfing!' cried one DR after he'd manoeuvred the motorcycle over a rocky path. 'It's easy. Get your arse off the seat, lean forwards, bend your knees and imagine you're on Fistral Beach in Newquay.' Afterwards, the phrase that most DRs used about the Matchless was that 'it felt part of you'; more than 80,000 were issued for army use. Herbert named his new machine Gracie, after his wife.

Chapter Eleven
Blown to kingdom come

———

The CO selected Herbert for a special mission. Herbert was delighted to be asked, and eager to please his superior. His notes about the assignment disclosed a willingness to accept responsibility, regardless of formal army rank, and revealed his paternal nature.

Now, the second night of our stop, I'd had just one hour of kip when the CO sent for me. He said he needed a DR to go back to B.R.A.S.B. at Hamont with a very important dispatch. 'Get me a DR Corporal right now,' he said. 'Right, Sir,' I responded. Going back to the barn, I found my boys fast asleep, nice and warm. I turned round, taking my riding gear with me. I went back to the CO and told him I would go. He said, 'You're a bloody fool, Corp.' I said, 'I know, but they're warm and asleep.' I told him it would take me a couple of days to get there and back in this weather. 'That's okay,' he said. 'Get this through to HQ for me. There'll be no medals, but it will be another job well done. And don't hurry back. Make sure you're okay before returning. I want you back here with me. I will see that the others do some work for a change, but we may have moved on.'

I did the 75 miles to Hamont. What a night. I was in first and second gear all the way, dragging my feet to save me falling from my bike. Tanks and guns were moving up ready for the Rhine crossing. We would have to fight before we got across, so we would need the guns, especially to hammer them on the other side. As the tanks passed me from the opposite direction, they were revving their engines, shaking the ground and the area around them. My head was going round and round, taking all my effort to stay on my bike. I dare not let myself slip or fall because I would have gone under their tracks. That would have been my last trip. A bit messy.

A trip of 75 miles was unusual for a DR. Most were a short distance, darting between camps and headquarters.

I had an important message to get through. I was frozen. It was sleeting and I rode through mile after mile of it, soaking wet. I had on my winter underwear, a shirt, riding trousers, riding stockings, boots, battle dress, jacket, leather jerkin, and a DR riding coat reaching to my ankles. I reached HQ. I was wet right through and frozen, and just about able to stop my bike outside. I had to be lifted off by two guards on duty at the entrance. I was carried inside and put on a chair, by a big white-hot stove in the middle of the room. They gave me warm cocoa. The officer in charge came out of his office to see what was going on. I asked him to unbutton my riding coat and take the dispatch from the special pocket. The dispatch was covered in waterproofing and was dry, but not me. I was soaked to the skin.

The CO gave orders for me to be taken care of. I was given a bunk and plenty of blankets. I took off all my clothes and they were taken away for drying. I had some hot food and drink, and plenty of kip. I was treated really well. The following morning, after a good eight hours sleep that did me a lot of good (the first proper rest for a while), I was given my clothing back. It was beautiful too, really dry and comfortable. I had a good breakfast, followed by an interview with the day officer, who told me the dispatch was being followed through and was quite an important one. He talked of how things were going and how rough it must be for all of us up at the front. I told him of the journey. He said, 'You have got one hell of a job, you DRs, haven't you?' 'I couldn't agree with you more, Sir,' I said. 'But there are a lot of boys up there having it a lot rougher than I am.' He agreed on that. We also had to agree that we all couldn't be doing the same thing, but whatever we were doing, it was all a means to an end – fighting a bloody war against evil gangsters.

I had a midday meal at HQ and left at 1300 hours in daylight because I would be able to travel better that way. I wanted to get back to our boys. They were glad to see me and had moved on another 20 miles. Jerry was moving back a bit faster than we imagined, but we realised they would make a big stand at the Rhine. The other DRs told me that the old man (our CO) had been on their tail a lot after I rode out. From then, we carried on towards the Rhine to meet the German army head-on. They were desperate now. On the other side of the river was Germany. That was their homeland and they were going to fight damned hard to stop us taking it from them.

All was still for a few seconds, very still. Herbert, ten months into active service, had experienced this preternatural calm several times. At nightfall, in their tents or wherever they had bedded down, soldiers often talked of it, how the birds fell quiet (did they really?) and the air was so tender that every sound – a breath, a footstep, the brushing of an arm against cloth on a jacket – bruised it loud. Herbert was standing on a hillside with other members of 35 Coy RASC, a mile or so from Wesel, a town at the confluence of the rivers Lippe and Rhine in western Germany. The corps had played their part in Operation Varsity, supplying provisions to the 16,000 paratroopers dropped behind enemy lines.

Wesel was a strategic target because it contained a German army supply depot and its 1,950m-long railway bridge was the last on the Rhine remaining under enemy control. The advancing Allied soldiers were supported by approximately a thousand planes that, over the next few weeks, would drop more than a million bombs. Herbert and his comrades had been spared the fine detail of the mission, but each knew it was a major undertaking and would be brutal; it was actually the largest airborne operation of the war. A phrase had come into regular use as they became increasingly aware of the vast firepower to be deployed: the weasel (as Wesel was jokingly known to the Allies) was about to be 'blown to kingdom come'.

> It was a mass of flames. All we could see was one big fire. The big guns on our side of the river had taken their toll. What a noise they made. It was deafening. Heads were 'buzzing'. I think that was the cause of my hearing to be impaired later in life. I am not entirely deaf, but I have a little corrector to help me now. From then I had to cross that river. A number of the troops went over by raft, or any way they could.

The attack began on Friday, 16 February 1945, and was relentless for four days and nights, and then on an intermittent basis. The Allied force, stationed or airborne along the Rhine, outnumbered the Germans ten-fold. Alfred Schlemm, Commander-in-Chief of the 1st Parachute Army, had been promised *Wunderwaffe* ('wonder weapons') but they did not arrive; they remained prototypes and were never used in combat. Schlemm, a career soldier with almost 30 years of service, was badly wounded in an air strike and replaced by another experienced operator, General Günther Blumentritt. Both men, with depleted resources and heavily outgunned, had known that resistance was futile but had been ordered to hold their position. Hitler had warned that any soldier who surrendered without suffering exhaustion or disabling wounds would be treated as a deserter, with payment and rations withheld from him and his family.

The military had three terms for bombing done over a specific area to inflict maximum damage – saturation, obliteration or carpet. Most civilians had been evacuated from Wesel to nearby villages but 2,000 died. More than 100,000 lost their homes and only three per cent of the town's infrastructure was left standing. In a message to Air Marshall Arthur 'Bomber' Harris, the Commander in Chief of Bomber Command, Field Marshall Bernard Montgomery wrote, 'My grateful appreciation for the quite magnificent co-operation you have given us in the battle of the Rhine. The bombing of Wesel was a masterpiece and a decisive factor in making possible our entry into that town.'

Soldiers in combat zones had to adapt constantly to extremes. Within hours of intense hostilities, the body surging with adrenalin, a soldier was back at headquarters, everything quiet and still, and usually among nature, hearing sounds evoking playing-out or camping-out days of childhood. Some could switch easily, as if merely walking from one frame to another in a comic strip, but others struggled. They were agitated. They paced. They wandered off to be alone. 'Leave him be' was the usual counsel, but occasionally their 'best buddie' was sent after him, offering a cigarette or arm on the shoulder: 'We'll soon be home, pal. Promise'. At different times, Herbert had found a colleague at a field's edge or crouched by a wall, trembling, crying, praying, or even singing quietly to himself. 'Don't tell anyone, Bert,' they'd implore.

At downtime, Herbert was surprised to discover unexpected facets of the men he was among. He read the handwritten poems of 'a lad no older than 21' from Blackburn and had marvelled at their depth and sensitivity. Another sketched drawings of figures set against tanks and trees and hedges, so real it seemed as if they might walk from the picture. Others had collected Perspex knocked out of crashed gliders and vehicle windscreens, and engraved them with churches, animals or countryside scenes.

Herbert had long accepted that it was not a soldier's lot to question or contemplate: he followed orders. At times, though, someone would mention the 'poor bastards' caught beneath the bombs. As Wesel burned, smashed to rubble, soldiers each had to support the other, eking out moral justification for such extensive destruction. Their efficiency and ruthlessness was bringing the war to an end, ultimately saving more lives and bringing peace to all: *for the greater good* became a mantra. At night, Herbert sometimes closed his eyes and dreamed of home – a walk in Alkrington Woods perhaps, where, about now, early spring, the snowdrops would be superseded by daffodils and then bluebells and, come June, a full-blown summer; he felt it drawing closer.

In the here and now, he looked across to the devastation inflicted upon Wesel. The surrounding fields were a pocked moonscape, the land effectively turned inside out so there was no grass visible, but craters of clay over which a grey dust had settled from blown-up buildings. Across the river, where the bombing had been more concentrated, trees had turned to spindly strands of charcoal, scratching at the sky. Fires were burning and a pall of smoke drifted over the rubble. Dogs barked. Herbert could not discern streets or paths; it was as if someone had crashed a fist on an architect's model of a town and left it in pieces. He wondered if he would be commanded to run messages and supplies to the advancing soldiers crawling over the debris, picking off the last of the Germans' resistance. He realised this was unlikely because without any discernible roads, it was virtually an impassable zone, even by motorcycle.

> Once over the river, we by-passed Wesel, ever onwards, following close behind our forward troops, who were really hammering away at the enemy, sometimes slowing up, sometimes a little faster. It was hard going. Remember, we were in Germany now. Jerry didn't want to give up ground, but had to. We knew these boys out front relied on us for supplies. It was a wonderful machine [the Army], well set up and it all helped to win that war.

Unusually, Herbert referred back to an earlier incident that had clearly stayed on his mind.

> Before going into Holland, our Captain H was somewhat not right for the boys in our platoon. We began to think he was crazy. He did a lot of silly things. One night in the camp, he came creeping round, watching the guard duty men. He was seen and challenged, but kept quiet. He was fired on. Next morning, he had the two men before him for firing on him; they had fired over his head. He had no idea who it was, so it got him nowhere. We told him we all knew what he was doing. No way could he blame the guard for firing, if

he didn't answer a challenge. Anyway, we got rid of him by complaining and got another captain. Captain S, his replacement, was a good bloke, right through to the end. On we went, stopping at various points near enough to the front to supply our boys.

Chapter Twelve
Proceed and enter

———

The 35th Company, with Herbert and two other dispatch riders forming a vanguard, pushed almost due east for about 20 miles until they arrived at the outskirts of Celle in Lower Saxony. The town sat on the banks of the Aller, a tributary of the Weser, and had a population of about 70,000. Its castle (Schloss Celle) had been built in Renaissance and Baroque styles, and the town centre (the Altstadt) had more than 400 timber-framed houses. Celle, the soldiers concurred, was *picturesque* – 'the sort of place you'd visit with your wife and kids at the weekend'. The peace and quiet was deceptive. Only a few days earlier, on 8 April 1945, a massacre had taken place at its train station. More than 3,400 internees from satellite bases of the Neuengamme concentration camp had arrived on a goods train, to be marched to another camp at nearby Belsen. The train was hit by bombs dropped by American airmen and a container loaded with munitions exploded. The prisoners were trapped in locked compartments and most died where they stood. A few hundred managed to escape but were hunted down by the

SS, police, members of the Wehrmacht and the Volkssturm (the German Home Guard), the Hitler Youth and residents of Celle; they were shot or beaten to death.

> At a suburb of Celle, we found some luxury houses, residential-type homes. Being Germans, we tipped a couple out of their big house and enjoyed a bit of comfort for a change, two days, and then on to Celle, arriving late evening, nearly dark.

As they proceeded through Germany, the Allies occasionally appropriated property on a temporary basis. They looked upon it as an opportunity to rest and refresh themselves. They bathed and shaved, and were delighted to have access to proper toilet facilities. They helped themselves to food and lounged on sofas, reading magazines and books they had carried in their kitbags. British soldiers were puzzled by the contraption positioned close to the toilet in some homes. They speculated on whether it was a children's drinking fountain or a foot bath; it was a bidet. 'You dip your backside in it when you've been to the toilet,' they were advised; 'it saves you having a manky arse.' They had spent months living under canvas or in dugouts carved into the sides of hills, riverbanks or ravines, enclosed by walls of turf or logs. They felt entitled to a touch of luxury.

American GIs, in particular, had a reputation for the petty looting of the homes where they stayed or passed. They viewed it as recompense for the hardship and losses they had endured in fighting a war, thousands of miles from home. They maintained that they needed items of clothing to stay warm, or a caste of jewellery as keepsakes. Necklaces and watches were taken from the bodies of dead German soldiers on the pretext that 'they were Hitler's mates', although many soldiers were superstitious of stealing from the dead and believed it might affect their chances of returning home safe and well.

> We came to a big meadow, surrounded by trees, good for cover. The idea was to check on the town next morning. While we were there, we came under shell fire from the Jerries, heavy stuff too. We lost one vehicle, not too bad, no injuries. Next morning, very early, after a talk with Captain S, I went out on patrol in the town, not knowing what I would find or come up against. Way back from the main part, I came across a factory. There was a lovely smell of cakes or biscuits. On entering the factory, I found it was biscuits. They were made there. There was plenty of everything required for the making of the biscuits. I went back to my CO double quick and told him they'd be good billets for us. We packed up and moved in there. While the men were settling in, I went out on patrol.

The streets around Celle were quiet; the German soldiers had moved on. James Hardman, a dispatch rider with the RAF, had been based in the area for a few days and, similar to the soldiers in Herbert's platoon, had found it a pleasant town, although he detected unease. In a letter to his wife back home in Hereford, he wrote:

Celle is a really lovely place, with several nice parks and swimming pools, but all its natural and architectural beauty is lost because of its atmosphere. I found the place streaming with lots of freed slave workers of various nationalities – Russians, Poles, Czechs, Greeks, Yugoslavs and others. Some of them looked reasonably well, but the majority were really pitiful to see, walking skeletons. The Germans in comparison are just like fat pigs. The younger women, from 15 to 30 years of age, are dressing up and walking about the place as though they're daughters or wives of millionaires.

Riding through the town, Herbert was at relative ease, enjoying the hush after the fury and desolation of Wesel. He tried to imagine that he was on a weekend ride to Macclesfield Forest, Edale in the Peak District or other beauty spots within easy reach of Manchester. He brought the Matchless to a stop at a junction and reached for a map in his pannier. He heard a rattling sound from behind, growing ever louder. He turned and saw a man approaching on a rickety bicycle. 'Hey,' shouted Herbert, as the man passed. Herbert pulled his Mauser pistol from its holster (he had taken it earlier from a surrendered German) and used it to wave the cyclist forward. '*Sprechen Sie Englisch?*' he asked. The man said he did but Herbert noticed that he spoke in a peculiar accent. 'I am from France but I worked for ten years in Glasgow before the war, selling newspapers,' he said. Herbert smiled at the absurdity: an Englishman in Germany talking to a Frenchman with a Scottish brogue.

The man said he had been a civilian worker for the Wehrmacht but with the war about to end, he was cycling home to France. 'On that?' said Herbert, pointing to the bicycle. 'It is old but reliable,' he answered. They shook hands and wished each other a safe journey. As the man remounted, he stopped abruptly. 'Do you know about the Belsen camp?' he asked. 'No, what's that?' responded Herbert. The man said he had heard that it was a death camp and was run by the SS, administered by a 'horrible' soldier (Josef Kramer, the camp commandant, later dubbed the 'Beast of Belsen'). The Frenchman said he had not been there himself but other workers had visited and told him there had been 'many killings, shootings and the prisoners were starving'.

Herbert asked the Frenchman to follow him to the platoon's headquarters at the biscuit factory. Soldiers had dispersed themselves throughout the various buildings of Harry Trüller Ltd, a major employer in the town, where rusks, waffles and chocolate was made, along with biscuits. Over a couple of hours, the Frenchman was asked to reveal all he knew about the camp, though much of it was hearsay. In gratitude, he was presented with a typed note explaining that he had greatly assisted the British Army. He was told it would serve as a pass at the numerous roadblocks he would encounter on his way back to France – a journey of about 350 miles. He was also handed a supply of biscuits which he placed into the deep pockets of his chore jacket.

I asked for maps covering the area – my own terminated at Celle. It was my job (among others) to lead our column because

I had already had a course in map reading previous to the invasion and it was known that I was good at the job. On checking, I traced a route with a little help from the Frenchman before he left. Our officers realised that if we were to find Belsen and take it, we would need plenty of something to give to the poor people (or what was left of them) in the way of food. So our vehicles were loaded with flour, milk powder and sugar, which was plentiful at the biscuit factory. We started off on our journey. I led the way, with my map and route card fastened in a special frame made to fit on my handlebars, so I could follow the right road.

A number of the platoon (in his notes, Herbert did not specify how many) were instructed to travel the 11 miles to Belsen and investigate what they had been told. On maps, they could see it was a rural village with a clutch of houses and a population of what they assumed to be a few hundred people. Along with 11 other parishes, it fell within the municipality of a nearby town of about 10,000, called Bergen. Herbert set off, followed by the others 'at a discreet distance'. If he needed assistance, he was told to fire his gun into the air three times. He carried with him a Sten submachine gun (with four magazines over his shoulder), the Luger automatic he'd 'taken from a previous encounter' and the Mauser. The early part of the journey was via a series of country lanes. Fallen branches and pine cones from the previous autumn snapped beneath his wheels. The pale sun refracted through the trees.

I stopped the column and talked with my officer. I told him that we had just a few miles to go and to take it steady because we did not know what road to take. He asked me to go ahead carefully. This I did with full mag on my Sten gun.

He met 40 or so 'uniformed men' led by a tall German officer ('well over six ft') standing at the front, carrying a long pole with a piece of white cloth attached. Herbert fired his Sten into the air, the blast echoing through the tundra.

Believe me, I was not too struck on the situation. But there I was, I was stuck with it until our boys got there. Somehow I was not afraid, but did wonder if it was me who was for it, or Jerry. One man against that lot was a bit much, but they behaved very well. They were men of the Wehrmacht, who, I learned later, were supposed to patrol the outer perimeter of the camp.

The German soldiers immediately put their hands behind their heads. The main officer said, in clear English, that they wanted to surrender and had left their firearms in their quarters. He stressed that what had occurred inside the camp had been carried out by the SS Commandant and his troops. Four other dispatch riders pulled up alongside Herbert until the CO arrived to accept the surrender. Herbert was told to 'mount up and carry on'. The camp was approached down a winding country lane with a ditch on both sides flanked by pine trees. He came to a tall continuous steel fence and, after about a quarter of a mile, arrived at what appeared to be an entrance. Herbert fired his Sten into the air again and was soon joined by his CO who gave the order to 'proceed and enter'.

> With full confidence in the knowledge that I was behaving correctly and carrying out an order, I debarred the gate that closed the road to intruders and rode into Belsen Concentration Camp, the first British soldier to do so. When I opened those gates it never entered my mind that I was doing something great or significant. It was a job I had to do. Leaving my motorcycle propped up outside the main entrance to the guard house with the other dispatch riders not far behind, I strode through the open main door. There were half a dozen SS men in the main office. Their rifles were stacked up in a corner and small arms were neatly arrayed along the counter at the far end.

Chapter Thirteen
Just skin and bone

The entrance gate at Belsen comprised two sections, each about 15ft across and 10ft high. The frames were wooden with a crossbar in the middle, supported by two pieces of timber leaning inwards to form an 'A' shape. They were criss-crossed with barbed wire, the holes large enough for a clenched fist to fit through. Another roll of barbed wire of about two feet in height was stretched across the top, buckled and skew-whiff as if it had been buffeted in a storm. Herbert would have seen similar fixed but flimsy gates before, around railway yards or building sites back home in Middleton.

This will shock you. People were walking around with a glazed, empty look in their eyes, so terribly thin that they looked like skeletons, and some who had simply dropped dead right in front of me. I saw thousands in such a terrible state. They were just skin and bone, not an ounce of flesh anywhere. Terrible to see. You are lucky you are reading this and not experiencing it. I saw a grave the size of a football pitch, stacked with emaciated dead bodies, eight feet high. What sort of fiends could do this thing? The inmates were not all Jews, as we are often led to believe. Perhaps they were in the majority, but there were also Polish, German, French, Danes and many others. We rounded up the SS guards, placed them under armed surveillance. I had to take a grip of myself to prevent me going berserk with my Sten as I faced them.

★

When Herbert pushed open those nondescript gates on Sunday, 15 April 1945, it would not be an overstatement to propound that he was about to suffer one of the greatest shocks of anyone who had ever lived. The scale of the atrocity – 60,000 'skeletons' and 13,000 unburied corpses – would not have been immediately apparent, but within seconds he saw hundreds of emaciated bodies and recognised the horror and cruelty that had been perpetrated at the site. The French civilian had forewarned him by terming it a 'death camp' and speaking of 'many killings, shootings and the prisoners were starving', but Herbert, in all likelihood, would have understood this to have been an exaggeration typical of 'civvies' and almost certainly limited to captured soldiers and not, as the military categorised them, 'non-combatants' – ordinary men, women and children; the inventory undertaken later revealed that three-quarters of the prisoners had been women. Beforehand, Herbert might also have assumed that the deaths and severe illnesses were due to a natural phenomenon such as an outbreak of typhus, rather than wilful neglect and malevolence.

I saw the prisoners shuffling along without hardly any energy in their body to move. That alone was a terrible sight, but there was worse than these poor bodies. They were just skin and bone. It made me wonder how the bones were left together. What had been muscle and tissue was faded ligaments like string, so terribly thin with no flesh to give bulk for support. Just as bad was the look on their faces, a look of despair and hopelessness, waiting for the end.

Understandably, Herbert and the other soldiers struggled to relate what they had seen on that first day. Major Ben Barnett of the 249 Battery, 63 Anti-Tank Regt, Oxfordshire Yeomanry, made pencil notes soon afterwards: 'The things I saw completely defy description. There are no words in the English language which can give a true impression of the ghastly horrors of this camp.' He wrote later: 'I find it even now hard to get into focus all these horrors. My mind is really quite incapable of taking in everything I saw because it was all so completely foreign to everything I had previously believed or thought possible.' Michael Bentine, the comedian and comic actor, served with the 22 SAS Regiment and was at the liberation of Belsen. In his book *The Reluctant Jester*, he wrote: 'Words alone cannot describe it. Many have tried to do so, and even inmates of that appalling place cannot succeed in conveying its full horror. I am not able to either. Only the photographs and the films of those scenes can convey a fraction of the spiritual nausea that gripped everyone who witnessed it. To me, Belsen was the ultimate blasphemy.' [2]

Lots of prisoners in a poor, poor state were trying to 'crowd round' us, to thank us for being there. Me and two other dispatch riders were told to ride around on a quick tour of the camp, to weigh up the situation and compile a report for the next day. It must be remembered that the war was not yet over. The advancing troops had to be kept supplied. And here at this terrible place quite a number had been diverted from carrying out their normal duties to deal with something beyond anything they had been trained for. This wasn't war. This was a nightmare. The gruesome sights and the smell. There wasn't much else we could do. Everything had been so quick, so unexpected. At least those poor unfortunate individuals were not harassed by the SS any more.

The smell emanating from Belsen was of faeces and decomposing flesh. Lieutenant-Colonel Douglas Paybody of VIII Corps described it many years later to his local newspaper, the *Warrington Guardian*, in 2001: 'What we saw was a nightmare which beggars description. Nobody should be allowed to see the things we saw: thousands of bodies lying all over the place. Excrement everywhere. The stench got into your clothes, your hair, your ears and your mouth. You could empty water over yourselves, but it took ages to get rid of the smell.' The soldiers instinctively recalled similar smells from their past. Captain Derrick Sington of the Intelligence Corps was typical: 'We reached a high wooden gate with criss-cross wiring. It reminded me of the entrance to a zoo. Once through the gate, this resemblance was strengthened. On the left of the thoroughfare stood row upon row of green wooden huts, and we came into a smell of ordure, like the smell of a monkey-house,'[3] he said. Brigadier Hugh Llewellyn Glyn Hughes, chief medical officer of the Second Army, also described the smell: 'There were faeces all over the floor – the majority of people having diarrhoea. I was standing aghast in the middle of all this filth trying to get used to the smell, which was a mixture of post-mortem room, a sewer, sweat and foul pus.'[4]

The liberating soldiers would say later they had felt to be 'wearing' the smell of Belsen or that it had 'got into them'. Memories evoked by smell are the most vivid and emotional. Odour receptors in the nose send messages to the brain's olfactory bulb, which forwards them to the amygdala – the brain's memory bank for emotional experience. Other senses have a more convoluted route to the brain, so arrive less pure and are more easily forgotten. In his book *Odour Sensation and Memory*, Trygg Engen, an authority in sensory perception, wrote that 'when future occasions present the same or similar odours, memory will bring back the early experience and directly affect the reaction to the new stimuli.' The soldiers and inmates of Belsen were fated, then, to revisit the camp psychologically whenever they were exposed to similar smells.

We discovered that the camp was divided into compounds or sections. There were five in all: A, B, C, D and E. At this point I think it will be necessary to stress that the speed of the advancing troops left the enemy bewildered. This naturally included the SS guards at Belsen who were consequently without orders from their hierarchy. They were caught, as it were, with their pants down. The camp staff was taking the surrender quite well. It seemed to me that mostly they were glad it was over, but a lot of them realised they would have to pay for their cruelty to mankind.

'A' compound was the first section to be entered by me and my CO. There was nothing to prepare us for the full horror that was soon to be revealed to the first of these British eyes. The illegal holding of many of these prisoners by the SS was the only horror so far encountered. Apart from the striped prison garb, the appearance of the inhabitants of 'A' section, whilst not too good, was not too bad either, considering what was to come. So, with great trepidation, 'B' compound was entered for inspection.

(I don't know whether I have mentioned the layout of the camp, so far. However, a little recap wouldn't go amiss at this stage. The four sides were roughly a mile long. The fencing was an awe-inspiring 20 feet high all round, including the gates, which was topped by rolled barbed wire, just in case somebody tried to break in or the inmates were strong and healthy enough to break out. Side one of the camp ran the length of A and B compounds; side 2 B and C; side three C and D; side four, D and A. Which left E. Yes, you have it – in the centre of the lot. Each compound had its own surrounding fence and two gates, one in and one out. The 'out' meaning the 'in', as no prisoner was ever released alive. Each compound had its quota of wooden huts, which would normally house 50 prisoners at a pinch, but, as time went by, the number of prisoners exceeded the amount of accommodation until, almost at the time of our arrival, owing to rations of food being so scarce and rare, the huts were holding roughly 150).

The experience of the camp from an inmate's perspective was presented by the Sarajevo-born author Hanna Lévy-Hass, who documented her time at Belsen in a diary:

> We have not died, but we are dead. They have managed to kill in us not only our right to live in the present and for many of us, to be sure, the right to a future life. But what is most tragic is that they have succeeded, with their sadistic and depraved methods, in killing in us all sense of a human life in our past, all feeling of normal human beings endowed with a normal past, up to even the very consciousness of having existed at one time as human beings worthy of this name. [5]

On first entering the camp, Herbert had instinctively rummaged in his pockets for any food he could find. He broke pieces from a chocolate bar and passed them to as many prisoners as possible. He regretted this because within minutes they were holding their stomachs and crying out in pain; the richness of the chocolate had caused severe cramp. Major Dick Williams, staff captain in the Supplies and Transport unit of VIII Corps Headquarters, recalled how they struggled initially to provide food for the prisoners. 'The food that we'd got, breaking open these compo rations wasn't right. Their stomachs couldn't take anything. The best we could do was the tea, and then we decided to open all the tins and make a big mess of it. We put as much boiling water in amongst it and made a thin stew. I'm afraid sausages and beef and everything, corned beef [this was a reference to it containing ingredients that did not conform to the Jewish dietary regulations of *kashrut*], it all got mixed up together, but at least it was some sort of liquidy food. Some of the people were still in the huts, where there were more dead than living. We would take a Dixie [cooking pot] of this broth and leave it at the door,' [6] said Major Williams.

The CO, with me in the lead, was making progress in compound B when a rattle of machine gun fire plus single shots from small arms weapons was heard coming from deeper inside the camp. This outburst was explained by the German Commandant as the action by his guards who were allowed to shoot prisoners for attempting to steal vegetables from the gardens, which they tended for their masters. The sheer desperation of their plight and state of malnutrition made those unfortunate beings easy targets for the armed gunmen. The CO ordered me to return to the Guard House entrance and round up as many British troops as could be spared. These were to be transported in their three-tonners further into the camp, in the direction of the shooting. In the vanguard of the CO was the Nazi commander who had to order his SS thugs to cease fire, surrender all weapons and place themselves under the orders of the British soldiers. It took some considerable time to get all the German troops under supervision and the weapons out of harm's way.

Herbert and the other soldiers knew nothing of the camp's history, of course. The first prisoners had arrived in late 1939. These were approximately 500 Jews from the Buchenwald and Natzweiler-Struthof camps, brought in as slave labour to develop a new site close to a large military complex in the hamlet of Belsen. Several sub-camps were established. The first was for the original prisoners – it closed in February 1944 and they were moved to Sachsenhausen, a camp 22 miles north of Berlin. The 'special' camp housed 2,400 Polish Jews who held passports or entry papers which they believed would see them quickly set free. They were deported to Auschwitz in late 1943 and early 1944, where most of them were murdered. About 350 Jews from neutral countries such as Spain, Portugal and Turkey formed the 'neutral' sub-camp. The 'star' camp was for Jews designated as possible exchanges for German prisoners-of-war. They did not have to wear prison uniforms, but had the Star of David fastened to their clothes; they were mainly from the Netherlands. Very few were actually 'traded' and by July 1944, 4,100 remained at Belsen.

Over the winter of 1944/45, Allied forces had encountered several near-deserted camps close to the frontline. Thousands of prisoners had been taken from them on 'death marches' (forced evacuation) to other camps deeper into Germany. The Nazis planned to use the prisoners for slave labour, and had moved them on because they did not want the Allies to bear witness to their appalling state. They were marched for miles without food and water to railway stations where they were forced into carriages used ordinarily to transport animals. The SS guards had orders to kill prisoners who could no longer walk. 'Anyone who dared to bend over, who stopped even for a moment, was shot,' said Iba Mann, who was 19 at the time. 'We walked through fields of ice, snow and blizzards. We saw ordinary Germans standing along the road, watching the prisoners go by. Unbelievable,' said Shmuel Beller, a survivor. Among those on the march from Auschwitz was Anne Frank, the Jewish girl from the Netherlands who documented life under Nazi persecution in her diaries. She died six weeks before Belsen was liberated, aged 15.

During the period July 1944 to April 1945, the number at Belsen expanded from 7,300 to almost 90,000. In crude terms, it had become a 'dumping ground' of the sick and malnourished. On a single day in March 1945, more than 2,000 arrived from Buchenwald. Abel Jacob Herzberg, a Dutch Jewish lawyer and writer, recalled it in his diary published as *Tweestromenland* [*Between Two Streams*] in 1959: 'The shouting, abusing, crying, taunting, groaning, cracking of the whips and thuds of the beatings could be heard throughout the night. The next morning, we saw hundreds of corpses being dragged onto a heap and stripped of clothing. All day, the heap of emaciated, naked bodies was left lying in the sun.'

Belsen did not contain the machinery of mass murder; there were no gas chambers. Instead, an estimated 52,000 died of starvation (no one had eaten for two weeks before the British soldiers arrived), disease or from violence inflicted by the SS. In the month before liberation, more than 18,000 had died. There was an acute shortage of food and water, no real sanitation and overcrowding had led to the spread of dysentery, typhoid fever and tuberculosis. 'Soon after arrival at Belsen, we found ourselves covered from head to foot with lice,' said Renee Salt, a Polish prisoner who was a teenager at the time. 'The camp was completely infested. No food was coming in and the water supply had been cut off. Like leaves that fall from a tree, people were falling down and dying. It was sheer chaos.' Renee (born Rywka Ruchla Berkowitz) had an archetypal backstory. The Gestapo had ejected her family from their home in Zduńska Wola, central Poland, stealing their possessions. She had spent time in Auschwitz and undertook forced labour at the docks in Hamburg before being transported to Belsen.

Unlike at most other camps, there was no established schedule at Belsen, which would have provided a daily routine for inmates. They were left to either sleep or hobble through the muddy lanes of the camp. Many lingered by the perimeter fence, staring out at the trees and fields beyond. The hunger was such that there were reported outbreaks of cannibalism. 'The doctors among the prisoners told me that cannibalism was going on,' said General Miles Dempsey. 'There was no flesh on the bodies, and the liver, kidneys and heart were knifed out.' [7] Harold Le Druillenec was thought to be the only British prisoner in the camp. He had been arrested in Jersey the day before D-Day, for helping his sister harbour an escaped Russian prisoner-of-war; Germans had occupied the Channel Islands during the war. 'Jungle law reigned among the prisoners,' he said. 'At night, you killed or were killed. By day cannibalism was rampant. All my time was spent heaving dead bodies into the mass graves kindly dug for us by "outside workers" [presumably local Germans], for we no longer had the strength for that type of work.' [8]

Prisoners had been kept in huts containing rows of three-tiered bunk beds. Each hut was designed for about 60 people but most held a great deal more, squeezed into beds or sleeping on the floor. They were called each day at 3am and made to stand for up to four hours. Until it ran out, the daily food ration was three pints of watery swede soup and a piece of black bread, brought to them in large dustbins. There were no eating utensils. 'At the time of the food distribution they behaved more like ravenous wolves than human beings . . . the inmates had lost all self-respect and been degraded morally to the level of beasts,'[9] wrote Captain Andrew Pares of the Durham Light Infantry. There were no toilets or washing facilities. They drank rainwater. A water butt from which some had been drinking was found to contain the decomposing body of a child. The floor, both inside and outside the huts, was said to have become a 'carpet' of dead bodies, excreta, rags and filth. Those who were fit enough roamed the camp, continuously looking for herbs and traces of food which they heated in a can over a fire made from a handful of twigs. As soon as they died, people were stripped of their clothing by others seeking to keep warm.

Chapter Fourteen
Incomprehension and rage

———

Josef Kramer, the camp commandant, had welcomed the British soldiers in a curiously formal manner, as if oblivious to the horror in which he was mired. He told officers that there were 60,000 inmates (of whom 10,000 were dead but unburied), 500 children, and the death-rate was running at approximately 500 per day. Until March, the dead had been cremated but a surge in mortality had overloaded the capacity of the crematorium. Bodies had been piled and burned on open ground within the camp for a few days, but soldiers at the Panzer training school two miles away had complained about the smell. Large pits had been dug using bulldozers but the internees were too frail to drag bodies over to them. Finally, bodies had been left in mounds ever closer to accommodation huts. Food and water had run out, which, claimed Kramer, was out of his control. He failed to reveal that there was a store at the training school containing vast amounts of potatoes, tinned meat, sugar, grain and wheat. The school also had medical supplies and a well-staffed bakery with the capacity to produce 60,000 loaves a day.

Typhus, much the same as starvation, had been used at Belsen as a de facto weapon. Without medicine or the facility to wash themselves or their clothes (to rid the lice), the disease had spread through the camp unchecked. Fania Fénelon (née Fanja Goldstein), a musician and member of the French Resistance, described the effect of typhus graphically in her book, *Playing for Time*: 'The illness took me over entirely; my head was bursting, my body trembling, my intestines and stomach were agony and I had the most abominable dysentery. I was just a sick animal lying in its own excrement. Everything around me became nightmarish. I merely existed as a bursting head, an intestine, a perpetually active anus.' On the day of liberation, Fania, aged 36, weighed under four and a half stones.

Only 75 SS guards remained at the camp, 49 men and 26 women. Most of the original 300 or so had fled in the preceding days. Those still at their posts were allowed to keep their guns initially because they said a riot would break out if prisoners saw they were unarmed. On the first few nights after liberation, the SS were themselves imprisoned and put on the same meagre rations endured by inmates. 'We left pieces of rope around and some hanged themselves. They knew they would have no chance in a war trial because their crimes were so great,'[10] said Sgt Norman Turgel of the 153 Field Security section of British Intelligence. In the official army report, one SS guard was recorded as committing suicide, two tried and failed, and two ran away 'but were immediately shot'.

Under cover of darkness, Russian and Polish inmates with

sufficient energy took reprisals on the kapos (prisoners working on behalf of the SS, usually violent criminals). More than 100 were thrown from the upper floors of the Panzer training school. Kramer was interrogated at the camp by Sgt Turgel of the Intelligence Corps. Turgel said later that, as a Jew, he was 'very proud to arrest one of the most notorious gangsters in Nazi Germany'. Before issuing an arrest warrant, Turgel locked Kramer in a meat refrigerator for a full day. He also revealed that any guards attempting to escape were shot on sight. 'When some of the SS tried to run away, they emptied their machine guns into them. These boys were so shocked that I think they would have killed any German they had come across,' he said. About 80 SS guards were thought to have fled into woods surrounding the camp. Most were apprehended by the Dutch Resistance secreted in the forest and 'strung up'.

Several mass graves were dug by SS guards under order of British soldiers. The task was so substantial that bulldozers were used to compact, scoop up and tip out bodies. Drivers steered and operated the bulldozers with one hand, using the other to hold a cloth soaked in petrol over their mouth and nose; the smell of rotting, broken flesh was unendurable. This image of desecration, human beings reduced to a mass of rubble, was among the most shocking at Belsen and became indelibly imprinted on the minds of soldiers and, later, the global population. The burials turned into a ritual gathering. A crowd congregated each morning in a clearing to watch the SS toil under the spring sun, shouting and mocking them. Emmanuel

Fisher, a radiographer with the Medical Corps, kept a diary. He wrote of the 'burial parties': 'The one thing I saw that pleased me was the SS men being bullied into work. All the time our armed troops shout at them, kick them, threaten them, never letting them stop for a moment. What a horrible type they are, these SS, with their Hollywood criminal features.' [11]

★

The tone of Herbert's notes had been broadly dispassionate until he arrived at Belsen. The same as most soldiers, he had become inured to acts of great hostility and resultant carnage. Though repugnant, he believed it was necessary and contributed towards a common good. He stated regularly that he was 'doing a job' or 'getting on with it'. This equanimity foundered at Belsen where he seethed with incomprehension and rage. Even if told beforehand, it was doubtful he would have believed in the existence of a mission as ruthlessly inhumane as genocide. Corporal Ian Forsyth, a wireless operator with the 15th/19th King's Royal Hussars, expressed this same incredulity: 'I couldn't believe what I was seeing. I couldn't believe people could sink to that level, and treat people the way they treated those prisoners. If you see a person who is a living skeleton, as these people were, it's difficult. It's astonishing that any human being could survive the terrible torture.' [12]

When the broadcaster Richard Dimbleby, the BBC's first war correspondent, filed his eyewitness radio report from Belsen ('I passed through the barrier and found myself in the world of a nightmare . . .'), it was not broadcast for four days. BBC editors said it was because of its graphic content but they were really seeking corroboration of its veracity: they too couldn't believe what they had heard. Dimbleby said he would resign if it did not run. The BBC relented. On finishing his ten-minute piece, he was reported to have broken down in tears.

The exactness of the description of prisoners as 'living skeletons' meant that the phrase would be repeated numerous times afterwards. An aura of otherworldliness prevailed, depicted by the Reverend Leslie Hardman, attached to VIII Corps of the British Second Army. He described a scene whereby two soldiers, new to the camp, were carrying potatoes that were spied by the prisoners: 'And then, almost as though they had emerged from the ground itself, a number of wraith-like creatures came tottering towards us. As they drew closer they made frantic efforts to quicken their feeble pace. Their skeleton arms and legs made jerky, grotesque movements as they forced themselves forward. Their bodies, from their heads to their feet, looked like matchsticks. The two Tommies must have thought they had walked into a supernatural world. They dropped their heavy sacks and fled.' [13] The shrunken size and state of prisoners caused the liberators to become psychologically disordered. James Hardman, an RAF dispatch rider, said: 'We went into a few of many huts of what I shall call the living dead. The inmates were lying there, the bodies so withered and thin that they looked like skinny babies on a full-size bed. They were all practically incapable of speech or movement. Lads of 20 years of age were so small that one could nurse them like a doll, and yet they looked about 100 years old.' [14]

My mind and heart was bitter, very bitter. If I could have had my way I would have lined all those cruel swines against the wall, or anywhere, and shot them down with my automatic. To me, this is what I thought would or should be done to them. But that would have been a too quick way to die after what they had done. I am not a cruel man, never have been. I was taught to kill in a war against enemies of my country. I was taught, as a soldier, to kill or be killed. That is a different thing than being cruel to a lot of innocent human beings. I am still against cruelty and try to help anyone in trouble or harm.

Herbert and the other soldiers showed remarkable self-restraint at a time of immense distress, and while in an altered state of consciousness. Witnesses, at the time and in hindsight, referred to it as Richard Dimbleby had done – 'like entering a nightmare'. The instinctive response was to seek vengeance but they largely resisted, under a strict directive from superiors. Lieutenant Colonel Leonard Berney explained in his book *Liberating Belsen*: 'We were, of course, shocked and horrified. What made it possible for us to do what we did was army discipline. All of us at that camp had, for many months, fought our way through France and were toughened soldiers. In the army, the man at the top makes a decision, men under him are given orders and they obey those orders. Whatever you were told to do, you got on with it.'

Sergeant-Major Reg Seekings of the 1st Special Air Service Regiment was among several to flout the official decree. His friend and fellow soldier, Johnny Cooper, recalled their arrival at Belsen:

'We stood aghast. We simply couldn't comprehend how it was possible for human beings to treat their fellow men in such a brutal and heinous way. The effect on Reg was one of utter rage.' While they were inspecting the camp, Sgt-Maj. Seekings saw an SS guard attack a prisoner. He asked Major Jon Tonkin if he could 'teach the man a lesson'. He was granted permission and punched the guard in the face. He fell down but dragged himself back to his feet. He was punched again and knocked unconscious. A week after its liberation, a British journalist visited the camp and reported that most of the SS were 'spattered with blood' and that the British soldiers were 'seized by a genuine and permanent anger'.

Belsen was not the first concentration camp to be liberated. Nine months earlier, in July 1944, the Soviet Red Army had arrived at Majdanek camp near Lublin, Poland, where approximately 78,000 had been killed, 59,000 of them Polish Jews; it had seven gas chambers. Auschwitz, a complex of more than 40 concentration and extermination camps, had been discovered by Russian soldiers in January 1945. These were major sites of the Nazis' 'final solution' – a euphemism for a plan to eliminate Europe's entire Jewish population. At least 1.1 million were killed at Auschwitz, most after being stripped naked and locked into chambers filled with Zyklon B, a gas containing hydrogen cyanide, described as smelling of bitter almonds.

An incident involving Heinrich Himmler, leader of the SS and overseer of the 'final solution', had prompted the decision to prioritise mass murder through gassing. He had visited a camp in

Minsk, Ukraine, in August 1941, where Soviet prisoners were incarcerated; more than three million Soviet prisoners-of-war would be killed before the end of the war. He ordered an execution of about a hundred inmates. An open grave was dug and they were made to climb into it and lie face down. As the rows of men were shot, others had to lie on top of the dead before they too were killed. Himmler was curious and stood at the edge to peer down. He was dashed by blood and slivers of flesh during the shooting. Karl Wolff, his deputy, reported that Himmler went 'very green' and almost fainted. Afterwards, Himmler said a less labour-intensive and 'less messy' process of execution was necessary; this was after more than two million people had already been shot dead at various camps.

A procedure was set down following each mass killing. The Sonderkommando – a unit comprised of mainly Jewish prisoners forced, under threat of their own lives, to assist with the disposal of victims – was ordered to remove jewellery from bodies. Gold fillings and crowns were pulled from mouths to be melted down into gold bars and sold to banks. Hair was recycled and used as mattress stuffing or in the manufacture of rope and carpets. Finally, the bones of victims were ground to powder and used as fertiliser or landfill, usually to level roads.

Four days before Herbert's arrival at Belsen, Buchenwald concentration camp near Weimar, Germany, had been liberated by the Sixth Armoured Division of the US forces; 50,000 people had been killed at the site. The scenes were similar to those at Belsen. 'As we came through the entrance to the main building, there were three trucks filled with naked corpses. Then I went into one of the buildings where there were furnaces and there was half a body lying in one of the furnaces. I also saw the hooks on the walls where bodies were hanged before burning,' [15] said Colonel Bernard Bernstein.

News of the discovery of these various camps was unlikely to have reached Allied soldiers based elsewhere through Europe. Few outlets existed for the transfer of information; letters to and from home were censored. In his notes, Herbert made no reference to being aware of such camps. Corporal Ian Forsyth was another among the first to enter Belsen. 'We weren't expecting to see anything – we didn't know there was such a place. We had been going ahead without any idea there was anything there. I think that was the worst part. My tank happened to be the lead tank on that particular day. But no one told us what to expect.', he said. Lance-Bombardier George Leonard of the 63rd Anti-Tank Regiment had marginally more information: 'We'd heard all these silly stories about the Germans and concentration camps – and we didn't believe it! We didn't! Nobody would do things like that! But of course, they did. And we walked into it.' [16]

The liberation of Auschwitz in January 1945 by Russian scouts from the 322nd Rifle Division had been by chance. 'We knew nothing,' Ivan Martynushkin, a senior lieutenant in the Soviet Army, told the *Times of Israel* in January 2015. 'We beat back the Germans in one village, passed through, and came out onto some kind of enormous field almost completely surrounded by electrified barbed wire fences and watchtowers,' he said. 'As we got closer, we began to see that there were people. We saw the inmates. I remember their faces, especially their eyes, which betrayed their ordeal.' Martynushkin said they were unaware that systematic murder had taken place. 'When we saw the ovens, our first thought was: "Oh well, they are crematoriums. So people died and they didn't bury them all." We didn't know then, that those ovens were specially built to burn those who had been gassed,' he said.

Among Allied soldiers it was known bluntly that 'the Nazis hated Jews'. Many believed this was without rationale and a manifestation of pure evil. Herbert, in the days after first entering Belsen, thought of those chats he'd had with older workmates, when they had explained how Hitler and his acolytes had manipulated the insecurities of a nation. They had offered strength, unity and leadership at a time of crisis – the end of the 'Golden Age of Weimar'; the Great Depression; the Wall Street Crash; Germany's ignominious defeat in World War One etc.

The wider population had also been united under a policy of scapegoatism. Propaganda had been used to advance a dogma that 'true' Germans were Aryans (a mythical master race) of biological purity – tall, broad, fair haired and blue eyed. The Nazis demonised and targeted groups classified as *Untermenschen* (sub-humans): Jews, Slavs, Roma, Sinti (a sub-group of Roma), blacks, communists, trade unionists, beggars, homosexuals, Jehovah's Witnesses and the disabled, of whom more than 200,000 were killed. The persecution of most of these groupings, while risible, was often on an arbitrary basis – they believed that homosexuality, religious or political views (and affiliations) could be abandoned or renounced. There was, however, no conceivable amnesty for anyone of Jewish ethnicity, and the stated aim was the extinction of the entire race. Over two decades, on an insidious basis that served to 'normalise' discrimination, Jews were branded as a devious faction of power-brokers, scheming to their own self-interest, a parasite within the body of Germany. They were reviled also for the Judaist belief that, via descent from the ancient Israelites as stated in the Book of Deuteronomy, they were *chosen*, and selected to be in a covenant with God. The Nazis portrayed this as conceit and a rival statement of ultimate supremacy that had to be vanquished.

In their state of shock, Allied soldiers voiced the same words repeatedly, describing the actions of the SS variously as senseless, inhumane, unbelievable, revolting, disgusting and 'beyond explanation'. They struggled to understand that to the SS, every deed had validation regardless of its barbarity. The British relief teams at Belsen saw incarcerated men, women and children, but the SS pictured vermin of different gender and sizes. Dr Fritz Klein, the camp 'doctor' at Belsen, précised this *Weltanschauung* (world view): 'My Hippocratic oath tells me to cut a gangrenous appendix out of the human body. The Jews are the gangrenous appendix of mankind. That's why I cut them out.'

As an elite corps, the SS (Schutzstaffel, meaning 'Protective Echelon') regarded themselves as 'political soldiers' of the Nazi Party and chief votaries of its doctrine; they swore absolute allegiance to the Führer. They had been indoctrinated in hate from an early age, enmeshed in a mass cult of ruthless, dogmatic imperialism. They were so absorbed in the industry and insouciance of killing that they believed *they* were the aggrieved; they were doing the 'dirty work' on behalf of the rest of Germany. They perceived themselves worthy of veneration for having the resolve to serve the Fatherland in such an essential way: they were ridding it of enemies and, in the killing of children, enemies of the future. They had few ethical misgivings or fear of reckoning because they were sponsored by the state, which had promised that their efficiency and ruthlessness would contribute to the *Tausendjähriges Reich* – a thousand years of peace and prosperity based upon global dominance, their birthright.

★

The various units of British soldiers returned each night to the requisitioned biscuit factory. The honeyed smell was a pointed contrast to the odours that had enshrouded them through the day. They were in trauma, so emotionally drained that their limbs felt dissociated from their bodies. They were offered food but couldn't eat. They slumped to the floor, knees drawn up, backs against the wall. They were unable to properly form sentences. 'Why, Bert? Why?' he was asked, probably because he was a few years older than most of the other soldiers. He relayed what he'd been told about Hitler and the Nazis while sitting on a bench amid the lockers in the rest room at work, hoping it might clarify why the SS had acted as it had; not that he really understood. He was interrupted. 'Hold on, you're not trying to justify what these evil fuckers have done, are you?' As Herbert struggled for the words, another spoke over him. 'I get what you're saying, Bert, I do, but, come on, however much they've been brainwashed and believe in all that Third Reich crap, when it comes down to it, everyone knows in their soul that it's fucking wrong, *very* wrong, to be killing women and kids. I don't know about you, but if I was asked to do it, I couldn't. I'd rather put a bullet through my own head.'

Another to whom they turned for insight was nicknamed Teach, a head of history at a private school in civilian life. They asked if it had 'ever happened before'. His response was ambiguous. He said that 'history was full of dark corners'. There had, in fact, been examples of mass murder based on conflicting ideologies, race and religion. The Holocaust was unique, though, in its scale and its aim to eradicate a whole genetic race.

Herbert and the other soldiers in the locale of Belsen were unaware of earlier atrocities. And, if they had known, they would have judged them to be macabre communiqués from an ancient past or remote corners of the world, a form of primitivism that existed before society had become ordered and sophisticated, and with that an assumption of broad morality. This catastrophic failure of humanity was happening *now* in a setting that could easily be a rural hinterland between two cities in Britain, and perpetrated by people who had been educated and held as cultured. Savagery had never before been so well dressed and spoken so eloquently. Within a few days, most of the British soldiers had started to drink heavily and smoke excessively; for some, the self-medication that would last a lifetime had already begun.

★

Back home in Britain, politicians had known about the existence of concentration camps four years before their liberation. The five-man war cabinet formed by Winston Churchill and its 'constant attenders' (other MPs and advisors) had been informed of organised mass killings in the summer of 1941. British intelligence agents had eavesdropped on German radio signals reporting mass murders by the SS in Lithuania, Latvia and, later, Ukraine; this information would have been shared with the military hierarchy. The first official confirmation came in December 1942 when August Zaleski, the Polish foreign minister in exile, informed the Allied governments: 'From all the occupied countries Jews are being transported, in conditions of appalling horror and brutality, to Eastern Europe. None of those taken away are ever heard of again. The able-bodied are slowly worked to death in labour camps. The infirm are left to die of exposure and starvation, or are deliberately massacred in mass executions.'

The British foreign secretary, Anthony Eden, read a declaration in Parliament condemning the treatment of Jewish people by the Nazis and an impromptu minute's silence was held in the House of Commons on 17 December 1942. The *Daily Mail* reported: 'One after another, MPs stood, until all, in their hundreds, sombre-garbed and sombre-faced ranks, were on their feet. I can tell you that there were many eyes which were not dry and there was not, I dare swear, a throat without a lump in it.' Another journalist wrote: 'I have never seen anything like this silence, which was like the frown of the conscience of mankind.' Within the cabinet, the response was much less sympathetic than had been portrayed. Oliver Harvey, principal private secretary to Anthony Eden, wrote in his diaries that, 'A.E. loves Arabs and hates Jews.' In a note to Harvey written in September 1941, Eden confirmed: 'If we must have preferences let me murmur in your ear that I prefer Arabs to Jews.' Three months before the liberation of Belsen, an internal memo of the Refugee Department of the Foreign Office, read: 'Sources of information are nearly always Jewish, whose accounts are only sometimes reliable and not seldom highly coloured. One notable tendency in Jewish reports on this problem is to exaggerate the numbers of deportations and deaths.'

News outlets in the United States were reluctant to report unverified claims of atrocities because similar stories had circulated in World War One but had later been invalidated. The chain-smoking Edward R. Murrow, a charismatic and esteemed broadcaster, broke rank on a live broadcast for CBS News in December 1942: 'What is happening is this. Millions of human beings, most of them Jews, are being gathered up with ruthless efficiency and murdered. The phrase "concentration camps" is obsolete, as out of date as economic sanctions or non-recognition. It is now possible only to speak of extermination camps.'

Files released by the United Nations in April 2017 revealed that a number of governments had known the true scale of the killings. They had been informed that two million Jews had been murdered in the first two years of the war and a further five million were at risk. These were remarkably prescient figures, for an estimated six million Jews were murdered in German-occupied Europe between 1941 and 1945, two-thirds of the continent's entire Jewish population.

Many MPs, both at the time and retrospectively, were outraged that Allied governments had not made the liberation of Jews a specific military objective. Some had argued against involvement in what they termed privately 'a Jews' War', implying that the Jews were complicit in their own persecution. Robert Arthur James Gascoyne-Cecil, the 5th Marquess of Salisbury, known publicly as Viscount Cranborne and 'Bobetty' to close friends, a member of Churchill's war cabinet and an avowed imperialist, had argued in March 1943 that Jews were not a special case. He said Britain had already taken in enough refugees. By September 1939 the country had accepted 70,000 Jews and another 10,000 arrived during the war, mostly on an unofficial basis. Other MPs were more supportive but felt that a distinct undertaking to the Jews would divert funds and manpower from the primary aim, which was to defeat the Nazis and thereby liberate millions, whether incarcerated in their own towns and cities, or within the perimeters of camps.

Chapter Fifteen
A prison frock, almost in tatters

Allied governments and military leaders had patently been alerted to the existence of death camps years earlier but, regardless, plans had not been made, nor provisions or resources set aside for the catastrophe. Soldiers and relief teams had to deal with it 'on the hoof', which meant that the days following the liberation of Belsen were long and arduous, with respite unfeasible amid such a colossal humanitarian crisis. The COs proclaimed: 'You've just got to KBO it.' They were mustering a phrase made popular by Winston Churchill – 'Keep Buggering On'. Initially, soldiers were too exhausted and mentally numbed to summon a grumble, even among themselves, let alone question army policy. The mood changed after a few days. 'Some fuckers knew about all this and they've let us walk into it,' was the protest. 'Why are we up to our knees in shit and dead bodies while politicians are sat at home by the fire?'

Another rally from the COs was, 'We've done it before, we'll do it again – remember Quetta.' They were citing an earthquake that had occurred a decade earlier, in May 1935, in the city of Quetta in Balochistan, British India (now part of Pakistan), when up to 40,000 people died. The occupying British forces had played a major role in the rescue operation.

Herbert and Teach, as senior soldiers, were asked: 'What's all this about Quetta?' News of the earthquake had been carried in newspapers for a few days, but, in a pre-television age, it had barely made public consciousness. Such was Quetta's geographical anonymity, most of the articles were accompanied by crude maps showing its location. The headline in the *New York Times* had been indicative of the grading of racial worth: '20,000 Die in Indian Quake; Wide Area is Devastated; 43 British Airmen Victims'. Herbert had only a vague memory of what had happened, but did not petition his superiors for fear of appearing ignorant. When fellow soldiers asked for the umpteenth time, he answered: 'I'm not sure now whether it was an earthquake, a heatwave, a storm, a flood, a drought or a landslide – there's always a lot of weather going on in India. Either way, us Brits pulled our tripe out and sorted it, and that's what we're being asked to do here.' The great distinction between Quetta and Belsen was that one was a natural disaster, but the other was implemented by man.

On 15 April and the days following, the RASC's battle log was updated on an almost hourly basis. At 15.40 on the 15th: 'Some of the inmates of Belsen camp are getting out and the guards are not preventing them.' At 17.45: 'The 63rd Anti-Tank Regiment arrived. They said they'd found all officials wearing white armbands and carrying white flags.' The next day: 'Conditions at Belsen

Concentration Camp worse than anticipated.' On the 17th: 'Began to feed inmates.' On the 21st: 'The Rev A C Austin delivered sweets, chocolate etc. to the camp for children.'

Over several days, Herbert returned to the camp.

Things began moving very early. On the face of it, the Germans appeared to have accepted their predicament with a certain amount of calmness, although the speed of recent events had left them a little bewildered. However, there were some of the upper-echelons (tough nuts who were dyed in the wool Nazis, utterly brainwashed bastards, cocky and arrogant) who found it difficult to accept their situation, to knuckle under as it were. They had to be dealt with accordingly. Members of the Liverpool and Scottish Regiment had been designated to deal with the German soldiers who were told to do all the work they had prescribed for their own prisoners, like cleaning up the camp and burying the dead.

These starving inmates – thirsty, poorly clad, filthy, lice infested, cruelly insulted by their captors – somehow managed to keep their dignity, which shone through like a small lamp in that dejection. I saw them shuffling around as though their ankles were chained together, allowing movement of only one inch at a time, as though the chains were too heavy. They were so weak. I looked into their eyes but they couldn't see me. There were some young prisoners with a stronger constitution who hadn't been there as long. They were queuing up alongside a water bowser which had been sent in with fresh water from outside. They were rationed to

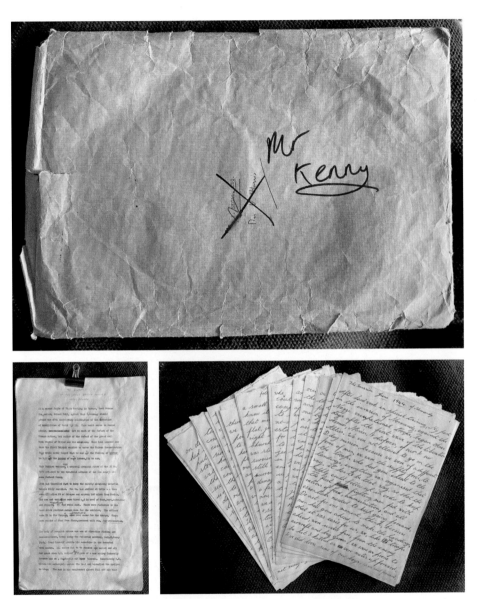

The original typed article that Herbert dropped off at the *Middleton Guardian,* along with the envelope in which they were contained, and his handwritten notes.

The block of maisonettes in Rhodes, Middleton, where the author conducted a newspaper interview with Herbert in May 1985, and Herbert's home for the last 25 years of his life.

The original piece about Herbert, written by the author in 1985.

Dressed in their Sunday best: Herbert (left, aged six)
with his brothers Leslie (standing) and Norman.

Ready for service: Herbert in army uniform,
about to embark for Normandy.

A rare moment of respite: Herbert on 'Grace',
his trusty Matchless G3/L motorcycle.

Internees waiting for a ration of potato soup a few weeks after liberation.

Belsen shortly after liberation.

British soldiers with rounded up SS guards.

Jewish Chaplain to the British 2nd Army, Reverend Leslie
Hardman, looks over a mass grave ahead of burial.

Piles of lice-infested clothing are burnt before being
buried by bulldozer to halt the spread of disease.

Grace outside the Kenny's first home in Australia, among the bricks where Herbert is laying a new patio.

Herbert and Grace in later life.

Courtesy of the Kenny family

One of the last photographs of Herbert (left), a reluctant musical accompanist to a Christmas sing-song with his pal Len Foulkes.

one cup each because any more at that particular time, according to the medics, would probably have killed them off. From then on, the British water tankers kept rolling in.

After assisting with the parking of these water tankers and preparing the trays of cups with which to issue the water ration, I stood back and watched the steady procession of grateful, thirsty unfortunates. I noticed one who looked like a young girl of about 17. You could tell the difference from the clothing the prisoners wore, otherwise they all looked the same – extremely undernourished, heads shaven etc. What caught my interest was the fact that this particular person, instead of moving off to drink this delightful, refreshing clear water, she carried her cup very carefully to the corner of a hut close by. She placed it on the dusty ground then proceeded to disrobe (if you can call it that). Her only clothing was a prison frock almost in tatters. As carefully as before, she took the cup with one hand and poured a little of the water into her other hand and went through the motions of washing herself. I blinked very, very hard (what could you do?). I shook my head to clear my vision and gripped my Sten to steady myself. I made my way to the side of this terrified poor girl who had known only brutality from the uniformed guards. She pulled back as if she had done something wrong, but I put my free hand gently under one of her tiny elbows, made what I thought were soothing noises to calm her fears, and gently led her back to the head of the queue for her to get a cup of water to drink. This was the reaction of a battle-hardened soldier who had seen other indescribable horrors all the way from those Normandy beaches.

'All right now, love,' I said. The words were spoken to test my voice more than anything else. Embarrassment isn't dealt with very easily by (tough) soldiers.

With that, I moved off purposefully on my rounds to possibly discover other hidden horrors in that camp. I was to see that girl later on before leaving Belsen, when she thanked me and told me a little about herself and where she was from in Poland. She had lived with her parents in a well-to-do area. She showed me a photo of her family taken in a well-kept garden of their beautiful detached stone house. The Germans had shot her parents and taken her into custody.

Among my other duties, I had to ride 50 miles to the main HQ to inform them of the discovery of Belsen and its appalling conditions. Also of the dire need for medical supplies and personnel. Tons of food was arranged to be collected from Celle's factory warehouses where there was a huge concentration of powdered milk, dried eggs and fruit of every description. Some provisions also found their way to supplement the rations of the British troops at the frontline. Why not? Who was there to complain? With expert care and attention by the medical staff many ex-prisoners survived, although huge numbers were too far gone to be given any useful help. When we left Belsen after three weeks or so, I was happy to see the progress that was being made.

More than 9,000 people died in the fortnight after the arrival of the British troops, and another 4,000 by the end of June. They had been too sick or malnourished to survive. Buildings within the complex were burned to prevent the spread of diseases. Two DP (displaced persons) camps were set up at the Wehrmacht Panzer training school, one for Jews and the other, Poles, mainly of Roman Catholic faith. Josef Rosensaft, the son of a scrap metal dealer, symbolised the resolve of the human spirit. He had been deported to Auschwitz in 1943 but escaped the transport by jumping into the Vistula river. He was shot and injured but made his way back to his home town of Będzin in southern Poland. He was recaptured, confined to a chicken cage and tortured for six months in the notorious Block 11, the 'Death Block', at Auschwitz. He later completed a death march to Belsen, where, when freed, he weighed five stones. He was elected chairman of the Central Committee of Liberated Jews.

Both DP camps were veritable townships. Jacob 'Coby' Lubliner, later a Professor Emeritus at the University of California, was ten when Belsen was liberated. He described the Jewish DP as 'a self-governing enclave', while Rosensaft referred to it as 'the last *shtetl* in Europe' (a *shtetl* is a small Jewish town or village in eastern Europe). The camp comprised 10,000 people and had a Yiddish newspaper (*Unzer Sztyme*, 'Our Voice'); schools; an orphanage; police force; court; theatre company and numerous cultural, political, youth and sports organisations. Hundreds of marriages took place and more than 2,000 babies were born. Effie Barker, a liaison officer at the British Red Cross Commission, was overjoyed to witness such a transformation, which may have accounted for the tone of the letter she wrote to her brother and father back home in Hurst, Berkshire, in June 1945: 'It is a privilege to have seen a miracle, and that is what Belsen now is. More like a Butlin holiday camp than a concentration one!'

The Polish DP camp was similarly organised, with a school for 600 children, two kindergartens, newspapers, a choir, brass bands and regular cabaret performances. By November 1945, prisoners had recovered sufficiently to take part in a football match – Polonia v the British Army. The presence of the Poles at Belsen was commemorated with a special Mass and installation of a tall wooden cross on the site. The Polish camp was dissolved in September 1946, and the Jewish in August 1951, with most survivors emigrating to Israel, the United States and Canada. Josef Rosensaft moved firstly to Montreux in Switzerland and then to New York where he became an art collector, owning paintings by Picasso, Monet and Renoir.

The utter desolation and despair of the Holocaust, perhaps understandably, stirred the media to search for fragments of hope, and focus disproportionately on narratives of resilience and triumph, such as Rosensaft's. The Centre for Holocaust Education ('the world leader in Holocaust education'), based at University College London, presented a stark assessment: 'It is often assumed that 1945 brought "liberation" for the victims of Nazism. This is, of course, naïve: you cannot easily be liberated from life-changing experiences of torture, slave labour and genocide, whose consequences lived on for victims and, often, affected the experiences of their families and the next generation.' Isaac Levy, the Jewish chaplain to the Second Army, said he was 'certain that

90 per cent of those who survive will never be normal. They have suffered too much.'

Dennis Forsdick was one of 96 medical students from London who volunteered their services to the British Army towards the end of the war. They had been told they were needed to treat Dutch soldiers who had become emaciated after the Germans had cut off food supplies. Instead, they were diverted to Belsen. 'The mental state of many of the prisoners was remarkable. Some did not know who they were, many had no idea whence they had come,' wrote Forsdick. Another medical student, Andrew Matthews, revealed the emotional impact of his experience shortly before his death in 1995, when he wrote: 'I faced the stark reality of life for the first time. I emerged unscathed but my beliefs did not. There is no God either in spirit or substance, only a Devil and that Devil is mankind.' [17]

★

In the autumn of 1945, members of the SS and kapos from Belsen were put on trial at a court staffed by the British judiciary held in a gymnasium in Lüneburg, 30 miles south-east of Hamburg. Although the SS was ostensibly a male-only organisation, women had enlisted as members of the SS-Gefolge (servants or officials who accompany a person of importance). They had worked as guards or 'nurses' – 16 were brought before the court. More than 450 SS had been 'employed' at Belsen but only 45 were charged – 11 were sentenced to death, 14 were acquitted and the rest given prison sentences which were customarily reduced on appeal; this reflected the move to a Cold War, where the Allies wanted to establish West Germany as a bulwark to the spread of communism in the Eastern Bloc. The 'denazification' policy, of which the imprisonment of SS members was symbolic, was relaxed because it was viewed generally as unnecessary and vindictive.

Josef Kramer was among those sentenced to death. Two days before Belsen's liberation, he had gratuitously killed 22 prisoners by firing at them from his office window with an MP 40 submachine gun. Such indiscriminate killing was a sick pastime of the guards. They would shoot at prisoners defecating because their white backsides formed an easy target. Irma Grese, a 22-year-old female guard, was also hanged. She was said to have randomly killed about 30 people each day. In an attempt to mitigate her actions, the court heard that her mother had committed suicide by drinking hydrochloric acid and Grese had been bullied at school. The SS members were executed by the famous British hangman Albert Pierrepoint, who later ran a pub called the Help the Poor Struggler, in Oldham, a few miles from Middleton. By 1955, all those imprisoned after the trial at Lüneburg had been released.

Chapter Sixteen
The most shocking scene

———

Herbert Kenny, aside from intermittent retelling of his tale in the *Middleton Guardian*, remained the Unknown Soldier. Among dozens of websites devoted to the subject, *The Liberators of Belsen Concentration Camp* is the foremost. It lists 1,244 men and women (a figure that continues to rise) who were involved in the emancipation. Herbert Kenny's name is not on it. The site is administered by Nick Price whose grandfather, Reg Price, of the 113th Durham Light Infantry, produced the famous sign that was positioned outside the camp: '10,000 unburied dead were found here. Another 13,000 have since died. All of them victims of the German new order in Europe and an example of Nazi kultur.' Since establishing the site in 2020, Price has made regular appeals: 'We're interested in all service and medical personnel who took part during the humanitarian effort at Belsen. Their roles and names are largely forgotten because many were too horrified to ever speak of what they had to do. This archive seeks to form a tribute to all those that were there, to find out more and to remember them.'

No one from Herbert's family has contacted the website; they are probably unaware of its existence. The Kennys belong to a social grouping much happier to defer, discomfited by attention. They are earthy, of their world. They mostly live in the same or similar houses to the ones in which they were brought up, and still reside within a few miles of one another, apart from Steven, Herbert's youngest son, who lives in Australia. Most have made their living through manual labour. The collective roll call of jobs they have each undertaken includes painting and decorating, cleaning, demolition, roofing, security, secretarial, engineering, bread delivery, mill work, and owning sandwich and chip shops. The happenstance of the renown brought upon them by Herbert's experiences at Belsen has prised them sporadically from the crowd scene but, to them, it was a single act in a life of many that they witnessed and shared. He is better defined to them as a father, grandfather and uncle, and, before that, a nephew, brother and son.

One or two in the family have kept cuttings from the *Middleton Guardian* but otherwise Herbert's connection to Belsen is seldom mentioned, nor considered. The Kennys get on with it – their jobs, their lives, their day. They do not indulge or sermonise, nor run to formality and ceremony. Chris Hoyle, Herbert's granddaughter, summed up their position: 'I don't really know what to say except that we are a typical Middleton family. We've never had much but we've always got by. We're not so close, now that we have all grown up and got our own families, but still love each other and would do anything for one another.' In another family, more assured of its place and of a higher social status perhaps, Herbert might have been exalted and commemorated, his story passed down through generations, and his memoirs, kept by the Kennys in a plastic bag and barely read, treasured as gold.

Based on the time I spent with Herbert in May 1985, he reminded me of others I had interviewed for the paper – Bill Marne, for example, who launched and ran an art gallery in Langley, opening with an exhibition of Henry Moore's work. And others keen to paste metaphorical sequins on the scars of the town, whether busy in amateur dramatics or similar creative and worthy projects. These were men – there were women too, of course – who, across two or three decades before and after World War Two, had generally embraced a certain trilby wearing, worsted clad, pipe smoking, medium-brow culture. They were earnest. They had hobbies. They listened to folk and classical music. They sought out pubs with flagstone floors and drank real ale or brewed their own in sheds kept in good order, creosoted once a year. They had allotments. They attended classes held by the Workers' Educational Association (WEA). They visited mechanics' institutes to read books or listen to lectures. Rhodes had its own reading room, donated by the Schwabe family, the founders of CPA. The more radical among them had taken part in the mass trespass at Kinder Scout in the Peak District in 1932, demanding the 'right to roam', knapsacks bulging with butties, a fold-away Bartholomew map in the side pocket. They painted. They had books in their houses, usually drawn from the Everyman's Library, a scheme set up in 1905 whereby world literature was made available to 'every kind of person'. Herbert didn't fully accord with every aspect of this caricature, but it formed an approximate classification of his personality. He was, in short, of the dynamic and culturally aspirational working class.

Sitting with him in the flat, there was a particular point when his mood dropped to its darkest. He stopped talking for a few seconds and I sensed that he was recalling a specific episode and deliberating on whether to reveal it, as if he had made a promise to himself of absolute secrecy. He moved his gaze to the window. His voice fell quiet, and he issued words not as sentences, but in single lonely fragments. He then divulged a piece of information that has remained with me all my life, which was far too grotesque to include in the original newspaper article. Similar to Herbert, I have been reluctant to curse others with the knowledge of this atrocity, but it has to be shared to understand the depth of his suffering. He told me that while most British soldiers had obeyed orders to spare the SS guards, there had been isolated but significant outbreaks of non-compliance. In one instance, a large group of prisoners had jostled Herbert and other soldiers, pleading that they be allowed to carry out their own retribution on the SS guards. They acquiesced. The notes I made at the time in my reporters' spiral-bound notebook are long gone, but Herbert's words and the hesitant way they were spoken are seared into my memory. He said: 'We handed over this guard to them and what happened next was almost impossible to believe. These skeletons who had been struggling to even walk, suddenly found a great energy from somewhere as they set about him. They ripped him to pieces.'

★

The discovery of Belsen, as related by Herbert and others, was a spontaneous and confused affair. By mid-April 1945 various sectors of the British Army had been advancing unevenly through northern Germany, their route and speed of progress dependent on combat engagement. The degree of communication between each was chaotic and sporadic, and it seemed to fall largely to chance which unit or individual would first reach Belsen. Unknown to many, a formal notification of Belsen's existence and whereabouts had been lodged with senior army staff a few days earlier, and this would later form an alternative 'official' narrative to the one experienced by most troops on the ground.

On retreat across several fronts in April 1945, Wehrmacht field commanders had broadly accepted the impending defeat. The administrative structure was falling into disarray and SS officers in particular could foresee a formal atonement for their involvement in war crimes. They each sought to destroy evidence and downgrade their own level of participation. Five days before the liberation of Belsen, Kurt Andreas Ernst Becher, the SS commissar with overall responsibility for concentration camps, had been ordered by Himmler to visit the camp. Himmler might have been considering burning it down with the inmates still present, or opening the gates, knowing that most would soon die in its vicinity from starvation or disease. He had earlier contacted both the Swedish Red Cross and representatives of neutral countries, seemingly to seek their counsel on how to deal with the prisoners but, more likely, to present himself as a conciliatory figure. He was in a quandary because he had a fierce loyalty to the Führer who wanted the prisoners to be evacuated and put on another lengthy death march. The high prevalence of typhus at the camp from an outbreak two months earlier complicated matters because, if prisoners were released, they could spread the disease to German soldiers or civilians – the mortality rate among the untreated ran to 40 per cent.

Kurt Becher recommended that the camp be handed over to the British Army, after the incineration of all files kept at the site. Becher was known for his guile, and envisaged that this gesture would be viewed as an act of benevolence. Earlier, he had arranged the safe transit of 1,685 Jews to Switzerland, but others said this came at a price – he embezzled their valuables. 'Becher was an interesting case because he *did* save the lives of a number of Jews,' said Aaron Breitbart of the Simon Wiesenthal Centre, a Jewish human rights organisation. 'On the other hand, he did it to save his own skin. And we'll probably never know the full extent of what he extorted from them.' Becher was not prosecuted later at Nuremberg and went on to serve on the board of many blue-chip companies. In 1960 his wealth was estimated at US$30 million, making him one of the wealthiest men in West Germany. Himmler, in great contrast, committed suicide by swallowing a cyanide capsule before he could be brought before the tribunal.

The process of handing Belsen over to the British Army evidently began on 12 April 1945. The VIII Corps of the Second Army was near Winsen, a city 18 miles south of Hamburg. Lieutenant-Colonel Schmidt of the 1st German Parachute Army and Lieutenant-Colonel Bohnekamp, along with a medical officer and translator, appeared before the frontline, travelling in a motorcycle with a sidecar, waving a white flag. In another reported version, this scene was played out at 159th Battalion's HQ and the two men stepped out of a large Mercedes car with a white flag fixed to the bonnet. They were blindfolded and taken to a caravan which served as the unit's headquarters. Schmidt told Lieutenant-General Brian Horrocks, the Corps Commander, that, as British soldiers made their way through Lower Saxony, they would encounter a prison camp where there had been an outbreak of typhus affecting about 1,500 people. This summit was presented as an act of goodwill by the Germans because it made the British aware of the possibility of contracting typhus and also allowed them a little time to prepare a semblance of relief aid. The true nature of the camp and the vast scale of wretchedness had, of course, been wilfully understated. A truce was agreed and an exclusion zone of 48 square kilometres instituted around Belsen; this was why soldiers from various British units had not met resistance.

The wider area of Lower Saxony was flooded with thousands of troops, either advancing, retreating or, in pockets, steadfastly holding their positions. They were heavily armed and fatigued after months of fierce warfare. The dispersal of German units represented a different threat from the habitual massed confrontation of artillery force. Now, they might be positioned alone or in small groups, firing salvos from amid the white-green blur of birch trees or lying flat to the ground over the next mound. The formal conflict was as good as over and soldiers on both sides recognised that a new atmosphere prevailed. In the rough-hewn language of the various battle logs, there was mention of 'mopping up forward areas', 'squashing' and euphemisms for sporadic skirmishes – 'we are having a certain amount of trouble'. According to the war diary of the 23rd Hussars, they were 'north of Walle' (a village near Celle) on 15 April and saw 'notices in English declaring Belsen area to be typhus infected and a neutral zone'. They 'passed the camp at great speed, little knowing what horrors it concealed'.

The liberation of mainland Europe had been a precise and resolute military campaign, but the arbitrary detection of Belsen was typical of the End Days of a war. The radio army bulletins that gave notice of a 'prison camp' in the proximity of Belsen was one of hundreds issued on various topics to scores of platoons in mid-April 1945; acting upon it would have been regarded as a task, rather than a mission. Consequently, the ad hoc, understated nature of Belsen's discovery was startlingly at odds with its impact, then and in perpetuity. In their book *Remembering Belsen*, Ben Flanagan and Donald Bloxham, two experts in Holocaust studies, concluded: 'The exact circumstances leading up to the surrender of the camp are difficult to establish.'

Chapter Seventeen

What did you do in the war, Daddy?

———

Amid the uncertainty and ambiguity, several soldiers or their advocates have laid claim to being the first liberators of Belsen. The most eminent was John Randall whose biography, *The Last Gentleman of the SAS*, stated that he was 'the first Allied soldier to enter Belsen'. The lieutenant, a member of 1 SAS (Special Air Service Brigade, a forerunner of the SAS), wrote that he was being driven by a corporal in an open-topped jeep 30 miles south of Lüneburg Heath, a large area of grassland and forest in Lower Saxony. They came to 'a pair of huge gates . . . which were wide open'. At first they thought they had discovered a 'country house' but, on driving down a rutted path, were overcome by a putrid smell and saw 'a tide of humanity as Dante or Hieronymus Bosch imagined them'. They were joined 30 minutes later by Sergeant Reg Seekings and Major Jon Tonkin, two more members of the 1st SAS. Inside the camp, they were approached by someone 'who looked a nasty piece of work'. Randall reports that this man told them: 'I am Josef Kramer. Welcome to Bergen-Belsen.'

John Randall's background was the antithesis of Herbert Kenny's. He was the son of a former army captain, and a mother who had trained as an opera singer in Brussels. He spent the first five years of his life in Kenya where his father ran a coffee plantation; he mixed with Masai and Luhya tribespeople. Back in England, he was sent to boarding school at nine years old, firstly the exclusive Arnold House preparatory school in central London (alumni: Lord Lucan, Jonathan Miller and David Say, Bishop of Rochester) and later the public school his father had attended, St Lawrence College in Ramsgate, Kent. In 1940, Randall, aged 20, joined the GHQ Liaison Regiment, known as 'Phantom', a special reconnaissance unit considered 'an army within an army'. The regiment comprised astute, valiant, athletic and often flamboyant men, drawn mainly from the privileged class; the actor David Niven was among its number. During the war, Randall courted an array of 'most charming' young women, known customarily by their pet names – Bunny Steele and Doodles Rayment, among them – and was described by his biographer, M.J. (Meirion James) Trow, as 'strikingly handsome, suave and sophisticated'.

M.J. Trow was sceptical of other soldiers making assertions about playing principal roles at Belsen. 'In the aftermath of the war, an astonishing number of men claimed to have been the first Allied soldier into Belsen. It's part of the "What did you do in the war, Daddy?" syndrome, where otherwise anonymous people saw the chance of 15 minutes of fame,' he wrote. These 'claims' may not have been deliberate acts of misrepresentation or exaggeration. The haunting images of Belsen were so vivid and so extensively published that many soldiers became mistaken about their level of participation. The film actor and author Dirk Bogarde was thought to be among them. He had served in the Royal Corps of Signals (eventually as a major) and spent much of the war studying aerial photographs – he had seen several of Belsen before liberation. In television interviews and newspaper articles he referred to 'entering Dante's inferno' and said he had 'gratefully followed the black and yellow signs to Bergen-Belsen. Where we lost our boyish laughter for ever.' In his autobiography, *An Orderly Man*, he wrote that witnessing scenes at Belsen was 'an internal tattooing which is removable only by surgery. It cannot be conveniently sponged away by time.' John Carey, *The Times* critic, questioned Bogarde's recollection. 'It is virtually impossible that Bogarde saw Belsen or any other camp. Things he overheard or read seem to have entered his imagination and been mistaken for lived experience.' Bogarde's official biographer, John Coldstream, set down a list of operational reasons why Bogarde could not have been at the site, and added: 'Given all that, what would Derek [Bogarde's real name] have been doing even at the gates, let alone inside them?' Afterwards it was commonly agreed that Bogarde, the same as hundreds of others, had been in the *vicinity* of Belsen.

Lt John Randall, according to Trow, did not embellish his standing in the liberation or question the declarations of others. 'John Randall has never contradicted these men because he does not have to and because of the kind of man he is [Lt Randall died in 2016, aged 96],' he wrote. Notwithstanding, a handful have queried Randall's account, which is not unusual among military afficiandos. Some have misgivings that a radio operator attached to the SAS HQ team would be patrolling in front of infantry units with the susceptibility of him being captured and codes seized by the enemy. The son of a soldier who also served with the Royal Corps of Signals posted on a military history site: 'I do not question the gallantry of Lt Randall nor his veracity, but if he was first, it was among several Tommies . . . it's odd to describe the camp entrance as though it were a couple of gates when, in fact, the camp outer perimeter wire ran for half a kilometre and could be seen from a distance. I know this because my father was a lorry driver for the Radio-Wireless section and was present three days after the camp's discovery.' In his book, Trow acknowledged: 'Because of the independent nature of SAS work, he [Randall] had no idea what had been going on in the previous days'. On a broader premise, the Belsen site was extensive and covered six square miles. While there was unmistakeably a main entrance, there was another directly across from it, in effect a rear entrance, close to the crematorium and site of mass graves. Other points of access and egress may have been formed as the SS deserted their posts, which included 23 watchtowers at the perimeter fence and within the camp.

Brigadier Hugh Llewellyn Glyn Hughes was another cited as being 'the first Allied officer to enter Belsen', often in official documents. Hughes, born in South Africa, had studied medicine at University College Hospital in London and was attached to the Royal Army Medical Corps (RAMC). He was undoubtedly *one* of the first senior officers to enter the camp but would have followed other advancing soldiers. The RAMC routinely situated itself behind other units, ready, if needed, to provide medical aid, or, in this case, humanitarian support. In his testimony at the War Crime Trials held in September 1945, Brigadier Hughes appeared to affirm that he had not been the first soldier into the camp: 'On 15th April Lieutenant-Colonel Taylor took over the administration of the camp and I followed him there'. Lieutenant-Colonel Richard Taylor was the commanding officer of the 63rd Anti-Tank Regiment and was acclaimed for his conduct at Belsen. Soon after arriving at the camp Lt-Col. Taylor had been greeted by a female prisoner. She called out, 'Mr Dick, Mr Dick' and asked if he recognised her. He didn't. She was extremely thin, her head was shaved and many of her teeth were missing. She had worked as a maid for his mother and had joined the resistance in Paris at the outbreak of the war before being captured and tortured by the Gestapo.

In the days following liberation, Brigadier Hughes had been an industrious and conspicuous figure about the camp. He had suffered curvature of the spine as a boy which meant he walked with a stoop. He was 51 years old, almost twice the age of many of the men with whom he served. After the war, Brigadier Hughes (known as 'Hughsie' and a keen rugby union player) was awarded the Order of St John of Jerusalem and the United States Legion of Merit for 'the care and rehabilitation of prisoners in Belsen'. He was also appointed Commander of the Order of the British Empire (CBE). He later became physician to the Queen and was a subject of the television programme *This Is Your Life* in 1959. He died in 1973, aged 81.

Major Dick Williams was another of senior rank reported to have 'discovered Belsen'; his journey to the camp was remarkably similar to Herbert's. Major Williams, a clergyman's son, was staff captain in the Supplies and Transport branch of VIII Corps Headquarters. In newspaper articles it was reported that he had been part of a 'small force' sent to assess the camp. He drove from Celle with only a map reference to guide him, passing white flags fastened into the ground. He came to 'a small cutting in a dense plantation of fir trees' before 'turning left down an unmarked track' where he arrived at 'a vast concentration camp surrounded by a 10ft high barbed-wire fence, and still guarded by armed SS soldiers'. 'We knew that it had dysentery and other problems, but we had no idea how big it was or how many people were inside,' he told the *Guardian* in 2005.[18] 'You couldn't understand that all those people could be there and yet everything was so quiet. It was this oppressive haze over the camp, the smell, the starkness of the barbed wire fences, the dullness of the bare earth, the scattered bodies and these very dull striped grey uniforms. The sun, yes, the sun was shining, but there just didn't seem to be any life at all in that camp. Everything seemed to be dead,' he said.[19] Major Williams died in 2012, aged 91.

All four men – Lieutenant John Randall, Major Dick Williams, Brigadier Hughes and Lieutenant-Colonel Richard Taylor – were verifiably at Belsen on 15 April 1945 and, according to eyewitness accounts, undertook their duties with exceptional diligence and compassion. Nonetheless, it would be almost unprecedented for soldiers of considerable senior rank in the British Army to have been sent to such an advanced position with its inherent risk, especially considering the volatility of the situation at that stage of the war. Unless there had been a temporary suspension of regular military protocol, the more likely procedure would be to send a 'scout' ahead of the forthcoming units to determine the level of threat or otherwise, before pressing onwards to the camp. Ordinarily this undertaking would be carried out by a private or NCO (Non-Commissioned Officer), much the same as Herbert Kenny.

★

The onerous task of filming at Belsen fell primarily to Harry Oakes and Bill Lawrie of the Army Film and Photographic Unit (AFPU) who worked alongside stills photographer, George Rodger – three men also mentioned as being among the first to set foot in the camp. They had resolved to record the scene 'as was' without artifice; 33 rolls of film were used to produce 200 photographs. 'I suppose you could make it more grotesque. For instance, when the SS guards were made to pick up the corpses, slung over their shoulders to bury the dead in the lime pits, you could make it a bit sick by doing a tracking shot of the lolling head in the foreground; that kind of thing would have been over the top, I think. I was very conscious of showing what it was actually like, but not making more of it,' said Sergeant Oakes.

Sergeant Mike Lewis was another cameraman with the AFPU. He was the son of Jewish Polish refugees who had migrated to Britain in the early 1900s. He pondered later on the nature of the evil he had filmed:

Why the Germans? They had their own culture, their own civilisation of a kind. They produced Beethoven, great scientists. How could it be? The terrible discovery came to me, this sort of revelation like a flash of lightning, because it penetrated these terrible scenes to make me think – all the stories I'd heard about the persecution of people from my mother and father, here they were true. But this had to be organised; it could only be done with modern administrative service. It could only be done by moving masses of people by rail. It had to be planned and worked for. It was a sort of death by administration.

Captain Leslie Hardman, a 32-year-old Senior Jewish Chaplain to the British Forces, attached to the 8th Corps of the British Second Army, was the first Rabbi to enter the camp. Born in Glynneath, South Wales, he was the son of Ashkenazi Jews, his father, Abraham, from Poland and his mother, Dora, Russia. They had anglicised their names from Hartmann. On arriving at Belsen, he recited Kaddish, the Jewish memorial prayer, over the dead. The most frequent petition he heard from prisoners was 'Tell the world, tell the world'. The plea would seem absurd in view of the scale of the atrocity, but in 1945 a global community had not yet been forged by television or, later, the internet. They genuinely believed that, in such a remote area, the vast number of deaths and the cruelty they had endured might go unacknowledged. The Revd Hardman honoured a promise: he told the world. In an interview with the BBC, he said: 'If all the trees in the world turned into pens, all the waters in the oceans turned into ink and the heavens turned into paper, it would still be insufficient material to describe the horrors these people suffered under the SS.' The deprivation he witnessed was reported to have caused him to lose his faith, but this was later refuted. 'I didn't lose my faith,' he said. 'But some of the words of the prayers I said at Belsen stuck in my throat. I couldn't understand how the God I worshipped could permit this.' He was appointed MBE in 1998 for his services to the Jewish community.

Chapter Eighteen
War is hell

———

The relief work undertaken by Herbert and others at Belsen had felt to signify an End of Days, the final cataclysmic episode after more than five years of war. The camp provided a curious sanctuary, and as they walked its narrow lanes, it was as if they were on an island, detached from the rest of the world. Herbert, when cycling through Celle – which now seemed months ago rather than a few days – had felt hopeful of returning home, but the war was still foaming, albeit in pockets of engagement. He had not been granted any special dispensation (or even recognition) for the specific and exclusive role he had played. He understood that this was emblematic of the army; you got on with it. In his case, it meant climbing back on to his motorcycle and doing as he had done before: everything had changed but nothing had changed.

We travelled north to catch up to our forward troops. From my maps, I found the shortest distance to the Elbe [a major river of almost 700 miles]. We came to a hamlet about 200 yards from the river where there were a small number of empty cottages. The bridge had been destroyed. We checked the cottages for booby traps, settled in and realised we needed a bridge, not only us, but for any other occupying forces and transport following later. We sent a message back for pontoon bridging supplies and engineers. While this was going on, we were visited by a Nazi aircraft observing the layout. We knew then that there would be some harassment from the enemy. In they came, one at a time, flying down the river, not in droves, but randomly – light aircraft with one bomb slung under their carriage, dropping the bomb as near as they could to stop us building our bridge.

It was decided that nighttime would be better. We made more progress under darkness. During daylight hours we lost one of our drivers. He had been through the desert campaign, but later came back with the others to join us for the invasion. I cannot remember his name, but he was a good man. A bomb was dropped and hit just behind the cab of his vehicle. We only saw what was left of him and his vehicle: not much. Eventually we made it across the Elbe, and then onward to catch up with some of our tanks. Moving forward, we came to the Hamburg–Berlin autobahn. We travelled with the tanks and then they set off across the open ground.

We carried on and found Lübeck [a city of more than 200,000 people], just off the autobahn. We took over a large petrol station. Second day there, we saw a long column marching along the highway. We set ourselves up and waited. They were German soldiers giving themselves up, surrendering to us. There were 200 of them, not a single gun between them. They had dumped them somewhere. They were thoroughly searched and put into a big compound at the rear of the petrol station. They made their own camp and were quite content that, for them, the war was over. We found out later that this was happening all over. We knew then that the war was almost at an end, but we had to go on.

We left the area of Lübeck, after the town had been checked (all was very quiet). We scouted Neumünster [town of 70,000 population] and Kiel [city on the Baltic Sea, 240,000 population] and arrived finally without further trouble. The Kiel Canal was our destination. There were ships there loaded with all types of canned food. We released some to civilians of different countries who had been made to work at the docks; they were in small huts here and there. Their conditions were terrible, the quarters unclean. They were poorly clothed and unhealthy. We took over and made the Germans unload food from the ships. This was distributed among the hungry people. Can-openers were found. There was meat, veg and fruit, so they were alright after that and were given clean clothing.

Two weeks later, we left Kiel in the hands of the occupying troops. I don't know actual dates. One day was like another, whether Monday or Sunday. We just went on and on, doing our job, the job we were trained to do. The things I saw, the sadistic cruelty of a regime that could not be allowed to take hold. The loss of life to our boys and allies was tremendous. So many had given their lives for the sake of others. All because of greed and brutality and gangsterism. I class myself as lucky. I went through hell, I know that. There were times when I think of the terrible time we had, when I thought my lot had come. Times when I was afraid. No man can tell me he was not afraid. Sometimes, you don't have to be a coward to feel a little afraid.

After we left Kiel, we returned to Neumünster. We took over a railway siding with trucks loaded with coal. The big signing was done on the 8th of May 1945 [Victory in Europe Day, VE Day, when Germany officially surrendered]. We still had work to do and carried on with it, organising labour for the German troops who had been using slave labour. The tables were turned. It was part of our job to see it was all done in a proper manner. Our platoon got ourselves fixed up with billets near to the working area.

★

Street parties to celebrate VE Day were organised hurriedly in Middleton. Rain fell in the morning but it became sunny and windy in the afternoon, causing bunting strung across streets to shudder and flap. Union Jacks and Star-Spangled Banners were run up flagpoles in Middleton Gardens. As night fell, Catherine wheels nailed to fence posts were set spinning. A charabanc bedecked in lights traversed the streets with the word 'Victory' burning bright. The wonky walls of the Olde Boar's Head pub, built in 1622, were set aglow by floodlights. Bonfires were lit across town. Free beer, limited to four pints per member, was on offer at the town's working men's clubs. Mr Harrison who ran the butcher's shop in Old Hall Street provided an ox, which was roasted on a spit in a field near Middleton Town Hall. A party was held in Chapel Street, Rhodes, where a maypole was fixed into a patch of grass for children to skip around. Harry Hilton, a keen pianist, asked volunteers to carry his piano out on to the street. He played at the kerbside while people sang and danced. A children's tea party was held at West Green, Rhodes, and they were serenaded by an impromptu performance from a brass band touring the streets. Mr Chandler, a coalman, gave rides to children on his truck. When the clock struck midnight in the town centre, people joined hands and danced around the civic fountain.

Venues capitalised on the mood of relief and triumph. In April, three weeks ahead of the actual VE Day, the Empire in Oldham had staged a twice-nightly 'Victory Circus'. Among the attractions were Fenella – 'see the children stroke this amazing full-grown tigress' – and Pom-Pom, a 'human pony'. Belle Vue Stadium reopened and held a 'Victory Whitsun Holiday Festival', boasting speedway and wrestling. The *Middleton Guardian* provided a gleeful summary of the revelry: 'It has been a momentous week and a very happy one. The town celebrated and made a thoroughly good job of it. There had been no elaborate civic arrangements but the desire of everyone to help assured the success of the occasion. The gloomy prophets of disaster who opined that many Middletonians would seize the occasion to become sottishly [stupefied] drunk were confounded. The thousands of people on the streets might have been gay and rowdy, raucous, and, at times, unsteady. But it was a very innocent, if hearty town of enjoyment.'

Albert Worrall was one of those raising a glass on VE day, with his wife and four children at their home in Morton Street. He was too poorly to make the short journey to join the throng in the town centre. Several soldiers from Middleton, as elsewhere, had returned home with permanent physical reminders of the war. Albert was badly injured while serving in France with the Lancashire Fusiliers. Before joining up he had spent 12 years as a member of the Territorial Army; he and Herbert were acquaintances. Albert had been taken prisoner and transported to the Stalag III-B prisoner-of-war camp in Lamsdorf (now Łambinowice, Poland), then in eastern Germany. The camp held up to 10,000 prisoners and they were forced to labour on farms, construction sites and tasked with clearing trees in forests. Albert, who worked in peace time at Tonge Dyeing Works, had been freed early because of his debilitation; he could no longer take his place on work teams. The letter sent home by the Ministry of Defence with details of his impending release incorporated a single line about his injury: 'He has lost his left leg.'

Towards the later stages of the war, Middleton people had been afforded a close look at the enemy. More than 6,000 German prisoners-of-war were based at a camp at the disused Glen Mill in Lees, Oldham. Most had been captured in Normandy as the Allies pushed through France. They were put to work on farms or at the allotment within the camp grounds. They were allowed to wear civilian clothes and took part in football matches between various regiments. They also played tennis on a court they had built themselves. Every morning, small groups were taken in jeeps and vans to work on municipal projects. One of these was the construction of a housing estate at Moorclose, Middleton; such developments were said to be 'Jerry-built'. Most of these soldiers were pleased to be out of the war, and relations with guards and local civilians were generally cordial. At the end of the war, almost 25,000 Germans chose to remain in Britain.

Earlier, Germans, in news reports throughout the war, had been referred to as 'Nazis' and depicted as being of considerable stature and cunning. An article in the *Rochdale Observer* recounting the capture of an escaped prisoner from the Oldham camp was typical. Erich Breuss, an Austrian seconded into the Wehrmacht at 16, was apprehended after being found sleeping on a railway bench, his clothes sodden. The piece carried the headline 'Nazi Storm Trooper in Escape Bid' and read: 'Police officers who interviewed the prisoner stated that he was a young man of magnificent physique but, during his detention, he did not display any trace of arrogance.'

Due to administrative protocol, hundreds of prisoners-of-war at the Oldham camp remained for months after the war had ended. By September 1945, the mood of magnanimity towards Germans was manifest, as shown in a light-hearted piece in the *Middleton Guardian*: 'The long-awaited invasion has come at last,' the article read. 'The streets and avenues of Moorclose echo with alien sounds. Not the sinister-sounding tramp of the iron-shod Jackboot, but the clang of pick and shovel, and the roar of mechanical tractors. The Germans are helping to straighten out the mess.' Reporters had been sent to appraise these work teams:

There was none of the blond Nordic giant among them, so extolled by the wee doctor [Joseph Goebbels, the Nazi Minister for Propaganda]. What we saw was of average physique and normal appearance. I asked one stalwart navvy what he thought of the prisoners. He said they were all right, a bit slow at first but they were getting better now. Finally, in Sandy Lane, we asked a Middleton housewife her humble opinion. She turned from her task of hanging out the Monday morning wash. 'Eeh!' she said. 'They don't seem a bad lot. But (pointing to the washing) – I've got the white flag out, just in case.'

A group of Middleton children were distinctly ungracious to the Germans in their midst. Teenagers from Mills Hill marched to Moorclose, intent on jibing the prisoners-of-war. They gathered at the perimeter of the building site and shouted, 'Jerry go home.' Elinor Wilson was among them. 'It was a rarity to see anyone from another country in our very young days,' she said. 'They were actually a pleasant bunch and just seemed pleased to see children and laugh at us. Now I'm in my dotage, I'm sure they must have been very homesick and perhaps some of them would have had no home and family to go back to, but as children we didn't realise this.' [20]

A disused mill at Stakehill on the Middleton–Oldham border was given over to the detention of British soldiers who had flouted army rules; they were widely viewed as ne'er-do-wells for undermining the war effort. Guards were accused of mistreating them and after several deaths and suicides, questions were asked in Parliament. Prisoners slept on beds without mattresses and were made to stand outside in their PE kits in freezing weather. They regularly went hungry. Albert Meltzer, an anarchist and conscientious objector, was taken there after serving time at a converted Butlin's holiday camp in Prestatyn, North Wales. 'Stakehill had the most notorious reputation in England. I was told of a parson who heard cries and rushed into a cell. Two warders had hit a man who was lying on the floor. One of them was saying to the other with heavy, sick sarcasm, "Kick him, Staff, he's still breathing."' Another soldier had died after being ordered to run a mile within seven minutes wearing full army kit. 'This man was dead after three days,' said the MP Tom Driberg. 'He was seen afterwards by his relatives with his forehead bruised and marks on his neck, and no inquest was held.' Dr Hyacinth Morgan, the MP for Rochdale, told Parliament that psychiatric help should be made available to inmates. Few newspapers reported this mistreatment of prisoners because it ran contrary to the mood of celebration at the war's end.

Allied soldiers in Germany were on a strict 'non-fraternising' order from their superiors after VE Day, but this was only nominally observed. They befriended German children, many of whom had been made orphans, handing them chocolate or chewing gum, and allowing them to help with the tidy-up of damaged sites. They saw the children's wholehearted enthusiasm as a sign of hope: a future generation without the scourge of Nazism. Allied soldiers had sexual liaisons with local women. A common ruse in rural areas was for women to 'sunbathe' in cornfields, where they would soon be joined by soldiers. A CO would give the order to 'flush them out' and a loud shrill of a whistle pierced the air. The corn would shake as if a sudden wind had blown, before men appeared on one side of the field, and women, the other.

Elsewhere in Germany, extreme acts of barbarism were being perpetrated, especially by the Soviet Occupation troops. The historian, Antony Beevor, described it as 'the greatest phenomenon of mass rape in history' and estimated that up to two million women were sexually assaulted. The soldiers' actions were carried out chiefly as retribution, but it was also said that they were driven by jealousy after seeing the splendour of many German homes and furnishings, in contrast to their own living standards back home in Russia. Joseph Stalin, the Soviet leader, said he understood 'if a soldier who has crossed thousands of kilometres through blood and fire and death has fun with a woman or takes some trifle'. In her book *War's Unwomanly Face*, Svetlana Alexievich included a quote from a former officer of the Red Army: 'We were young, strong, and four years without women. So we tried to catch German women. Ten men raped one girl. There were not enough women; the entire population ran from the Soviet Army. So we had to take young, twelve or thirteen-year-olds. If she cried, we put something into her mouth. We thought it was fun. Now I cannot understand how I did it.'

Herbert, meanwhile, had fallen ill.

In September 1945 I began losing my appetite for food and drink, gradually getting worse until finally I could not eat, drink or do anything. I was losing weight and feeling really sick. It was a matter for the MO [medical officer] who sent me away to hospital in

Hamburg, some distance away from where we were stationed. Once there, I went through lots of tests, together with special feeding to keep me alive. I was finally taken to another part of the hospital. There must have been at least six doctors and four nurses in this private room. I was given an injection and remembered nothing until sometime later when I found myself back in my own bed with a nurse standing by.

I was told that they had at last got to the bottom of the illness. It seems that the drug they pumped into me made me answer all of their questions. They found out the kind of field work I was involved in, including the Belsen episode. They diagnosed that the tension had gradually built up inside me and, because of my job, I had pushed it inside rather than letting it go as soon as the war came to an end. At that point, I had more time to myself, instead of always being on the move, and letting the other DRs rest up instead of me. I had a delayed reaction and my nerves started. The whole of my body system had given way and wasn't working as it should. It just went all wrong. They had not heard of this before.

While Herbert was in hospital, the British soldiers still in Germany were given a special supplement of *The British Zone Review*, a pamphlet published fortnightly detailing 'the activities of the control commission for Germany (British element) and military', the body of civil servants and army personnel set up to administer a large area of northern Germany. The eight-page edition, published on 13 October 1945, was titled 'BELSEN' with the sub-heading: 'An account, based on Official Reports, of the uncovering by the British Army of the Belsen Concentration Camp and of the actions taken during the vital days to minimise the suffering of 60,000 inmates'. The opening paragraph defined the episode as 'that greatest of all exhibitions of "man's inhumanity to man" ', and carried details of the genocide with photographs of scattered and piled corpses. The British Army, probably under a government directive, had released such an explicit document to avoid a repeat of the disgruntlement after World War One, when soldiers had returned home sceptical of its real worth in view of the great cost in lives and suffering: 880,000 British soldiers were killed. On this occasion, the message was unequivocal: this is the evil over which you have triumphed.

On a similar theme of moral justification and blame apportionment, nine days after the liberation of Belsen, Colonel Spottiswoode, the military government commander, had addressed an invited audience of burgomasters local to Belsen, and told them: 'What you will see here is the final and utter condemnation of the Nazi Party. It justifies every measure which the United Nations will take to exterminate that Party.' The Allies had earlier fastened photographs of scenes from the camp on gateposts and trees around villages near Belsen. Many locals expressed incredulity. They were brought to the camp and made to view the mounds of corpses. The Army Film and Photographic Unit filmed the responses – people hurrying past unable to look, some holding handkerchiefs to their mouths, and others crying.

The discovery of Belsen and other concentration camps framed the war as a righteous crusade and deflected criticism of the Allies' own conceivable transgressions: had it been necessary, for example, to saturate Dresden with bombs, razing the city and causing the deaths of at least 25,000 citizens, most of them women, children and the elderly? In Norway, German prisoners-of-war under British supervision were reportedly forced to clear minefields – 275 died and 392 were injured in an act that breached Geneva Conventions. There were other isolated retributive acts of murder, violence, robbery, looting and torture.

Retrospectively, historians and politicians would dissect the war and find mistakes and miscalculations, evidence of institutionalised apathy, self-interest, misrepresentation and jingoism, occasionally with wide-ranging consequences. The censure, however, was squarely of governments and generals. The British soldier, aside from a few incidents of misconduct, had remained free of reproach, especially the liberators of the concentration camps. Joachim Gauck, the then-President of Germany, reaffirmed this in April 2015 in a speech given at a memorial service on the 70th anniversary of the liberation of Belsen:

> The liberators did everything in their power to save lives and ease suffering. They provided medical care and ensured a functioning water supply. And they looked after the many children who had been orphaned in the camp. Despite all their efforts, however, thousands more died after liberation as a result of imprisonment

and starvation, abuse and forced labour. But eventually the day came when there was a halt to the deaths of the sick and starving, and the board by the entrance to the hospital said 'First day with no death'.

In attending this memorial service today, I feel a profound need to express heartfelt gratitude to the British liberators. They came here at a time of inhumanity. They came in a spirit of humanity. With their actions and their attitude – thoroughly rooted in human kindness and decency – they ushered in a new epoch: people, even members of the so called 'master race', were to learn anew that it was indeed possible to put care for one's fellow human beings into practice.

And the British soldiers were ambassadors for a democratic culture which focused not on gaining revenge on the enemy, but on creating a new and sure foundation for justice and human dignity in Germany. Moreover, they came with express instructions from their Government to show fairness to the defeated nation, so that the Germans would themselves find their way back to fairness, too.

At the war's end, more than 380,000 British soldiers and 67,000 civilians had lost their lives. In total, at least 70 million died from all sides. Many years earlier, William Tecumseh Sherman, an American Civil War general, had summarised the futility and barbarity of conflict: 'I am tired and sick of war. Its glory is all moonshine. It is only those who have neither fired a shot nor heard the shrieks and groans of the wounded who cry aloud for blood, for vengeance, for desolation. War is hell.'

Chapter Nineteen
Not attributable to war service

———

Army psychiatrists tendered the slogan 'every man has his breaking point' to reduce the stigma and garner more public sympathy for ex-soldiers with mental health problems. The understanding of psychiatric issues caused by combat had advanced greatly on that experienced by the 'shell-shocked' of World War One. Nevertheless, attitudes of 'pull yourself together' and 'get on with it' still prevailed. Mental illness was predominantly viewed by both the sufferer and the wider public as a sign of 'weakness'; it would be several decades before the various elements of war trauma were categorised as Post Traumatic Stress Disorder (PTSD). The affliction, in formal terms, was said to affect a person's social interactions, their ability to work and 'other important areas of their lives'. Symptoms included disturbing thoughts and feelings, mental or physical distress, unexpected changes in behaviour and an increase in the fight-or-flight response.

I finally finished up in hospitals back in England, in Birmingham and Manchester and was then discharged unfit for further service. That was February 1946, after being hospitalised from October 1945.

Herbert was not alone in suffering an extreme physical response to the horrors of Belsen. Sergeant Norman Turgel of British Intelligence had spent three days at the camp when he returned to barracks. 'I woke up and could not get out of bed. I was paralysed. This happened to two or three of our chaps. We simply could not walk. When the doctor came and stuck pins in our legs, we felt nothing. This lasted for 24 hours, and they put it down to shock on our nerves from the horrific sights we'd seen,' he said. A handful of soldiers reported temporary blindness and speculated that 'their eyes had turned off' as if protecting them from witnessing further hideous images. These syndromes were put down to 'nerves' but were later formally recognised as 'sensory conversion' or 'conversion disorder' – 'a condition in which a person experiences physical and sensory problems, such as paralysis, numbness, blindness, deafness or seizures, with no underlying neurologic pathology.' On a much happier note, six months after the liberation of Belsen, Sgt Turgel married a freed prisoner, Gena Goldfinger. The wedding was held in Lübeck, in a synagogue that the Nazis had used as a stable; Gena's wedding dress was made from parachute silk.

The time in hospital cost me my stripes [soldiers wore a 'stripe' on the left sleeve of their jacket to indicate length of service].

You naturally lose them after a period of time like that. I came out grade E, but got no pension. The pension people said it was not attributable to war service, although I was an A1 plus when I entered the army, the highest grade.

★

Footage shot at Belsen was shown on news reels at British cinemas. The Nuremberg trials, which began in November 1945, also received extensive coverage throughout the world. A film showing scenes from the camps was played in the courtroom as evidence. Before the lights were dimmed, Thomas Dodd, the US prosecutor, said: 'This film we offer represents in a free and unforgettable form an explanation of what the words "concentration camp" implies.' The candid material validated the Allies' efforts to bring the Nazis to justice and also harvested great sympathy for the prisoners and the personnel involved in the liberation. Much of this was of little individual worth because many – military, cleric, medical, photographic, journalistic, administrative etc. – had chosen to conceal their experiences and remain anonymous within their communities, even keeping it from their families. Herbert was among them.

Photographs and film footage from Belsen and other camps would have varying psychological impact on the public over the decades. Colour photography was invented in the 1860s but did not come into widespread use until a century later because it was an expensive and complex process involving plates, flashbulbs and a certain level of expertise. The AFPU used black and white film; colour images of Belsen are not thought to exist. In the 1940s and '50s monochrome was considered the true milieu of photography and the public became accustomed to seeing this depiction of war and concentration camps. The introduction of the Kodak Instamatic 50 camera in 1963 had a profound effect on the perception of time. The camera was inexpensive, easy to use and, within months, as millions clicked away, it seemed as if life itself had changed from black and white to colour. Relatively recent episodes shot in black and white – news items, sports events, feature films, two world wars, the Holocaust – suddenly seemed dated beyond the actual years, as if they belonged to a different epoch.

Colourisation, a process where colour was added to monochrome or sepia images, dated back to the early 20th century. Initially they were saturated in fulsome tones and resembled paintings done in oils or pastels. When applied to war photographs, especially from World War One, the process fashioned a dream-like element that veiled the abject horror. The introduction of digital image technology in the early 2000s meant that existing monochrome film could be 'coloured' more subtly, to an astounding level of realism. *Auschwitz Untold in Colour* was a two-part television documentary broadcast in January 2020. David Shulman, the producer and director, had undertaken the colourisation with 'a great deal of reservation'. 'I thought it could be perceived as incredibly crass, given the context,' he went on. 'It was a far cry from colourising World War Two, and the narrative and diversity of the footage you would have, versus the Holocaust and the camps.' The approach was vindicated: 'It's amazing what colourisation does to a photograph. In black and white, it seems so distant and abstract, something from "back then", but in colour you start to realise that they are people. Flesh and blood, human beings, just like you or me. It really drives home the sheer horror of what you are seeing.' As a child and teenager, Shulman had imagined the Holocaust to be 'long ago and far away'. 'Today, it's a complete paradox,' he said. 'It feels much more recent and much more relevant than it did then.'

Tom Marshall, one of the country's leading colourisers, produced a series of striking images to mark Holocaust Memorial Day in 2020. They have been viewed more than a million times online, with many commenting that they 'brought people back to life'. 'They were close to death by the time of their liberation, so painting skin tones was completely different. In colour, you can see the bones and the bloodless skin, and even young men look older with greying hair and dark patches around their eyes,' said Marshall. The work came at an emotional cost. 'This is the most harrowing project I have ever worked on. It was upsetting because the images are so shocking. I had to give myself time to do something else and try to switch off. I felt more sick as the pictures came to life and I was also becoming angry,' he said. Marshall's great-grandfather, Charles Martin King Parsons, had been a chaplain in the 9th British General Hospital of the British Army, and had entered Belsen in April 1945. While at the camp, he had taken photographs, including some of the mass graves. 'I did not want to colourise these,' said Tom. 'It didn't feel the right thing to do, but generally I think it's important to remind people – especially younger generations – that this happened and it's not really that far back in history.'

More than 75 years after the liberation of Belsen and almost 20 years since Herbert's death, technology and digital craftsmanship had finally allowed the world to see the scenes in a way that most resembled those he had witnessed. The earlier fitful footage and flat, shadowy monochrome photographs had badly served the soldiers, making the camp and those within it appear unreal, lost souls at the edge of the world. To Herbert and the others, it was in colour, three-dimensional and all around everywhere, then and for the rest of their lives.

> I went back to work at my civilian job, but could not do a full week's work owing to my health. My nerves were in a terrible state. I could not control my emotions, forever breaking down and feeling ill. More than a year afterwards, someone told me that the British Legion would have fought the pension people for me, but at that time I could not think straight, could not concentrate on anything. It was hard going. Somehow I had to earn cash to look after my wife and children. We had to live.

Herbert had not wanted to *burden* his family and friends with what he had witnessed at Belsen. He didn't want them soiled by the images and memories. He was supposed to be his family's protector, the head of the house: the strongest. He tried to view it as a 'test', holding it in, managing it. He imagined that talking about it, finding the words to relate its magnitude, might make it worse and bring it closer still. And if he did tell others, he would lose sole ownership of the memory: who knew when they might bring up the subject, perhaps at a time when it had momentarily slipped his mind. June, his eldest daughter, was nine years old when he returned from the war. 'I know it had a devastating effect on him,' she said. 'Although I knew my dad was different, kids of that age don't really understand. He would never talk about it, even when we were adults. It was too painful and we understood that.' Many years later, when other liberators had resolved to finally speak out – sometimes on their death bed – they described the effect it had on their lives. They said they had 'never been the same again'. They had been left 'changed' or 'broken' and 'it had never left them'.

While Herbert internalised his distress, some found it beneficial to share their stories and attempt to self-heal through communication. The global success of *Schindler's List* in 1993 had a remarkable impact and acted as a catalyst for many to break a silence they had upheld since the Holocaust. The film, directed by Steven Spielberg, was based on a novel called *Schindler's Ark* by Thomas Keneally, which had won the Booker Prize a decade earlier. Survivors and liberators were prompted to contact museums and organisations, or finally share stories with their families. In the words of a Holocaust expert, 'the floodgates opened'.

Corporal Ian Forsyth was 21 when he drove a tank into Belsen. He dedicated his later life trying to ensure that the Holocaust would never happen again, revealing his experiences at schools and events organised by the Holocaust Educational Trust. He appeared on a video with the then-prime minister, Boris Johnson, on Holocaust Memorial Day (27 January) in 2021, aged 96. He said he still woke at night 'with it going through my mind and every detail still clear'. As a teacher in civilian life, he said his job made him better able to speak to groups, but many soldiers 'had been less successful in their struggles with the past'. He became tearful on film and explained: 'Sorry, I get very emotional when I talk about this. It shows just how low mankind can sink.' Ian, from Hamilton, Scotland, died in December 2021, aged 97.

Herbert, in his dotage, spoke of returning to Belsen, perceiving it as part of a resolution that had begun when he made his notes in the mid-1980s and revealed his story to the *Middleton Guardian*. On the 50th anniversary of VE Day, in June 1995, the paper carried a follow-up story headlined, 'Evil and Horror of Nazi camp left me a Broken Man'. Herbert, 82 at the time, told the reporter that he was still hopeful of going back to Belsen. 'I would like to see what has become of it. Although it would be painful, it might help me lay some of the ghosts to rest,' he said. He didn't undertake the trip but most that did said it had a therapeutic effect. Bernard Levy, a corporal in the British Military Government, was 19 when he entered Belsen, one of several Jewish British soldiers. He returned in January 2015. Speaking at the site to ITN News, he said: 'I'm glad I'm back because it's the last time I'll be here. I just feel like I've come to say goodbye to all that, and I hope that they all rest in peace.' Bernard had refused to be defined by his wartime experience and, despite being 5ft 4ins, he founded the High and Mighty chain of retail stores, specialising in clothes for men of a large physique. He died in May 2022, aged 96.

Throughout his life Herbert remained alert for 'triggers' that might send him spiralling back to Belsen. If the war or Holocaust was mentioned, family members were used to him snapping off the radio or television. He told the *Middleton Guardian* in 1995 that he had turned off a television programme marking the anniversary of VE Day. 'I can't bear it,' he said. Other families reported similar behaviour: their loved one abruptly leaving the house to take a walk or retiring early to bed, leaving them unsure what had sparked an upsetting memory or mood. Many cited the release of *Judgment at Nuremberg* as a particular nadir, a film released in 1961 based on the trials of former Nazi leaders, exploring the complicity of the German people in crimes committed by the state, including the Holocaust. Two years before, the film *The Diary of Anne Frank* won three Academy Awards.

Films about the Holocaust appeared on a consistent basis during Herbert's lifetime, among them *The Pawnbroker* (1964), *Holocaust* (1978), *Sophie's Choice* (1982) and *Life is Beautiful* (1997). The television series *The World at War*, made by Thames Television in the early 1970s, spanned 26 episodes, one of which, episode 20, first broadcast in March 1974, was titled *Genocide: 1941–1945* and featured footage and interviews with SS officers and camp survivors. In the original opening, the series narrator, Laurence Olivier, made his only on-screen appearance, warning viewers of the disturbing content; it wasn't included in subsequent TV screenings or video/DVD releases. Herbert eschewed these films and documentaries, but it was difficult avoiding the publicity and news that they engendered.

The smell of burning was particularly synonymous with Belsen and a 'trigger' for many. Small fires had been lit throughout the camp by the prisoners. Soldiers reported that they could also smell burning flesh when they first arrived; corpses had been incinerated in the camp's crematorium furnace, which had a tall brick flue and was housed in a plain wooden shed. A poignant photograph taken at Belsen was of a workman's coat hanging on a peg fastened to the wall of the shed, close to the furnace. Images of such an everyday approach to mass death later prompted the philosopher Hannah Arendt to write her influential piece in the *New Yorker* in 1961 yielding 'the banality of evil': can one do evil without being evil?

Fires had raged for days after liberation as lice-infested huts and piles of clothing were set alight to stymie the spread of typhus. As an act of symbolism, the last remaining hut was set alight, this was done on Monday, 21 May 1945. Long licks of fire were discharged from a Wasp IIC flame-thrower manned by three soldiers from the 4th Battalion Somerset Light Infantry. An Imperial German flag was fastened to a side of the hut, with a large banner portrait of Adolf Hitler at the opposite end. As flames took hold at the bottom of the hut, it seemed for a few seconds as if it was being lifted by a giant fiery hand. Former inmates, soldiers and relief teams looked on as a funnel of black smoke briefly shut out the sky. At 6pm a ceremony was held in which the Union Jack was raised for the first time; it had not been done before, for fear of associating it with the amorality of Belsen. Soldiers from the Durham Light Infantry fired a salute to the dead. Afterwards it was said that birds would neither settle nor fly over Belsen; this was untrue. Moreover, visitors to the site commented that they found solace in hearing birdsong. It was a sign of hope and renewal.

Belsen, more than any other camp, became embedded in the collective psyche of the country because the British had played such a predominant role in its liberation. British soldiers and medical teams had been supported by organisations such as the British Red Cross and the Friends Relief Service, a volunteer force made up largely of pacifists and conscientious objectors, providing humanitarian support. Within days, hundreds of relief staff had arrived at the camp offering specific assistance: laundry teams, laboratory workers, microbiologists, sound engineers (to maintain the mobile speaker systems), food hygienists, mechanics etc. Initially it was believed that the operation was conducted wholly by the British, but this was inaccurate. The Royal Canadian Air Force (RCAF) provided more than a thousand airmen for several weeks after liberation. The coding of 'B118' indicating the airfield close to Belsen was later discovered in many personal and unit diaries of the RCAF – its 437 Squadron was flying out survivors and carrying high-ranking Allied officials. The 42nd Tank Battalion, as the only American unit attached to the British Second Army, was also on site, along with about 70 American Field Service (AFS) ambulance drivers from C and D Platoons of 567 Company; they spent seven weeks treating prisoners at Belsen.

Over time, Herbert developed coping strategies. He did not seek formal medical assistance and was sceptical of what he called 'happy pills' (anti-depressants). No one in the family had any knowledge of him seeking counselling. In all likelihood, he was in a state of melancholia most of his life, with frequent bouts of acute depression. Although he was considered even-tempered, he was sporadically prone to outbursts. 'My mum [Freda] told me that grandad was a bit nasty with me and my two older brothers when we were little,' said Chris Hoyle, one of Herbert's granddaughters. 'He used to shout at us and tell us what to do, before my mum and him argued over it and she told him she was the only person who could tell us what to do, not him. I think his wartime experience had a lot to do with his temper.'

Unlike many of the liberators and ex-soldiers generally, Herbert did not 'self-medicate' with alcohol; he barely drank. Many turned to drink to help them sleep – persistent nightmares were a symptom of trauma, along with 'night terrors', a disorder where a person awakes suddenly in a terrified state. Across websites dedicated to the liberation of Belsen, heavy drinking was a feature mentioned by relatives and friends. One contributor recalled a man from his village: 'His wife and children moved away and he spent the rest of his life a lonely man who could be seen crying while he worked at a local farm. I saw him several times breaking into the hymn "The Old Rugged Cross" as he nursed a pint in the local pub. He died alone in the 1990s. Very sad'. Another wrote of an ex-colleague: 'As a student in the 1960s I worked with an ex-soldier who had been present at the relief of Belsen. "Jock" had never recovered from the shock and horror. An intelligent and sensitive man, he depended on alcohol and never married. His fellow workers respected him and showed touching understanding of his trauma.' Another lamented on his great-uncle: 'He was an army truck driver who was sent to Belsen to help. Since that day, he became an alcoholic. He tried to block out the horror.'

Back at work, Herbert dutifully fed his card into the clocking machine at the start and end of his shift, but the monotony was starting to tell. The noise and the heat at CPA was stifling and some days he barely saw daylight. The war, and Belsen in particular, had left him damaged but, paradoxically, it had furnished him with a hankering for freedom – those days on the Matchless, the rolling fields of France, moments of profound quiet amid the fury. And if not freedom, the outdoors at least. He left his job as a welder and became a delivery driver for Hulbert's Coal and Iron Merchants, a long-established Middleton company. 'Dad went where the work was,' said Herbert Jr. 'He wasn't particularly ambitious.' Herbert called each morning at the depot in Mill Fold Road, Alkrington, or, more usually, the yard based at Middleton Railway Station, to load up his flatbed lorry with bags of coal.

Whether alone driving the lorry or lugging hessian bags of coal in the yard, Herbert sometimes became engulfed by grief. His workmates, though they were unaware of the details, knew that he'd had a 'bad' war and were sympathetic. If they saw him fall quiet and move away from them, kicking his feet at the perimeter wall, they shouted after him: 'Get yourself home, Bert. We'll sort this lot.' When he arrived home, the best way of 'settling his nerves' was to play records on the gramophone. Grace would join him in the living room. They pushed the settee against the wall and lifted the coffee table out of the way to set up a tiny dance area, careful not to knock over the standard lamp. They danced cheek to cheek as the orchestrated refrains of, among others, Jimmie Grier ('Stay As Sweet As You Are'), Joe Reichman ('Because It's Love') and Angelo Ferdinando ('Kiss Me Goodnight') filled the room. Nearly 50 years later, Herbert would tell the *Middleton Guardian*: 'I was a broken man and would cry with my wife all day. It has been with me all my life . . . the shuffling people with barely any flesh on their bodies and great stacks of bodies piled on top of each other.'

Chapter Twenty
A handful of friends

———

The Royal British Legion has more than 2,500 branches in Britain and overseas. The charity provides social, financial and emotional support to veterans of the British Armed Forces, their families and dependants. Every second Monday of the month, members of the Middleton branch (No. 1529) meet at the Olde Boar's Head in Long Street. The branch has a chairman, vice-chairman, secretary, treasurer, branch community support rep, poppy appeal organiser and standard bearer; several combine more than one role. They range in ages from their mid-thirties to early eighties and have 53 members, although only about 15 routinely attend the monthly gatherings. 'At our meetings, which are minuted, we discuss the business of the branch, problems in the area, veterans who need help etc. Then it's beer o'clock and a social natter,' said secretary, Glynis Duffy. None of them remembers a former soldier from their town called Herbert Kenny or knows anything about him.

Phrases used most commonly to describe Herbert are 'he liked his own company' and 'he kept himself to himself'. No one is alive who knew him before the war, so it is difficult to determine whether his introverted nature was attributable to Belsen, although his family has assumed this to be the case. If Herbert, health permitting, had been more sociable and joined organisations such as the Royal British Legion or shared his story with even a select few, he might have been surprised to find others from his home town who had undergone remarkably similar experiences.

Fred Standring served with the 113th Light Anti-Aircraft Regiment and had been based a few miles from Belsen in April 1945; soldiers had asked about the foul smell and locals told them it emanated from an abattoir. Fred's unit was called in to assist with the relief of the camp, but he did not speak of what he encountered there until almost 20 years later. His daughter, Margaret, born ten months after the end of the war, had met a young German, Joachim, while on holiday with a friend in Yugoslavia in 1964. They exchanged letters and Joachim asked if he could visit Margaret in Middleton. 'At first I asked my mother if this was okay but she said I'd better speak to Dad about it – this was something that never happened in our house,' she said. 'I was 18, keen, and I tried to persuade him. I could tell it was something about the war and I said, "Come on, Dad, it's a long time ago."' Fred agreed that Margaret could see Joachim but the suggestion that he might stay with them for a few days brought an unexpected response. 'He suddenly said, "No German is staying under our roof" and I noticed tears streaming down his face. Until that point, I'd never seen him act like that. He kept saying, "You've no idea, you've no idea,"' she said.

Rising from his armchair in their terraced house in Ash Street, Mills Hill, Fred placed a footstool against cupboards set into an alcove by the hearth. He brought down a biscuit tin from the top shelf and pulled out a booklet. He passed it to Margaret, telling her, 'This is your worst nightmare.' The booklet was 'an account of events which took place at Belsen Concentration Camp between 13 April and 21 May 1945'. The text had been written by Captain Andrew Pares, an adjutant (an administrative assistant to a senior officer) of the Durham Light Infantry. The repugnant detail of Belsen was set down in cool, chilling prose. The pictures had the most lasting impact on Margaret: rows of withered naked bodies, a mass of tangled flesh and bone in a huge pit, and triangular stacks of flesh deposited randomly around the camp.

Margaret listened as her father recounted all he had experienced; it would be the only time he broached the subject. 'He told me he knew he would never get over it. He said they had an inkling of what had been going on but had no idea of the scale or that people had basically been sent there to die. The first thing he saw was the wire fencing and bodies piled up against it,' she said. The soldiers, she said, were made to stand in line with only one in every ten allowed to keep his rifle, presumably to reduce the risk of more bloodshed. 'He said he was glad that he had been asked to hand over his gun. I asked why and he said because he didn't trust himself not to shoot every German there. This was a man who would never hurt a fly in civilian life. I realised how much it had changed him, that I'd not grown up with the dad I should have done. I was grateful that he had told me, though. It brought me closer to him. I adored my dad and, in confiding to me, it helped him get it off his chest,' she said. Margaret recalled later that, as a young girl, she had heard her father sobbing when she was in bed at night. 'It all made sense after what he told me about Belsen,' she said. Margaret did not respond to subsequent letters from Joachim, out of respect for her father's feelings.

Fred spent his working life at Ferranti, an electrical engineering company, at its plant in Hollinwood, Oldham. When he started work there, he was told it was expected that he would become a member of the Amalgamated Engineering Union and the Labour Party. He signed up to the AEU but, although he voted Labour, refused to join the party. 'They kept telling him that he *had* to join but he wouldn't have any of it. He didn't want to be part of a political party or forced to do anything because it felt as if he was being dictated to – he knew where it could lead,' said Margaret.

Much the same as Herbert, Fred found it difficult forging relationships and had only a few friends. 'He had been through something so overwhelming and I think it made him feel different to other people, as if you had to go through the same thing to start to understand,' said Margaret. 'He was something of a loner.' Fred was a regular in the Old Cock and the Rose of Lancashire pubs in Middleton, where his bulldog, Judy, would sit at his heel. One evening, he had a chat in the pub with Father Christie from St Peter's RC Church. They struck up a friendship and the pair would meet on a regular basis. 'This happened about two years after Dad had told me about Belsen,' said Margaret. 'Father Christie acted as a sort of counsellor for him and afterwards Dad seemed happier and more outgoing.' Fred had been an Anglican but converted to Catholicism.

On the rare times Fred found himself in close proximity to Germans speaking in their own language, he would move on. 'It used to bring back those awful memories,' said Margaret. 'It's easy for people to say he shouldn't have been this way, but they hadn't been through what he had.' More usually, Fred confronted racism whenever he encountered it. Margaret remembered walking through Middleton and seeing rooms offered for rent with posters in the windows declaring, 'No blacks, no Irish, no dogs'. 'He used to knock on their doors and ask them to take them down. He'd tell them he'd served with Irish and black people in the war and they'd helped fight for this country,' she said.

After the war, some ex-soldiers, especially those who had liberated death camps, held vehemently anti-German sentiments but Herbert had always differentiated between Germans and Nazis. He told the *Middleton Guardian* in 1995: 'Someone said that it was not the German people that we wanted to beat, but the evil of the Nazis. And I agree with that.' Fred Standring died in 1973, aged 59, after a heart attack. Margaret donated artefacts from the biscuit tin to the archive of the Royal Regiment of Artillery.

Frank Watson, 'Big Frank', was a well-known character in Middleton. He had started work at Middleton Baths on 11 July 1927 – the day of the 'Middleton Flood' when a storm caused the Rochdale Canal to burst its banks and leave parts of the town almost 12 feet under water. He taught generations of the same families to swim, firstly at the 'fill and empty' baths in Manchester Old Road (the water was emptied each week, the pool scrubbed and filled again) and then at the 'new' baths, now demolished, in Fountain Street, opened in 1940 with the outside walls sandbagged to limit any damage, should it be bombed.

At the outbreak of war, Frank joined the Scots Guards and became a security officer for various COs, travelling extensively through Europe. Frank, though he was usually chatty, was another who barely spoke about his war service. He featured regularly in the *Middleton Guardian*, notably when he was made deputy baths supervisor in 1948, and main supervisor in 1965. One piece carried a mention of his time at Belsen, almost as a footnote. He was quoted as saying that he had seen 'bodies heaped five feet high'. He had remained in Germany for a few months after the war, acting as chauffeur for an officer; it meant he was given a rare glimpse of the country in peacetime. 'The Germans are well dressed, well-mannered but very short of food. They dig up their potatoes before they are fully grown,' he told the paper. He said he had been offered as much as £7 10s for a pound of coffee or 20 cigarettes. He returned to his job at the baths which he ran to military precision, his voice reverberating under the domed roof. At the end of swimming lessons, he had a favourite saying to children from Rhodes: 'Now get back to the other side of that big chimney!'

Sammy Greenwood was a member of ENSA (Entertainments National Service Association), the organisation that provided entertainment for British soldiers during World War Two. He was with a concert party based in Celle at the end of April 1945. While there, he wrote a letter of great contrasts to his grown-up daughter back home in Middleton. He opened by acclaiming the 'delightful little town' of Celle, specifically its centuries-old castle surrounded by a moat. 'As you look down some of the streets you imagine you are looking at a pantomime or Hollywood set,' he wrote. After several paragraphs on the splendour of Celle, he mentioned: 'On Tuesday morning we went to the prison [presumably Justizvollzugsanstalt Celle, a high-security prison completed in 1724] three miles from our billet, to see the women SS and men SS prisoners from Belsen.'

As a propaganda exercise, Canadian soldiers had invited people to witness members of the SS who they were guarding at the prison. Sammy and his colleagues were escorted on a tour where they were encouraged to look through peep holes into the cells. They were allowed entry into some to ask questions of the prisoners. 'I will not pretend that I enjoyed looking at the wretches. There are certain things I will not put in my letter but will tell you about one day,' he wrote. A concert planned for the same afternoon was cancelled at short notice, allowing Sammy to revisit the prison. He observed the SS, men and women, in the exercise yard. He wrote of 'a fair-haired, small, 23-year-old girl, SS leader, who had three murders proved against her'. She had tempted children with a piece of chocolate and then 'beat them to death and burned them'. Sammy had been determined to record what he had seen at the prison. 'Other spectators had their cameras, so I slipped out for mine, but was too late to get the women, but I got some pictures of the men parading around,' he wrote. He revealed: 'The treatment of these prisoners is not exactly kid-gloves. I will say no more.' A few days afterwards, he was taken to Belsen and shown around the camp. He closed his letter: 'Don't think I am glorifying in the horror of all this. It was something that should be seen by everyone, or at least never be forgotten by anyone.'

Lawrence Frattaroli spent time at Dachau and Buchenwald concentration camps as a member of the army medical teams sent in after liberation. The experience did not appear to affect him greatly, though a few years afterwards, he and his family was involved in an unnerving incident. They had travelled to Torquay for a holiday and had an outing to Plymouth. The Armed Forces was staging an Open Day and the Frattarolis joined others on a barge in Plymouth Sound. 'Everything was going fine,' said his son, Tom. 'We were taken around the various navy ships and then we heard this noise overhead. It was a group of planes doing a re-enactment, swooping down as if dive-bombing the harbour. Dad grabbed my mum, me and my two brothers, and was in a real panic. Mum called him a "stupid bugger" which I realised after was unfair because he was doing all he could to protect us and it had obviously brought back memories of the war.'

On D-Day, Lawrence had been part of the landing forces at Arromanches, where Herbert would land a few days later. Lawrence's unit was met with gunfire from a sniper positioned in the spire of a church, the Église St-Pierre. 'He told me they sent for a tank and blew the top off this church and the sniper with it. It's the kind of incident you see in a film but then you realise it really happened,' said Tom. Lawrence made his way through Normandy with the 1st Battalion RAMC, tending wounded soldiers in Caen and Falaise. While making camp one evening, he found a pair of Canadian Army-issue boots positioned upright in a field. He took them as his own. When he tried them on later, he realised flesh and bone was inside; the soldier had been blown up while wearing them.

Lawence seldom spoke about the concentration camps but disclosed scraps of memories to Tom. 'He said he saw what he assumed to be a pile of clothes. He looked again and saw that it was moving – people were still alive but laid on top of one another,' said Tom. Lawrence was told to 'root among them' and select the ones 'worth saving'. He picked out six and helped them into an army ambulance to take to hospital. A few miles down a dirt track, they were stopped by Russian soldiers. As he greeted them, Lawrence put on a greatcoat that had been left in the vehicle by a CO. The Russians ordered that the sick prisoners be taken from the vehicle; they said they would 'deal with the problem'. The British soldiers were told to drive on. 'They had not got far when they heard machine-gun fire,' said Tom. 'He was convinced that if the Russians hadn't seen the pips [slang terms for the stars worn to denote a military rank] on that coat, they would have shot them, too. He always held that the Russians were particularly ruthless.'

Much the same as Herbert, Lawrence distinguished between Germans and the SS. 'He liked Germans and thought they were great but said that the Nazis were horrible, arrogant bastards,' said Tom. Lawrence was in attendance once when an SS officer was being treated by a British Army surgeon. The officer's arm was mutilated after a shooting and barely attached to his shoulder. The doctor was about to administer an anaesthetic before amputation when the SS officer spat in his face. 'My dad said the surgeon just yanked his arm off,' said Tom.

Lawrence's younger brother, Thomas Frattaroli, whom Tom was named after, was shot and killed while on patrol, aged 21, on 18 August 1944, a day before his platoon of the 5/7th Battalion, Gordon Highlanders helped liberate Paris. Lawrence returned home to Miles Platting, Manchester; Thomas was buried at Saint-Désir-de-Lisieux War Cemetery in Normandy. 'In Dad's later years we went with him on one of those war tours,' said Tom. 'We were in a little museum and this Scotsman had been listening to him talking to me about what had gone on when he'd been a soldier. My dad wasn't one for fuss but this fella asked if he could shake his hand, as a thank-you for what he'd done. It made me realise the role he'd played. I still fill up now thinking about it, and also the uncle I never met but whose name I carry.'

After the war Lawrence worked at a traction maintenance depot in Newton Heath, Manchester. The family moved from their two up-two down terraced house to Langley, Middleton, in December 1956. A keen singer, Lawrence would take the microphone when he and his wife, Gladys, spent evenings out at the Woodside Working Men's Club or the Dyers and Polishers Club. 'I don't think what he went through in the war affected my dad, really,' said Tom. 'He came from poverty. His own dad had died when he was a boy [from tuberculosis], his brother had been killed. I think this all contributed to making him want to live his own life as much as he could. He didn't dwell on matters or bear grudges. He lived in the moment and his attitude was always, "Just get on with it." ' After retiring, Lawrence worked as a bus driver for social services. 'He absolutely loved it. He was taking kids with Downs syndrome to and from school and was always saying how great they were and how much he enjoyed it. That was my dad all over,' said Tom. Lawrence died in July 2006, aged 88.

Chapter Twenty-one
No longer their true and proper selves

———

The Kenny family moved to a council house in West Green, Rhodes. The Municipal Borough of Middleton, known to almost everyone as Middleton Corporation, had a progressive housing policy, of which West Green, built in the early 1930s, was a fine example. The properties were mostly semi-detached and built to a high standard, each with a good-sized back garden. The houses on the cul-de-sac were positioned around an oval-shaped piece of grassland 'as big as a cricket pitch'. Locals had their own names for nearby landmarks. The rugby field near Broad Street was 'the rec', the land behind West Green was the 'top hill' and the ginnel (narrow passage between houses) leading to the cul-de-sac was 'the Lambeth Walk' – many years earlier a family had returned from a night out and were heard singing the song from the musical *Me and My Girl* at the top of their voices; the name stuck.

Children ran errands to Doris Hamilton's greengrocer's shop, or the newsagent's run by Bessie and Leslie Elliott. The Elliotts' shop was popular because, beneath the sign for Woodbine cigarettes, the window was filled with an array of brightly coloured toys. Most teenagers in Rhodes had a spell working for them as paper boys or girls. They were permitted occasional free dips into the penny and halfpenny sweet box and taken on a once-a-year outing to Blackpool. At Christmas, to help amass more tips, they were given a card for every customer with the message: 'Weather good or weather bad, don't forget the paper lad.' Children helped with the haymaking at Clayton's Farm and learned how to milk cows and tend sheep; the rural heart of Rhodes was still beating.

The Kenny family home, a three-bedroom corner house in a block of four, formed part of this close-knit community. Herbert Jr recalled his growing up years as 'absolutely amazing'. 'People were always there for you, willing to help. As kids, we knew everyone as either Mister or Mrs. This was a mark of respect; we'd never refer to an adult by their first name. There felt to be plenty of optimism around, everyone more hopeful after getting through the war. We were proud to come from Rhodes and definitely wouldn't say we were from Middleton,' he said.

While Herbert had been away, either in mainland Europe or, before that, at training camps in Britain, the Kenny household had run to a pattern set by Grace. The children had been born over a short period of time: June (June 1936), Freda (June 1938), Edith (October 1939), Herbert Jr (September 1941) and Linda (November 1944). Grace was a hardworking and devoted mother who, the same as many during wartime, had undertaken roles traditionally regarded as maternal *and* paternal. Herbert had returned home on leave occasionally but was mostly absent for the vital first few years of the children's lives. 'He came up the street and was wearing khaki and had this little army cap on,' said Herbert Jr. 'Someone said to me, "That's your father" and he stooped down to pick me up. That was the first time I remember properly meeting him. He was a smart chap, very handsome with a pencil moustache. People used to say he looked like Errol Flynn.'

A strong bond had developed between Grace and the children, especially the two eldest, June and Freda; this would remain all their lives. The family dynamic was changed again when, 17 years after the birth of their first child, Steven was born in September 1953, when Grace was 38 and Herbert, 41. Until the children each left home, space was at a premium but none of the siblings remember it ever being an issue. Grace largely presided over this busy, lively household, a position she embraced wholeheartedly. She was a chain-smoker and the children were sent regularly to the Elliotts' shop to replenish her stock. They recall having to clear the smoke from rooms with a broad sweep of their arms, as if swimming through the haze. She was self-assured and resolute. One week, she was unhappy with the weekly portion of potatoes. She'd asked for 10lbs worth, delivered to the front door in a basket from George Starkey's horse-drawn cart. She marched down the garden path and told him she wanted 'spuds not clay'. He dutifully cleaned them with a wire scrub before weighing them again, adding more in the process.

Herbert played a peripheral role, an accord that was easily delineated in a family unit dominated by females – he often referred to 'the girls' and this included Grace. 'Dad was always happy in his own company. He never had a lot of mates. In fact, I can't think of him having any at all,' said Herbert Jr. 'He didn't go to pubs and didn't drink at home apart from a whisky on Christmas Day. My Uncle Les, Dad's brother, couldn't have been more different – he was always on the beer, and the pub was his second home. Dad was happy tending the garden and he always walked everywhere. He'd think nothing of strolling to Manchester and back [a round journey of about 12 miles] instead of getting on a bus. Actually, he didn't stroll – he marched everywhere. He didn't hang about: he just went.' Herbert combined his love of walking with earning extra income when he worked as an agent for a football pools company. He called door-to-door on his 'round', collecting betting payments, picking up and dropping off coupons; almost one in three adults gambled on the pools in the 1940s.

Family members sensed an air of detachment about Herbert and noted that he was frequently 'in his own world'. While he was usually passive, he sometimes had 'screaming rows', mainly with Grace. She would seek to end them with a plea that he 'forget it', but he was persistent. 'She did well to cope with it, really,' said Herbert Jr. 'She must have been a strong woman to put up with his moods.' Grace generally dealt with minor family infractions but if matters escalated, Herbert was called upon. He possessed a stern 'look' that stood as a warning, but he went further on one particular occasion. Herbert Jr, as a teenager, was arguing with Grace and began using bad language. She shouted over to her husband: 'Did you hear that, Herbert?' (he was known generally as Bert, so using his full name was a sign of gravity.) He lunged at Herbert Jr. 'Bang, he whacked me with his forearm. It was a hell of a blow. I tried to get away and sort of crouched against the wall behind the settee. It was really heavy, this couch, made from horsehair, and he just lifted it up and shoved it aside; he was that strong. He went for me again and my mum had to drag him off. It was the only time I ever saw him lose his temper like that,' he said.

On the surface Herbert and Grace's marriage was a cordial bond; it produced six children, numerous grandchildren and would last for more than 40 years. Grace, although primarily a 'home bird', embraced Herbert's greater spirit of adventure, forged principally by his army service. Although family members were reluctant to speak on the matter – their loyalty was commendable – it was clear that Herbert's experience at Belsen had affected his personality on a deeper level than the occasional bouts of depression and irritability. He was sometimes violent to Grace. She was known 'to give as much as she got' but this was in verbal spats; he was the taller and stronger and, very occasionally, had been known to lash out physically. 'I'd be in the other room and would hear them going hammer and tongs,' said Herbert Jr. 'Once or twice he slapped her. It wasn't as if he stood over her and beat her up but he definitely struck her; you could hear it.'

Sadly, Herbert's conduct was not uncommon in the strongly patriarchal times in which he lived, and the prevailing social mores. In many households, wives were routinely given 'a slap', 'a winger', 'a tickle' or 'a straightener' by their husbands – the prosaic depiction of assault reflected its habitualness. Herbert had been traumatised by war and first-hand experience of genocide. He was among thousands of men who had returned confused and troubled, no longer their true and proper selves. The brutalised becoming brutalisers was a depressing pattern of behaviour. 'I'd hear him saying to my mum afterwards, "I'm sorry about that, love" and he was tearful and full of regret. It sounds awful now, but this was going on all over. If I called at a friends' house, their mum and dad would be arguing and it would usually end up with the mother being knocked about,' said Herbert Jr. Much later, Herbert Jr came to better understand his father's sullenness and bouts of rage. 'He must have had all sorts of things on his mind. He kept it all in. My mum would have known, and probably our June. It upsets me to think about it, but his life was ruined, really.'

At the age of 14, Herbert Jr began work as a painter and decorator, alongside his cousin, Roy Kenny (the son of Herbert's brother, Les) and his business partner, Jack Isaac. Soon after starting, Herbert Jr was made aware of how his father held to convention. 'Every Friday one of us would go to the chippy and pick up a cracking tea for everyone, and we'd all sit round and eat it together. I always shared a meat and potato pie with our Linda. Anyway, my dad announced this time, "You're a working man now, you can have a full pie all to yourself", and from then on that's what I had.' Herbert Jr was told he could remain at the family home on condition that he handed over his wage packet to Grace each week. She deducted an amount to cover 'board and lodgings' and handed back to him what she and Herbert dubbed 'spending money'; this arrangement continued until Herbert Jr left home at the age of 19 to marry Beryl Crossfield, in July 1961. On first hearing that Beryl was 'stepping out' with

Herbert Jr, her father, James, had asked: 'Does his dad have the same name?' When Beryl told him that he did, James said he was reassured because he knew Herbert and that, 'his lad will be a good 'un if he's anything like his father'.

As a promising footballer, Herbert Jr received letters from Football League clubs inviting him to attend trials. He played for local teams on Saturdays and Sundays for many years, but his father attended only one match, a cup final. 'He turned up about a minute before the kick-off. It was nice that he came but I wasn't really bothered. He wasn't interested in football, and that was it. That's how my dad was,' said Herbert Jr. A rare occasion that piqued an interest in football for Herbert was in the formation of a women's team, the Luscious Ladies of Rhodes FC. While a lot of men mocked the women, Herbert thought it was a 'grand' idea; he admired their pluck. The club had been set up in 1947 by Sarah Tatlow who worked at CPA at the same time as Herbert. Matches were organised against 'anyone who could raise a team' – this included RAF men at the Bowlee base. The club lasted for four years, with the players using the Gardeners Arms as their headquarters and dressing room.

Chapter Twenty-two
The war against ill-health

_____

The frequency of what Herbert called 'one of my turns' became more intermittent. He was able to go a month or two without having to leave work early. Some mornings Grace would wake to find him in the kitchen, frantically doing the washing up, putting plates away and then mopping the floor, whistling all the while. 'This lad's full of beans this fine day,' he'd tell her. She was confused. 'I know. It's odd, love. I go to bed feeling rotten and I wake up almost giddy,' he explained. Although undiagnosed, he was probably suffering bipolar disorder, known previously as manic depression. The condition caused extreme mood swings, embracing emotional highs classed as hypomania, and lows (which were much more common) that left the sufferer feeling sad or hopeless, with a loss of interest and pleasure in almost all activities.

Before the war Herbert had possessed an itchy energy that, according to workmates, had him 'flitting about like a blue-arsed fly'. At home, he could seldom settle to watch television or read and told everyone that he 'liked to be doing'; this meant undertaking menial jobs, such as digging over the garden or household chores. He was aware that he had to harness the fidgetiness heightened by the upswings of bipolar. He hit upon a solution: he would return to the supreme fitness of old. His notes revealed a man keen to take charge of his life once more.

> Eventually I decided to get my health back. As I had done PTI [physical training instruction] in the army, I began to use my knowledge and drove myself on, gradually getting fitter. It took a long time before I was fit again, more than a year.
>
> Later, in 1948, I started teaching younger men (teenagers) to get and keep fit, using weight-training schemes. I built up some strong teenagers, then I went for my certification in 1951 and got it. I won my war against ill-health that World War Two had brought on to me. I was one of the lucky ones who came back, even though my health was impaired. I will never ever forget that war, mostly the Belsen horror camp. That is something one could never forget. It eases for a while, but never fades. It was evil. I firmly believe in saying that. Seeing what I did see in Belsen, on top of a build-up of tension, was the cause of my breakdown.

The PE routines practised in the army had become popular in peace time as soldiers carried on their personal regimes. Men and women, usually wearing white vests and shorts, were seen in parks or on wasteland, running on the spot or carrying out star jumps, toe touches, press-ups and sit-ups. The main fitness trend after the war was stretching exercises to enhance flexibility. People fastened elasticated belts to doorknobs or garden fences and pulled against them to strengthen their backs and stomachs. Herbert saw the value of these but had grown up during an era when the 'muscleman' Charles Atlas was popular, turning himself from a '97 lbs weakling' to the 'world's most perfectly developed man'. Herbert endorsed the pay-off line in adverts carried in comics, that, 'You can do these exercises almost anywhere' but recognised that another of the claims was an exaggeration – 'seven days is all you need'. He knew from his own experience that keeping fit took great dedication over a long period of time.

He visited boxing gyms and lads' clubs in nearby Collyhurst, Ardwick and Salford, and noted that they were frequented by men of all ages keen to use the equipment – punch bags, dumbbells, barbells, medicine balls, skipping ropes – to build up their strength and physique, rather than taking part in actual boxing. Training had become staunch and gritty with great emphasis on lifting heavy weights. Many had adopted 'hypertrophy training' which, through repetitive squats and curls, developed pronounced muscles in specific areas of the body such as thighs, calves, biceps and the back; they were said to be in search of the 'body beautiful'. Herbert Jr believed his father's approach was more practical. 'He liked all that stuff, reading about these musclemen – he used to subscribe to the magazines – but he was a tall, lean bloke himself and was probably just keen to get fit and feel as healthy and look as trim as he possibly could,' he said. Herbert described himself as a 'sun worshipper' and stressed the importance of absorbing UV rays to generate Vitamin D, a nutrient that was good for the bones, blood and immune system. 'Get out in that sun,' he'd say. 'It'll do you the world of good and see off any chills or colds. But don't burn yourself while you're doing it, that's no use to anyone.'

Few shops sold training equipment, so Herbert devised his own, employing his engineering skills and resourcefulness. He filled hessian carrier bags with stones and fastened together house bricks to provide weights for his bicep curls and lateral raises, drills he'd found in magazines such as *Health and Strength* and *Muscle Builder*. His most ingenious innovation was a pair of lead-lined boots. 'He had these old pair of boots and somehow he'd fastened lead to the soles,' said Herbert Jr. 'We asked him why he'd done it and he said he wanted to get his legs going! This went on for quite a while, him wearing them around the house and in the garden.' At first, Herbert exercised in the kitchen where he was joined by two local men, Eddie Plumridge and George Norman. Eddie Plumridge was a psychiatric nurse at Prestwich Mental Hospital; Herbert's family speculated whether he had shared details of his experience at Belsen with Eddie: they didn't ask.

Herbert was eager, constantly declaring the value of fitness to his children, singing out rhythms as he worked out: 'One-two, good for your heart. One-two, good for your soul.' His enthusiasm was infectious. They joined in occasionally but couldn't match his commitment to a daily routine. In a bid to show them what could be achieved, he took them to body-building shows at the Free Trade Hall in Manchester. 'I was a teenager then and not really interested,' said Herbert Jr. 'It was at the time of Mr Universe and all that.

Charles Atlas was still going – I remember lots of his books around the house.'

Under gentle chiding from Grace to 'clear off', Herbert moved out of the house and rented a large shed at the back of the Wilton Hotel, a half-mile or so away. He saved to buy conventional equipment and invited others to join him but didn't set it up as a formal organisation; it was usually referred to as 'Bert's Club'. 'He got quite a few people from Rhodes dropping in and kept it going for a number of years,' said Herbert Jr. 'I'll never forget, my dad told me this story about a bloke turning up and my dad said to him, "You're not joining." The fella had a fag in his hand and my dad said he'd have to stop smoking if he wanted to come in. The funny thing was that my dad was smoking at that very moment and this bloke obviously pointed this out. My dad said, "I don't any more" and stubbed it out. He never smoked again. It was as if he'd seen how bad it was at that very instant.'

Herbert no longer left work early in a distressed state. In fact, he realised that he was now being perceived in a completely different way. As he loaded up the wagons, he would joke with the men working on the railway line that ran from the nearby Neva Mills to Middleton Station. 'Put your back into it, lads, it'll do you good,' he'd shout over as they lugged bales of cotton. 'We're not all as fit as you, Bert,' they'd shout back. He enjoyed this endorsement and was proud to be regarded as fit and nimble in his early forties. He'd set about his tasks – shifting coal bags on to his back, strapping down the ties and manoeuvring in and out of the cab, with even more relish. He found his working day passed more quickly and with better cheer if he treated it as if it was a fitness routine, undertaken with gusto. The coal was delivered throughout Middleton and neighbouring towns but Herbert sometimes travelled further afield for Hulbert's, dropping off ironwork. In the school holidays, he invited his son, Steven, to tag along. 'The run I remember most was to the Lake District. We used to sing songs from *Oklahoma* and other musicals. He was the most loving, caring dad anyone could ever ask for, who would go without to make sure we didn't,' said Steven.

In his notes, Herbert occasionally professed his vigour and physique, and it could be construed as a rare example of hubris from a man of otherwise great modesty. He was comparatively tall for his generation at about 5ft 10ins, had a 'good head of hair' and presented himself well; he paid close attention to his 'Errol Flynn' pencil moustache. He took pride in his appearance and, when he had been tending the garden, would change out of his 'scruffs' to a collar-and-tie, even if merely calling round to the corner shop. 'I suppose you might say he was a little bit fond of himself,' said a family member.

The work at Hulbert's became less reliable and Herbert found himself laid off occasionally. He disliked any degree of insecurity and didn't feel he should have to inform his employers of the necessity for regular pay: it was obvious. Work was always available at the Calico Printers Association (CPA) in Rhodes and Herbert returned there more than 30 years after first starting at the company. During its heyday of the early 1900s, CPA had more than 1,000 staff but in the late 1950s, when Herbert went back to operate a machine cropping metal, it employed about 300.

Within the first few weeks, Herbert was told the same two stories that he had first heard three decades earlier. He didn't mind; he enjoyed a good yarn. The firm had been set up originally by a local man of German-Jewish descent called Salis Schwabe, whose family held to benevolent principles, funding schools, libraries, hospitals, etc. One of his sons, Edmund Salis Schwabe, came to a grisly end while on a world tour recovering from gout and depression. A man occupying an adjoining room at the Windsor Hotel, Montreal, Canada, heard a gunshot. On entering Schwabe's room, he found the 51-year-old with a bullet wound to the head. A verdict was recorded of suicide while in a temporary state of insanity. The other tale, repeated often, was far less solemn and Herbert broke into laughter in the retelling. A textile buyer from overseas, Mr Yussef El Gammal Pasha, had been waved off from Rhodes on his way to Manchester to catch a train. He hailed a horse-drawn cab, but, reportedly weighing more than 35 stones, his girth caused the floor of the cab to splinter and give way. The horse bolted and, to keep up, Mr Pasha had to run as fast as he could while within the frame of the vehicle.

The enlightened working practices of the Schwabes had largely been abandoned by the 1950s but workers were grateful for moderately small concessions – the plant was kept clean and attention paid to health and safety, which wasn't the case at many other companies in Middleton. During the week, the working day was 7.30am to 5.30pm with, on Saturdays, a compulsory shift of

8.30am until noon. A meter was fixed to looms, measuring the amount of cloth running through. Fast workers could, after reaching daily targets, augment their earnings under a bonus scheme. Jacqueline Smith worked as a wages clerk at CPA at the same time as Herbert. 'You couldn't compare it to working life today,' she said. 'You were told what to do and you got on with it. There was little chance of promotion and there was no real training. I remember a comptometer [a key-driven metal calculator] being plonked on my desk and I was expected to learn how to use it myself.' Senior bosses had the mien of military personnel. Leonard Fox, the general manager, would amble through the workshops and across the site in a flying jacket.

CPA was a noisy place with a constant din of machinery. Ear protectors were available but wearing them was optional and many regarded them to be – in their words – too much of a *faff* (an over-complicated task); they also made it even more difficult to communicate with one another. The demarcation was well-established: women worked in the offices with their friends, mothers, daughters or aunties, while men either laboured, operated machines or worked as engineers, tending or repairing the heavy equipment, often alongside friends and family. Herbert soon discovered that it was a village within a village, teeming with gossip and innuendo, half-truths and whole truths. He kept his counsel but surreptitiously enjoyed the badinage.

The same as Herbert, most of the 'old boys' had served in the war. The lads aged 17 to 21 left regularly to complete their National Service, an edict that lasted until 1960. 'What's it like in the army,

Bert?' he was asked. He'd shake his head and purse his lips. 'Keep your head down and whistle a happy tune and you'll be right,' he replied. What more could he say? After a medical and six weeks of basic training, they were sent to take part in military operations in countries such as Malaya, Korea, Cyprus and Kenya.

Herbert Jr was laid off as a painter and decorator and advised by friends to 'get down to CPA and sort yourself out'. He was taken on as a 'jacquard lad', minding the jacquard machine, a contraption with perforated cards fitted to a loom that wove brocade fabric. He worked at CPA at the same time as his father, though their contact was limited because he was based elsewhere on the site and did shift work. Herbert was the organiser of the weekly football pools syndicate at CPA, incorporating about 20 of its staff. One week, Herbert Jr did not have the half a crown needed for his weekly payment. He asked his father to lend him the money. 'He told me that if I couldn't afford it, I'd have to miss out, that it was my fault for using up all my spending money.' That week, the syndicate had a jackpot win. 'It was a really nice pick up,' said Herbert Jr. The Kenny family also had a syndicate and they won, too: about £200 each. Herbert Jr missed out again because he had not paid his weekly subs. 'On both occasions, I didn't get a fig out of either win,' said Herbert Jr. 'My dad just said, "You didn't put anything in, so you're not getting anything out." He was a stickler like that.' Herbert Jr did not bear any ill-will to his father. He recognised that, although it was a particularly harsh lesson, he was being taught to take responsibility for his own life. 'It made me very independent. I've never asked for anything from anyone and just got on with my own life. I was pleased for those that won and thought, "Good on 'em."'

While at CPA, Herbert Jr was able to see how his father was viewed and treated by people other than family members. 'I could tell he was well-liked,' said Herbert Jr. 'My dad was a gentleman. He dressed smart, as if he was going out somewhere. I think he got this from the army. I never saw him in the canteen. He took his own butties and a flask and did his own thing, which was typical.'

Chapter Twenty-three
Jews for breakfast, Poles for dinner

_____

The Holocaust had been a hugely extensive undertaking, carried out at 23 main camps and almost 900 sub-camps across mainland Europe. At the war's end, tributaries of pain, suffering and loss flowed from these sites and elsewhere as more than 50 million people were dispersed throughout the globe. Their homes had been bombed to rubble or seized, and many of their neighbourhoods still seethed with antisemitism; the scourge did not expire with the war. In Britain, almost 200,000 Poles and 35,000 Ukrainians were housed in former army and air force bases, before moving chiefly to urban areas in search of employment. They had come as part of the European Voluntary Workers scheme to support post-war labour shortages in British industry. Middleton, with its mills and workshops, and close proximity to Manchester, was a prime destination. Herbert, had he been inclined, could easily have found others who had also witnessed and endured genocide. These people were literally on his doorstep.

Rosaria Sityk was a Polish woman who, in her later years, lived directly across from Herbert in Croft Gates Road, Rhodes.

She had been imprisoned in several concentration camps. Her home-help, Wendy Lord, remembered seeing weal marks on Rosaria's back from where she had been whipped by prison guards. They had also shattered her kneecap. Rosaria was a familiar figure in Rhodes because she toured the streets with a shopping trolley, collecting wood, and she regularly threw sweets down to children from her flat window. She died in October 1986, aged 72. PC Alan Grocott, the community police officer for Rhodes, was called to her flat after being told of her death. He found her life savings taped to her stomach beneath her clothes. A suitcase was on top of a wardrobe in her bedroom. The officer expected to find personal papers or clothes inside; it was full of sugar, which had been rationed after the war.

Emila (aka Emilie) Bendasiuk (née Trojan), another Polish woman, lived a few hundred yards from Herbert, in Manchester Old Road, Rhodes. As a young teenager she had been force-marched with approximately 700 other 'foreign and German persecutees'. They were held captive at a camp established in a prison at Straubing in Lower Bavaria, southern Germany. After the war she moved to Rhodes with her husband, Fedor Bendasiuk, a Ukrainian, and raised three children, Peter, Michael and Pamela. 'They were lovely people, the salt of the earth,' said neighbour, Phil Gaunt. 'Ferdy [Fedor] used to drive a coke wagon for Middleton Gas Works. They had a bit of a poultry farm at the back of West Green. I used to see this number tattooed on Emila's arm. I asked her one day what it was and she told me the Germans had branded it on her in the camp.'

A Polish couple, Albin and Irena Lasowski, moved into the house in West Green, Rhodes, that had previously been occupied by Herbert's older brother, Leslie, and his wife, Bertha. Albin had been brought up in Władysławowo, a town on northern Poland's Baltic coast. He was among 225,00 Poles forcibly conscripted into the Wehrmacht. Although they had no say in the matter, these men were stigmatised and ostracised in Polish society; the slur 'grandfather in the Wehrmacht' was still vented nearly 80 years after the end of the war. Albin had been taken to Stalag V-A, a German prisoner-of-war camp in Ludwigsburg, north of Stuttgart, from where inmates were transferred to labour camps to work in factories or repair roads and railway lines. In July 1943 Albin was moved to a camp in the German city of Ulm, close to its border with Bavaria. 'My dad was always vague about what had happened to him in the war,' said his daughter, Janina Haslam. 'He didn't want to talk about it. It must have been a horrible thing, being made to join an army that was against his own people. He told me that he'd been sent to Siberia for a while. One time, we had a map of Europe in the house and he drew lines on it of all the places he'd been taken.'

Irena Lasowski (née Soltysik), was born in Wolbrom, a small town in southern Poland. The Gestapo called at her home and ordered her to carry out forced labour. Her parents protested that she was only 16 years old; they were threatened with being shot. Irena's papers were falsified by the Gestapo to make her eligible for work. She was marched to railway sidings and led with others into an open truck. Ingrid, her best friend, was with her but became overcome by grief. She said that she wanted to go home and was unable to stop sobbing. Irena tried to help her fall quiet, telling her to cover her mouth with the cuff of her coat. The Germans were vexed. Ingrid was lifted back down from the truck. A few seconds later Irena heard a gunshot. She never saw her friend again.

Irena was transported to a rural location in Austria where she was made to do agricultural work for a German family. She slept in a cowshed. She complained and the family reported her. The Gestapo paid a visit. She was beaten and pistol whipped. After the war she moved to England and worked in the mills in Oldham and Rochdale. She met Albin and they married in the summer of 1949. 'They were both from rural places in Poland and, although they got on with it, I don't think they ever adapted to the noise of the mills and being indoors all the time,' said Janina. At first, they lived in houses shared with other immigrant families but moved to Boardman Lane in Rhodes and later, West Green. They were occasionally subject to racism. They were called 'Polish pigs' and their front door window smashed. The couple had seven children, but it was often a troubled home. Albin, a regular at the Polskie Koto (Polish Circle Social Club) in Cheetham Hill, drank excessively. 'He took to drink and we all suffered as children. He was quite feral really and we had to parent him as much as he was our parent,' said Janina.

Albin's behaviour led to a separation but Irena still cooked for her husband, with family members dropping off pans of stew at West Green, where Albin had remained with his son, Albin Jr. One day, Albin Jr found his father slumped on the settee in front of a fire with the heating turned up full. He had committed suicide with an overdose of painkillers and whisky; he had made previous attempts on his life. He was 59 when he died in January 1985. At the inquest, the coroner speculated that his wartime experiences had contributed to the frequent bouts of depression and volatility. Albin Jr was afflicted by schizophrenia; he also died at 59. 'Mum used to say how horrible it had been in the war. "Horrible" was a word she used a lot,' said Janina. 'She would hear the news about disagreements between countries and say, "I hope it's not all going to happen again." She never lost that fear.' Another of their daughters, Irene Williams, a junior school head teacher, posted on a public Facebook group on the 75th anniversary of VE Day in May 2020: 'My mother. Irena Soltysik. Another name to remember on VE day. Ripped from her family aged 16 in Poland to work as a slave for the Germans. She came to England after being shot, starved and beaten by Germans to settle in Rhodes. She had 7 children and many, many house moves. Loved a spring roll, Kenny Rogers and "Jolene" [the Dolly Parton song]. She taught us all to keep going and to be independent and strong. Love and miss you. Xxxxx.'

The ill-treatment of Albin and Irena Lasowski, and tens of thousands of others, had been habitual during wartime. The Nazis regarded ethnic Poles as *Untermenschen*; only the *Volksdeutsche* (those with German origins) were spared, about two per cent of the Polish population. Many Poles used the aphorism 'Jews for breakfast, Poles for dinner'. Approximately three million Polish Jews and two million Polish Gentiles were killed in the

Holocaust. Mateusz Morawiecki, the then-prime minister of Poland, said in 2022: 'From a Western perspective, the conflict can be seen as a series of battles, troop movements and political decisions. For us, it was primarily a set of crimes, atrocities and destruction. From the very beginning, World War Two was a cold-blooded crime planned with the goal of the physical elimination of entire nations and destruction of entire countries. Nazi Germany regarded us as a race of slaves on whom horrific crimes and experiments could be carried out with impunity.'

Henry West gave decades of public service to Middleton. He was a Labour councillor and chairman of the town's main forum, the Middleton Township Committee. He was also governor of the Middleton campus of Hopwood Hall College, where a building was named in his honour in May 2006. Henry's family had fled Nazi persecution before the war. He spoke publicly about the Holocaust and said he had 'avoided it rather than survived it'. His father, Paul, had been a journalist, working as a foreign correspondent for German newspapers, and had seen first-hand the growing antisemitism. The dissenting tone of some of his articles had been noted and he 'quaked every time the front doorbell rang', expecting the Gestapo. Paul's wife was English and a Gentile – Orthodox Judaism follows matrilineal descent. The family was able to leave Berlin in December 1938 on the sovereignty of her British passport. Henry was ten years old when they moved to north London and then Middleton. The family changed its surname from Wegner to West, after eight years in England.

Henry found out later that many of his relatives had been killed by the Nazis. He visited his grandfather's home city of Drohobych in Ukraine where 14,000 Jews had been murdered by Ukrainian nationalists, aided by the Wehrmacht. On Holocaust Memorial Day in 2015, Henry spoke at a special remembrance service: 'It's still happening now, that people are discriminated against simply because of their ethnic origin. It's important to remain constantly vigilant, so that our society does not degenerate into anything like that, and we make sure our efforts go towards uniting people, not dividing.' Henry lived for many years in King's Drive, close to Herbert's flat in Croft Gates Road.

During the mid-1980s the Carters Arms in Rhodes became an unlikely setting for regular discussions about the Holocaust. Jim Allen, the playwright, had a daily routine which incorporated a walk through Alkrington Woods to the Carters for a lunchtime session, often stretching into the evening. Allen was among an assembly of writers, producers and directors established in the 1960s and '70s through work featured in left-field television series such as *The Wednesday Play*, *Thirty-Minute Theatre* and *Play for Today*. His drama, *Perdition*, was centred on an episode whereby Hungarian Zionists had allegedly been complicit with the Nazis in the death of 800,000 Jews at Auschwitz, on an understanding that, in return, 1,685 prominent Zionists would be granted unhindered passage, at a price of $1,000 per person, to neutral Switzerland and onwards to Palestine. The genocide would provide a mandate for Zionists to convince the world that a Jewish state was vindicated – an 'ingathering of exiles'. 'Israel was founded on the pillars of Western guilt and American dollars' was a line from the play. And another: 'Israel was coined in the blood of Hungarian Jewry.'

Allen defended the play vigorously, whether in the tap room of the Carters Arms or on national television, where he refused to demur or alter his dishevelled appearance. Allen had moved to Langley from Miles Platting as part of the slum clearance in the 1950s; he had worked on the estate as a labourer while it was being built. Two of his works, the television play, *The Spongers* (1978) and the film, *Raining Stones* (1993), directed by Ken Loach, were both set there. *Perdition* caused an international furore. Allen agreed that he was anti-Zionist, viewing the movement's leaders as he did the elite self-serving overseers of industry in his other work, but he objected strongly to being labelled an antisemite. 'My record as an anti-Fascist goes beyond writing letters to the *Guardian*,' he said. 'When I was a docker and a miner we just stopped them whenever the scum turned out. The streets ran with blood.'

In January 1987, two days before a preview performance at the Royal Court Theatre in London, the play was withdrawn. Max Stafford-Clark, the theatre's artistic director, said he did not want to 'offend sections of the community'; there were claims that he had yielded to pressure from the theatre's funding bodies. A single one-off performance was staged at the Edinburgh Festival in the summer of 1987, before a revised version ran at the tiny Gate Theatre in Notting Hill, London, in 1999, produced by Elliot Levey, the son-in-law of Ken Loach. Levey told the *Guardian*: 'It is not historically inaccurate. It's very much a pro-Jewish play. My hope is that it won't be sat on, as it was in the 1980s.' While the controversy raged, Allen had been advised to be more 'balanced' in his output. 'But I don't accept the position of balance,' he said. 'People who sit on the fence only get splinters up their arse. You have to take a position. Knock me down, argue, but don't drown it.'

In his home town, Allen was viewed as 'typically Middleton'. 'Jim could be challenging and contradictory but he was the real deal,' said a friend. 'It wasn't an affectation; he was genuinely at his happiest in the Carters with a few pals.' Allen died in June 1999 but lived long enough to see *Perdition* performed at the Gate Theatre. Paul Bond, in *World Socialist* – a media outlet favoured by Allen – wrote: 'What strikes the viewer finally able to see *Perdition*, after all the attacks and slanders, is its burning humanity, the belief in a better world, something that marked all of Allen's work.' Two cast iron plaques to Allen's memory were set into Yorkshire stone paving in Middleton town centre in 2010. One read: 'Trade unionist, socialist and writer whose work celebrated the strength, humanity and vision of working-class people.' A blue plaque in his name was fixed to the wall of Middleton Library, featuring his quote: 'My only regret when I die will be the books I have not read.'

Chapter Twenty-four
Build a new life and start again

———

Over a nine-year period, Herbert and Grace grew accustomed to rooting out their best clothes and attending their children's weddings. The first to wed was their eldest daughter, June, who married Jack Clark in July 1955. Jack worked at the Ciba-Geigy dye works in Rhodes; he used to joke that he came home a different colour after every shift. In October 1958, Edith married John Williamson, an engineer at CPA. John, sometimes known as Jack, was a keen angler and said to be 'very fond of a pint'. Just three months afterwards, in January 1959, Freda married Albert Hoyle, a scrap man who worked at Albert Burton's yard in Rhodes, operating machinery to crush cars and cut up boilers. Albert, described by his family as 'a hard grafter but not a good mixer', had wanted a low-key wedding; it was held at Holy Trinity Church in Parkfield, Middleton, at 9am with only a single photograph taken. Herbert Jr married Beryl Crossfield in July 1961, and Linda married Ivan Kernaghan in October 1963; Ivan worked in the building trade. The birth of Steven in 1953 meant that Herbert and Grace effectively experienced two versions of family life. The first had been a busy, chatty household with five children born over a short time span, but once Linda had married, Steven, aged ten at that time, became in essence an only child, which made for a much quieter household.

Amid the flurry of weddings, Eliza, Herbert's mother, became a widow again. Her husband, Clement Jackson, died in August 1958, aged 85. Eliza continued to live at their home in Trinity Street, Rhodes, where visitors usually found her drawn close to the fire, sitting up straight in a tall chair, wearing small, dark, round glasses – no one was sure whether they were prescription lenses or an affectation. She later moved to Schwabe Street, also in Rhodes, named after the founders of CPA. Herbert Jr would visit with Beryl and their young daughter, Janet. 'I loved her. She was so talkative and interested, whether it be about the family or life in general. She had something about her,' said Herbert Jr. 'She listened to the radio a lot and wanted to learn things. She was kind and never criticised people. My dad was very much like her. She'd brought him and his brothers up on her own. She was strict but a lot of people were in those days – she'd been through two world wars.' The conviviality towards Eliza was not shared by Herbert's sisters, June and Freda, or their mother, Grace. 'They thought she was snotty-nosed, a bit above herself. The great shame with Grandma Jackson was all that stuff about being a bastard and wanting to be part of the Kilvert family. She was adamant, and remained bothered about it until the day she died,' said Herbert Jr.

Now that five of his six children had married, Herbert felt he had 'done his best by them' and could remodel life to make it better for himself, Grace and Steven. His outlook was much changed from before the war. He'd been a soldier, part of the communion of an army – told what to do and where to be – but, at the same time, he'd frequently travelled solo perched upon his motorcycle. He'd noted the changes of scenery as he passed over smooth roads, gravelly paths, shuddering down dirt tracks and slipping through fields, feet stabbed to the ground to stay upright. At full pelt, with the grip in his right hand tilted to its furthest point, he had felt as if he was racing away from himself – that withdrawn, cautious chap from Middleton becoming a speck in the rear-view mirror. He had seen a bigger, wider world. France, Holland, Germany – even the writing on street signs was different. Whenever he recalled what the other soldiers called DRs, he'd break into a crescent-moon smile: *glamorous bastards*. Back home in Middleton, everything seemed built from the same carmine-coloured brick while, *in Europe*, the buildings were a mismatch of shapes and colours, cream to pink to gold. Once, he'd tried to describe all this to a pal at work. He was quickly put right: 'Go and write a bloody poem about it.'

Before, his life had seemed small and narrow: husband, father, worker – everything plotted out to the end of his street and back, and maybe a daytrip here and there to Manchester with, if he could afford it, an annual holiday to Blackpool or Rhyl. He knew he wasn't gifted with words; few people were, from his background and level of education. Nevertheless, the one word that lit up shiny bright in his mind whenever he tried to categorise this new disposition was *worldly.* He daren't volunteer this aloud, though: he didn't want to appear conceited.

Another distinct memory of the war and his time on his motorcycle was the weather. They had landed on the beaches of France in early June and, as much as he remembered the smell of burning, the scrabbling and blasting, the granules of sand gritty between his teeth and eyelids, he also recalled the heat and light – not on the actual day of landing, when it was cold and overcast, but soon afterwards. He thought of the times when they had made camp or he'd parked up by the road or turned through a gateway into a field for a rest and some *snap* (food). He and the other soldiers all agreed that the heat was different from back home, but struggled to describe the distinction. 'It's dryer, somehow,' said one. 'No, fresher,' said another. Whatever, Herbert had enjoyed the warmth and the wider, open skies. On returning to Manchester he had quickly felt to be nailed down, fastened in. Darkness would settle over the streets soon after dinner time (as the midday meal was known), and most days, even in summer, carried a shiver or portent of a downpour. Herbert saw this climate reflected in the people. They were tense. They scurried here and there, buttoned up. He was growing restless.

Adverts encouraging people to emigrate to Australia had been appearing in the *Manchester Evening News* and other newspapers since the end of the war, but their frequency increased throughout the 1950s. Australia, with a population of 7.5 million, had adopted a policy to swell its workforce known as 'populate or perish'.

Workers were needed to move the country away from a rural economy, with jobs available in manufacturing, construction, transport, mining, steel and as factory hands. The Assisted Passage Migration Scheme offered a deal whereby adults from Britain could travel to Australia to take up a job for a fare of £10 each (the average wage in Britain in 1950 was £7 per week) with children free of charge and 'minors' (14 to 19 years old) paying £5 for a ticket. The cost, if unsubsidised, would have been about £100 per person.

The campaign was widespread and persuasive, focused unremittingly on the sunshine and opportunities offered in Australia. 'NEW LAND – NEW LIFE!' was the motif on an advert carried in newspapers, with, beneath it, a mother holding aloft her smiling, well-scrubbed young son. In another, featuring a smiley baby with ruffled hair, the strapline was: 'His future in your hands. Take him to Australia.' Coupons were issued to request a 'free wallet of info' – a set of booklets about life in Australia. Most adverts had been placed by the Australian government, but some were taken out by private companies. Melbourne Tramways, for example, offered jobs as conductors with a wage the equivalent of £24 per week. Successful applicants were promised 'A sunny life in a land of opportunity', exemplified by a line-drawing of a young woman in a bikini sitting beneath a parasol, a beach ball at her feet. Aspiring tram conductors were asked to meet with Mr J Keith Allen, a 'Tramway representative' at Liverpool YMCA, between 1pm and 7pm, any Saturday. The hyperbole was mirrored on television, with commercials set to a soundtrack of jaunty music and footage of happy, busy emigrants. Australia had 'room to move and space to grow' and was 'the country for get-up-and-go people'.

British workers taking up the offer became known as 'Ten Pound Poms'. They had to be nominated by a friend or relative already living in Australia, or endorsed by their current employer. The only stipulation was that they must spend a minimum of two years in Australia or they would have to reimburse the £10 fare and self-fund the journey back to Britain. Australians were encouraged to support this immigration with slogans on posters such as, 'Make it easier . . . help build Australia. Bring out a Britain.'

Herbert was rapt from first seeing the adverts. He could do that, he thought: move to the other side of the world, build a new life and start again. And it would be under a burning sun, the days long and flushed with light; maybe memories of Belsen could be bleached away. He knew it would take charm and chicanery to persuade Grace. She was a homegirl, happy with her lot. 'My mum dug her heels in because she didn't want to go,' said Herbert Jr. 'He kept telling her that it would be a much richer life out there. I'm sure now that being in England reminded him of his war years and he felt sort of unhealthy living here.'

The distance from Manchester to Adelaide, South Australia – a city where many British people had settled since the 1830s – was more than 10,000 miles, but when Herbert began mentioning it as a possible place to relocate, his family considered it to be 'on a different planet'. 'There was obviously no internet then and phoning one another was difficult with the line always breaking down. Actually, I don't think we even had a telephone back then. All you could do really was write, but letters took ages to arrive,' said Herbert Jr. At the time, foreign travel was so uncommon that anyone undertaking it was sometimes featured in the *Middleton Guardian*. Mrs Jenny Newton of Mill Fold Road, for example, informed the paper that she was going to spend Christmas with her two daughters in Florida, prompting a story with the headline: 'Jenny (79) is Off to Enjoy Herself'. The exorbitant cost of travelling to and from Australia, outside the £10 fare scheme, meant that families knew they would not be able to afford to see one another for many years, or in some cases, ever again. Herbert was patient. He was aware that Grace would not have contemplated the move while most of the children were young or settling into their lives as young adults, but that period had passed.

The harsh winter of 1962/63 served to do the bidding on Herbert's behalf. Snow began falling on Boxing Day of 1962; it felt an especially joyous Christmas after the peaceful outcome to the Cuban Missile Crisis two months earlier. The powdery snow falling on Middleton caused great excitement as children hunted out sledges from cellars and sheds. Roads were iced over and closed to traffic. The No. 59 bus became stuck in snow near Boothroyden Road. The lodges in the grounds of CPA froze and intrepid children ventured out across the ice, crouched into bread trays, wooden beer crates and orange boxes. The cold weather remained for weeks, barely climbing above freezing point in January and February. Blizzards caused snowdrifts, blocking lanes and hiding garden walls. 'It's bloody horrible, this,' Herbert would say to Grace as he prised open the front door to break the seal of ice and battle through the wind to call at the newsagent's. 'It's not doing anyone any good, this weather,' he added. 'It gets in your bones.' During the Big Freeze (as it became known), pavements froze over, making them almost impassable; for a few weeks it meant Herbert missed out on the work-out sessions at the shed behind the Wilton Hotel. 'This awful weather means you can't plan for anything in this country,' he grumbled.

Grace fretted about how a move to Australia might affect Steven, aged ten, having to leave friends behind and interrupt his education. 'Kids love it out there,' reassured Herbert. 'They can play out in the sunshine all day. He'll be fine.' Steven believed his mother was 'a little unsure but happy to give it a go'. The Kennys were 'nominated' by Wasyl (known as Bill) and Doreen Chemny, a Middleton couple who had already moved to Adelaide with their children, Peter and Linda. Herbert announced their intentions to the children who, by 1964, had young families of their own. 'I knew that once Dad had made his mind up about anything, it would happen. I don't recall there being a going-away party or any kind of celebration,' said Herbert Jr. He was especially upset – 'gutted' in his words – to be parted from his brother, Steven, to whom he was close despite the age gap of almost 12 years. Most weekends, Steven had stayed over with Herbert Jr and his wife Beryl at their home in Highfield Street, Middleton. 'He was a belting little lad and we both looked forward so much to him coming over. I'd wait for him at the bus stop and then put him on the 59 back to Rhodes the next day. It all happened so quickly. One minute they were here and then they were gone.

Steven had been such a big part of our lives.' The next time the brothers met was decades later.

Only weeks before they were due to emigrate, the move was almost thwarted. An offer for their house had been accepted, but while the paperwork was being undertaken the purchaser told them he could no longer meet the asking price. 'This came at the last minute. Everything had been set for us to move – dates, flights, everything,' said Steven. 'So Dad had to accept less than originally agreed to avoid our plans being thrown into chaos. Mum and Dad were pretty angry and upset about it all.' Herbert and Grace had bought their council house at 17 West Green, using a good portion of the pools-win money. The Housing Act of 1936 had made this possible for tenants, although very few took it up before the 'Right to Buy' scheme of the 1980s. The decision had been characteristically astute and farsighted of Herbert.

Chapter Twenty-five
Pottering in the garden

Most Ten Pound Poms travelled to Australia by sea, a journey that could take up to six weeks, but Herbert, Grace and Steven flew. Their household items following on by sea a few weeks later. Beforehand, they were inoculated against cholera and smallpox; Steven remembered his arm 'feeling like lead'. They travelled by train from Manchester to London, visiting Buckingham Palace – Herbert was always keen to make best use of time – before boarding at Heathrow. They left for Australia on Thursday, 14 May 1964, on a BOAC airliner; it was the first flight for each of them. Herbert was 51 and Grace, 48. The plane refuelled in Karachi at the southern tip of Pakistan where they disembarked for a few hours. 'Boy, it was hot,' said Steven. 'It was like stepping into an oven from the air-conditioned plane. We had to walk across the tarmac into the airport building. I saw an amazingly dressed fellow. He looked like a Maharajah – all flowing, brightly-colourful robes and a feathered turban.' Back on the plane, after the thrust of take-off they were travelling over a mountainous region at a constant velocity, giving the impression of stillness. Grace remarked, 'Oh, we've stopped moving.' Herbert responded: 'You better hope we haven't or we'll be on the ground sooner than expected.' Grace laughed and poked Herbert in the ribs.

The plane called at Singapore and Darwin before arriving at Sydney where they changed to a smaller aircraft. Within minutes of boarding, Herbert began to feel ill. He was extremely pale and had sunken eyes. Flight attendants helped him off the plane, with Grace and Steven following closely behind. He was checked over by a doctor and diagnosed with 'flying sickness'. He was given an injection – they weren't informed what it contained. The three of them were put up in a boarding house. 'By the time we got there, the injection had taken hold of Dad. He was acting as if he was drunk, which the landlady wasn't happy about. Mum put her right and explained what had happened. She warmed up a bit after that. We got Dad into bed and he was out like a light,' said Steven. Grace and Steven were hungry and called at a café, a ten-minute walk away. 'It was full daylight when we went into the place, but when we came out it was totally dark. Mum was surprised. Unlike in England, there had been no twilight at all. Everything looked different and she was completely lost. I knew the way, so we walked back and went to bed,' he said. Herbert awoke the next morning in good health, immediately orientated to his surroundings. He wanted to maximise their day in Sydney, hurrying Grace and Steven out of the boarding house. They took a ferry across Sydney Harbour and spent several hours at Taronga Zoo. The day afterwards, Herbert reported fit to the doctor and was permitted to fly to Melbourne, and then on to Adelaide.

The Kennys knew they would be spending time initially in temporary accommodation at Adelaide. Brochures had listed this as a 'luxury camp' and 'miniature suburb'. Gepps Cross Migrant Hostel was based on open plains in the district of Gepps Cross at a major road intersection in the north of Adelaide, close to a huge abattoir. The 'hostel' was essentially a camp to house approximately 2,000 British people, comprising rows of Nissen and Quonset huts – prefabricated structures made from corrugated iron or steel which had been used as barracks in World War Two. The site included hospital wards, a post office, crèche, shops, banking facilities, and had communal toilets, showers, laundry and dining rooms. When the Kennys arrived, Linda Hakes's family had already been living there for several years. She later wrote of the experience: 'It was a dreadful place. I wouldn't put my dog in a Nissen hut where there wasn't heating or cooling. It was like living in an oven. Putting migrants into sub-standard housing was not the way to endear them to Australia. It would not be tolerated nowadays.' Cheryl Burman, an Australian-born author, later reflected: 'Can you imagine travelling 10,000 miles to be set down on an arid brown plain in a hot Nissen hut, sharing bathrooms and having to eat what's given you? Some went straight back to England and who can blame them?'

Unbeknown to the Kennys, rent strikes had taken place over conditions at Gepps Cross, and a year before their arrival the Australian government had tabled plans to shut it down. Grace was adamant: she wasn't going to live there. 'We were shown into the hut that we were supposed to be staying in,' said Steven. 'Mum took one look at the place, especially the kitchen – which was filthy even through *my* eyes – and said, "NO, I will NOT be staying in this dump" or words to that effect.' Herbert was relieved, though he kept his counsel. As much as he wanted to begin a new life in Australia, the fence at the perimeter, the lay-out of the camp, the buildings, the smell of the abattoir – it evoked memories of Belsen.

The Chemnys, Bill and Doreen, invited them to stay at their home for a couple of weeks. The house was small and Steven had to share a bedroom with his parents. A near-neighbour had two spare rooms and offered these to the Kennys while they found their own place to live; this arrangement lasted for a few months. Grace found a job assembling television sets at Phillips Electrical Industries in the suburb of Hendon. The company was based in a former World War Two munitions factory and employed nearly 2,000 people, most of them women. Herbert returned to engineering, working at Tecalemit in Cavan, north Adelaide. Grace and Steven used to joke with Herbert that they didn't properly understand what he did at work. 'I weld and I graft and I get covered in muck,' he told them. The company's brochure, presented to staff on joining, offered little further insight: 'We design and manufacture lubrication equipment, fluid transfer, fluid measurement and workshop equipment for the agriculture, automotive, industrial, mining and transport industries around the globe.'

Scores of housing estates were being built to meet a population explosion that saw 4.4 million arrive in the country from 1945 to 1985, 40 per cent of them from Britain and Ireland. The Kennys were able to choose the lay-out and design of their house in Seaton, five miles north of the city centre and a mile or so from Grange Beach, overlooking the Gulf St Vincent. Until the early 1950s, Seaton had been given over to agriculture with poultry farms and land set aside to grow lucerne (also known as alfalfa), a plant used in animal feed. The new estates featured mainly detached houses with low roofs and large windows, set back on expansive front gardens with long driveways, reached via roadways mapped out to a neat grid pattern. The Kennys' new bungalow was in McMurtrie Place, a cul-de-sac in Seaton; the contrast with north Manchester could not have been greater. 'It was good to finally move into our own house. It sat on about a quarter acre of land. My dad planted fruit trees. He was in his element,' said Steven.

While still in England, Herbert had enthused to family members about the impending move and some had expressed an interest, hinting that they might 'follow on'. June (Clark), his eldest daughter at 28, was most enthusiastic and within weeks of the Kennys settling into their new home, she confirmed that she would soon be joining them with her husband, Jack, and their five children, Valerie, Karen, Lynn, Robert and Anthony. Herbert was delighted and had an extension built so they could live together. The Clarks arrived and after five months with the Kennys they moved 12 miles across the city to a suburb called Modbury. 'After that, our house felt too big for us and we sold up and moved into an older one.

I'm really fuzzy on timelines at this stage. We moved so many times it's hard to keep track of where to and when,' said Steven.

The family settled in the 'City of Elizabeth', a satellite 'city' of Adelaide built on 3,000 acres of rural land as part of the wider development of South Australia. At first this new administrative region was to be known as Munno Para, a Kaurna Aboriginal term meaning 'golden wattle creek'. The name 'Elizabeth' was chosen instead to appeal to British families new to the area – Queen Elizabeth II and the Duke of Edinburgh had visited Adelaide in February 1963. Herbert, Grace and Steven moved into a newly built house in Searle Road on an estate similar to the one in Seaton. 'I loved it there. My mum and dad liked it, at first. One of Mum's cousin's [Alice Williams, married to Les – they had three children, Maureen, Jean and Peter] lived just down the road. I enjoyed being at Elizabeth West High School and was doing really well, for a change. I never liked school. Not from the get-go, back in England. My teachers used to say I was too easily distracted. The classes were actually interesting at my new high school,' said Steven. 'I have always been a bit of a loner all my life, even as a child in England – happier in my own company and very shy. I still don't like crowds or gatherings where I don't know many people. I never feel lonely now, when I'm on my own. So I guess moving away from friends didn't affect me quite as much as it would someone else. Moving houses was always a royal pain, but Mum and Dad bore the brunt of all that. Work and finances probably played a role in the amount of times we moved.'

On one occasion Grace returned to England on her own for what Steven remembered as 'many weeks'. 'Dad was at work full time, so it was a bit difficult for a while with me being at school and him not getting home till it was nearly dark. We managed, with help from Uncle Les and Auntie Alice. It was sometime later that mum got unsettled,' he said. Herbert and Steven were often together in the late evening and at the weekend, pottering in the garden or chuckling at the inane news items on the local Adelaide channels, ABS2 and ADS-7. Now that Steven was a teenager, Herbert might have deliberated about sharing his wartime experiences. 'He *never* talked about the war: not to me, ever,' he said. 'Maybe he did to Mum in the past, but that was about it. Me and Dad had a special bond. He was always just . . . Dad. He got on with it as best he could, for both our sakes. He knew Mum had just gone away on a holiday, so he was okay with that.'

On her return to Australia, Grace said she was missing friends they had made while living at Seaton, so they moved to a suburb called Woodville about two miles from where they had first lived in Australia. Steven was unhappy at his new school, Woodville High. 'It was a God-awful place. The teachers were awful, too,' he said. 'I had lost my friends from Elizabeth High and I was probably rebelling about having to leave there. You know, 14 years old, teenager and all that.' Steven dropped out of school early and began work as a trainee second-class sheet metal worker ('basically a labourer' – Steven) at Tanks Sheet Metal Holdings in Woodville, making rainwater tanks, downpipes and guttering.

They rented a house in Woodville and then a ground-floor flat, before moving to another house, which had an eerie atmosphere. 'A mechanical bell was on the front door with a T-shaped lever that had to be twisted to ring a dome-shaped bell inside. Every time we went to answer, there was nobody there. It happened in daylight and after dark,' said Steven. In other episodes, on two separate mornings they awoke to find Grace's 'knick-knacks' (ornaments) lined up in a row on the dining table; they had been on the mantelpiece when they went to bed. Another time a pendant went missing from Grace's 'fancy tin'. Steven took out every item looking for it and put them all back again. 'Next morning, Dad and I were sitting at the dining room table when Mum came in holding the pendant with an amazed and very puzzled look on her face. She had opened the lid and found it sitting on top of everything else. Dad wasn't really a believer in such things – not a denier, just not convinced – so he really couldn't understand why stuff was happening. Mum, on the other hand, was a big believer, as am I, and always have been. We believed it was a child's spirit. When I think back to that time, I still imagine a little girl in a blue dress. Weird, I know. There was never any feeling of malice and nothing to fear there. Out of curiosity, a few years later I drove past to see if the house was still there. It had been demolished and a block of flats built in its place. I've often wondered if the tenants have had any strange things happen.'

Grace occasionally hosted Ouija sessions at the house. 'I'd hesitate to call them séances,' said Steven. 'Now and then, even when I was small, she'd invite friends and family around. She'd cut out letters of the alphabet in a circle, using an upturned glass as the planchette.' Herbert declined to take part. 'He wasn't really a believer, and usually went out when Mum was doing her "circles". She felt his *non-belief* may block spirits from coming through, so he happily did other things,' said Steven. He felt his mother had a remarkable ability to 'read' people. 'If she liked them straight away – they were good people. And if not, then: probably not so much. She was rarely wrong. Her first impression was usually correct, in other words.'

While at the 'haunted' house, Steven met his first wife, Fiona, who lived nearby with her parents, Nan and Doug, after emigrating from Coatbridge in north Lanarkshire, Scotland. Doug had refashioned his life principally for reasons similar to Herbert. He had been one of the rescuers called to a mining disaster at Knockshinnoch, Ayrshire, in September 1950 when the pit flooded, trapping 115 miners underground. The rescue team had dug for three days in poor air quality under threat of being engulfed in sludge; they saved all but 13 of the miners. Doug rarely spoke about the disaster but, when asked, said it was 'horrific'.

The Kennys' next move was to a semi-detached house in a neighbouring suburb, Woodville West. While there, Grace worked at ACTIL (Australian Cotton Textile Industries Limited), a company with historical links to Rhodes, back home in England. During the war, CPA had planned to establish a mill in Java, Indonesia. The ship carrying machinery was diverted to the Outer Harbour at Adelaide, to avoid Japanese gunships. Tom Playford, the premier of South Australia, offered to build a mill on 34 acres of grazing land to accommodate the machinery; it was completed within ten weeks. Grace worked there with about 1,000 others, turning raw cotton into pillowcases, nappies and sheets.

Herbert and Grace appeared to be enjoying life in Australia, especially Herbert. They were keen ballroom dancers, which underwent a boom in Australia in the 1960s. Adelaide had scores of ballrooms, such as the King's, the Windsor and the Wonderland, while local town halls at Norwood and Glenelg held Saturday night dances. These events regularly attracted more than 1,200 people, with Herbert and Grace often among them.

Jack Clark found work at the huge ACI (Australia Consolidated Industries) glass factory in Croydon, Adelaide – hundreds of Australian place names were of English origin, commemorating the birthplaces of original settlers in the 1800s. While living in Australia, the Clarks had another daughter, Caroline, but began to pine for England. They left Australia in 1972 but returned three years later; this toing and froing was typical of many Ten Pound Poms. They emigrated back to England in 1977 although, years later, Caroline would return to Adelaide with her husband and son.

The Kennys received dreadful news from England in January 1973. Herbert and Grace's five-year-old grandson, Neil – born to Edith and her husband, Jack Williamson – had drowned in the River Irk, close to their home in Dalton Street, Rhodes. Neil had been playing out with friends on a Sunday afternoon, promising to return home by 5pm. At first his parents thought he was at a friend's house but after learning that he wasn't, they formed a small search party. Within a couple of hours his body was found in the river which had swollen because of melting snow. Neil had slipped down a muddy bank and fallen in, close to an iron bridge near Boothroyden Road. He was swept 200 yards downstream to a weir. His cousin, Steven Kernaghan (born to Herbert's daughter, Linda, and her husband, Ivan Kernaghan), also aged five, had tried to save Neil by holding out a tree branch. 'Steven came home in a terrible state but said nothing,' his mother Linda told the *Middleton Guardian*. 'I knew something was wrong but it was not until 9.45pm that his father got it out of him. We have warned him time and again not to play near the river and I think he was afraid of getting smacked for disobeying us. He was also very shocked.' Edith said afterwards that the tragedy might have been avoided if the river had been fenced off. 'Although it might not prevent such a terrible thing happening again, it would certainly lessen the chances,' she said. A year earlier, a boy of a similar age to Neil had died at the same spot.

Grace wrote often to her children in England and received scores of letters back, learning of their news and growing families. In contrast, Herbert's letters were 'few and far between'. While the Clarks had lived in Australia, Grace had grown close to her grandchildren and was missing them now they had returned to England. She began to feel increasingly that the family was riven and she should be with the greater number in England; an inclination exacerbated by the death of Neil. She suffered a mild stroke. 'She told my dad that she wanted to return to England,' said Herbert Jr. 'She knew how much he enjoyed living out there, and said she understood and it was fine if he wanted to stay.'

Grace attended Steven and Fiona's wedding in April 1974 and left for England a few months later. 'It was hard to take,' said Steven.

'Dad was going to follow her on after settling things up in Australia, which took several months. My wife and I moved in with Dad for the duration – it helped us, and him. He wasn't at all happy. He loved Australia but he loved Mum, so he wanted her to be happy. A year or so after they left, they came back saying they were *considering* returning, but it was more of a holiday than anything – they spent about two months in Adelaide. Dad was never really happy back in the UK, but had no choice. After they'd gone, Doug and Nan treated me even more like their own son, as they always had.' Steven had two children, son Shane, born in April 1976 and daughter Erin, September 1977. He later remarried and had two more sons, Christopher, born February 1995, and Darien, November 1996, before he was divorced from his second wife, Jenith. Steven remained in Australia, living in Walkerville, Adelaide. Retired, he devotes his time to the paranormal, astronomy, photography and creating AI-generated artwork. He has his own YouTube Channel, 'Magick & Mystery Tour' on which he uploads videos of the ongoing modifications to his Winnebago Kirra. He has another channel dedicated to ghost hunting.

Chapter Twenty-six
A beautiful man

Grace and Herbert had become 'Boomerang Poms', returning in the spring of 1975, 11 years after first leaving England. They were among 250,000 Ten Pound Poms who did the same, although half later changed their minds again and went back to Australia. Grace lived for a few weeks with Eliza, Herbert's mother, in Rhodes. Herbert followed on and a delegation of Kennys assembled at the barrier at Manchester Piccadilly Station to meet him off the train, the last leg of his journey from Adelaide. 'I knew straight away that he wasn't happy,' said Herbert Jr. 'He could barely raise a smile. Most of the family had turned out but he knocked all that happiness on the head. It really upset me. You could just see that he didn't want to be in England.'

Herbert had arrived back a few weeks after the death of his older brother, Leslie, in January 1975, aged 66; he was survived by five children. Herbert Jr had always detected a strong bond between the brothers, though they had few common interests. 'I don't know for sure, but it wouldn't surprise me if Dad had confided to my uncle

Les about all that he'd gone through in the war,' he said. 'Les, when he wasn't in the pub, would pop round to see us. Him and Dad would nip out into the back garden and I often saw them talking out there.' A year later, in August 1976, Herbert's mother, Eliza, died at the age of 91. She had lived alone for 18 years after Clement's death, still brooding on the family legacy she felt she was due, briefing various solicitors but achieving naught.

Herbert was surprised to learn that he had to apply to a body known as Rochdale Metropolitan Borough Council to be put on the list for a council property in Middleton; his home town had been subsumed by Rochdale in the local government shake-up of 1974. Their first choice was a flat at Croft Gates Road, Rhodes, a small development for mainly older people built in the 1950s, very close to West Green. None was available and they moved into a flat in Larkhill Court, close to the centre of Middleton. The new flat fell under the shadow of Warwick Mill, especially in the late afternoon. The mill, built in 1907 from Accrington brick, and five storeys high, was the largest building in the town and a landmark known to everyone. Herbert seldom passed by without stopping to look at the sheer face of its sandy-red walls; he felt his time in the army had given him a more acute sense of seeing, a capacity he relished. If he was with anyone, he invited them to share his awe. He'd point to the spire at the end of the building and tell them it was similar to the captain's quarters on the bridge of a cruise ship. 'Just look at the size of it,' he'd say and add, 'it didn't just appear overnight, you know. It had to be imagined, designed, every brick lugged there, hoisted up and put into place – how incredible is that?'

The return of his parents delighted Herbert Jr but he rued the years he had not seen them. 'It made me realise all I'd missed. I'd recently married when they went to Australia and, if they'd not gone, me and Dad could have become mates rather than lad and dad. I felt like I'd lost out, but I know why they went out there. Dad was trying to forget. He set out on a dream of Australia and thought to himself, "I want a bit of that before I snuff it." He also missed out on our children Janet [born 1966] and Joanne [born 1969], and didn't have them in his arms when they were babies.' Herbert Jr and Beryl also had a son Steven born in 1976. They often visited Herbert and Grace at Larkhill Court. 'It was odd because despite not seeing them for such a chunk of years, it soon started to feel as if they'd never been away,' Herbert Jr said.

Grace suffered ill-health for several years. The stroke had left her with compromised use of her left arm and leg; she used a walking stick. After a heart attack at home, she died later in Oldham Royal Hospital on New Year's Day, 1978, aged 62. Herbert was by her side.

A few days after Grace's death, Herbert received a letter informing him that a property had become available at 30A Croft Gates Road, a first-floor flat on the edge of the estate, close to the grounds of North Manchester Golf Club. The flats were based on a piece of land known locally as the 'croft', where a bleach works had stood for many years. As he moved in, northern England was hit by tornadoes and heavy snow. Storms continued throughout January and snow fell intermittently until April; it was the coldest winter since 1962/63. Herbert was 65 but whenever he ventured out and met anyone he knew, they invariably told him that he looked younger. He'd been away for more than a decade and was surprised at the different ways people responded to meeting him again. Some were nonchalant, as if they had last seen him a week earlier, and often didn't acknowledge that he'd been away, choosing instead to talk about the weather or local gossip. Others said they had heard he'd emigrated ('Australia, was it?'), but guessed that it had been for only two or three years. When he confirmed that, yes, he'd been to Australia, he knew what they would ask about next: the heat, the spiders and kangaroos. 'It wouldn't do for me,' was the customary response as they shuffled off gingerly, careful not to slip on the ice.

Rhodes had barely changed while Herbert had been away. Glimpses of its rural past were still visible along the A576. He occasionally ventured out into what he called 'the wilds' on either side of the main road. Alkrington Woods swept down from a hillside swathed in trees, with waterways and meadows zigzagged by footpaths. A group of five lodges, formed originally to supply water for industry, ran parallel to the main road. On the other side of Manchester Old Road, the golf club stretched wide across the slope. The rest of the valley was dotted by piecemeal housing developments that reached a quarter-mile or so up the gentle incline of the hillsides. The quantity and quality varied, from neat streets of sturdy redbrick terraces to low-cost council property, where, here and there, fences were kicked down and the odd upturned settee lay on a scrubby patch of lawn. The same as the rest of Middleton, Rhodes comprised a long-established white, working-class community; for many years there was only a single black family in the neighbourhood.

Herbert was bemused to find that the municipal status of Rhodes was still a topic of discussion. He thought it futile to constantly discuss whether Rhodes was a village or not, when it could easily be resolved. On a rare day without rain or snow, he walked across town and settled himself down in the local studies section of Middleton Library. He discovered that the definition of a village was imprecise, though the consensus appeared to be that it must have no more than a few thousand inhabitants and have both a place of worship and central meeting point. At that time (the late-1970s), Rhodes had a population of approximately 2,500 and a church (All Saints, where Herbert and Grace had married) but it was without a 'central meeting point', although it had what locals called a 'drag' – an aggregate of shops and businesses stretched along Manchester Old Road. He had done the research to satisfy his own curiosity and hardly shared it with anyone, though he occasionally revealed what he had learned if he trusted that it wouldn't lead to an argument – life was too short.

Soon after arriving back, one of the first pieces of local news imparted to Herbert had been about a 'sting operation' carried out at Little Heaton Social Club. Two undercover police officers had visited on a regular basis and their evidence led to more than 50 people summoned for 490 offences, most of them minor, from after-hours drinking to failing to keep proper accounts. On his walks, which he did more frequently now Grace had died, he would stop at the club to read the noticeboard outside, noting the 'turns' booked to appear. He had rarely visited the club himself but was pleased that Rhodes had such a lively social hub. Back in the 1960s, the committee was known for its enlightened policy, booking a range of acts, from choristers to comedians. Jimmy Tarbuck had appeared while still working as a car mechanic during the day; it was said that he'd changed out of his overalls in the toilets. Herbert's grown-up children would enthuse about the music and the atmosphere, but the best part of the night, they said, was the arrival of George Lowe, the local seafood vendor. He weaved among the tables with his wicker basket, selling whelks, cockles and mussels.

Rae McGrady worked as a 'walk-about' warden and made daily visits, checking on the wellbeing of about 60 elderly people living on the estate along Croft Gates Road and Armitage Close. Years earlier, as a young child, she and her friends had put on singing and dancing shows for residents, who would bring out chairs from their flats and sit by a pear tree on the grass verge. 'How could I ever forget Mr Kenny?' she said. 'And I always called him that. As a mark of respect, I suppose. I couldn't refer to him as Herbert or even Bert, if I tried. He was a beautiful man.' She remembered the day she started her new job in the winter of 1982. 'He invited me into his flat and said he hoped I'd enjoy the work. He was such a nice man. His house was smart and he was always smart in appearance, too,' she said.

In her early thirties Rae had been diagnosed with multiple sclerosis. She told Herbert that she was often in pain. He said that he had a good understanding of reflexology and offered to apply pressure to her feet. After finishing her daily round, she began calling back at Herbert's flat for regular sessions of reflexology. None of Herbert's family was aware of where he learned the therapy, but he had frequently expressed an interest in alternative and naturopathic remedies. On one occasion, Rae was ill and confined to bed. 'Mr Kenny must have heard and came knocking at our door,' she said. 'He asked my husband, Chris, if it was okay to see me. He massaged my feet and it was lovely and relaxing. It worked – I started to feel a lot better.'

Rae often shared Herbert's company and viewed him as a 'deep' person, although he didn't divulge any personal information or mention the war. 'Mr Kenny seemed to know everything but he was reserved when it came to talking about himself. He wasn't cold, though. In fact, I sometimes felt like cuddling him,' she said. The only time she sensed he was becoming reflective was when he asked her once to look out from his window to a grove of trees at the back of the flat. 'It was wintertime and there were no leaves on the branches,' she recalled. 'He said he could see a shape – I can't remember now what it was – and asked if I could see it, too. He said it reminded him of something. In itself it wasn't anything really but, to me, it revealed his imagination and that he was thinking beyond whatever small talk we would have been having at the time.'

Phil Gaunt was another who visited Herbert at Croft Gates Road. He worked as a butcher but supplemented his earnings by tending the gardens of about ten people in Rhodes, including Herbert's. He had been in the same class as Herbert Jr at school. 'We used to talk about me knowing his lad and he mentioned a few times that he'd lived in Australia,' he said. 'He was friendly enough but we didn't have many conversations. He'd watch the telly and leave me to cut the grass.' Phil had heard rumours of Herbert discovering Belsen. 'I was told that he'd shot the bolt off the main gate but this wasn't something I discussed with him. He paid me a couple of quid and sometimes gave me a pat on the back. He was friendly enough. I never had the impression that he had something particularly on his mind.'

Although past retirement age, Herbert took a part-time job working for Mars, the confectionery company, at its packing and storage depot in Baytree Mill at Middleton Junction. Mars advertised regularly for staff: 'We are offering light, clean work in a pleasant working atmosphere' was its petition to locals, some of whom had been employed at the mill previously when it was full of heavy textile machinery. The main line of work at Mars was packing Christmas stockings and selection boxes. On one floor hazelnuts were stored, an ingredient of Topic bars ('a hazelnut in every bite'); workers referred to this area as 'the nut house'. 'I'm not sure exactly what Mr Kenny did at Mars,' said Rae McGrady, 'but I think he might have been a nightwatchman. I know he was working shifts. When I called round to see him, he used to give me chocolate bars for my sons.' As part of the security team, Herbert monitored fire escapes at the rear of the mill. A common ruse was for staff on cigarette breaks to throw chocolate bars down to their friends waiting below on the towpath of the Rochdale Canal.

★

Herbert suffered the grief of being pre-deceased by a grandchild for a second time in February 1985. While Herbert preferred to stay in watching television or listening to the radio, the night-time ritual for many locals in the 1980s was a tour of the pubs in Rhodes, especially at the weekend; some even went out straight from the factory gates in their overalls. Memories of those days and the warm communality was still being celebrated many years later, in rhyme. 'Every week would end like this, Friday tea-time, on the piss,' wrote a contributor to a local Facebook page in December 2019.

Robert Clark, Herbert's 21-year-old grandson, was a regular visitor to the pubs in Rhodes, chiefly to play pool. He was a keen and competent player, representing both the Carters Arms and the White Hart in the Middleton and District Pool League. He had spent the evening of Friday, 15 February 1985, in the Waggon and Horses with his mother, June, and friends – their drinks passed to them through a serving hatch by Roy 'the Boy' Barry, who was considered a 'turn' as much as he was a landlord. An ex-Royal Marine, Roy was comically mean, reluctant to put coal on the fire or new records in the juke box. Robert and his pals enjoyed the joshing. An hour or so would pass cheerily whenever anyone proposed, 'Do you remember that time . . .?' A favourite story was when Roy asked a hairdresser to give him the 'curliest, frizziest perm' in Manchester. He claimed later that people were driving from as far as Rochdale and Bury to see his hair, 'and they all feel obliged to buy a pint!' he said. He hosted 'matinee afternoons' on Saturdays when video recorders and tapes first became widely available. Regulars were told they could watch 'any film they liked, as long as it's *Zulu*'.

Although Robert had left Middleton at the age of two and lived for nearly 14 years in Australia, he had adapted well on returning in 1979, attending Moorclose Senior High School. He had worked as a wood machinist at FD Kitchens in Prestwich but had been laid off at Christmas, 1984. He spent most of the night of 15 February 1985 in the Waggon and Horses playing pool, before telling June that he was going across the road for last orders at the Carters Arms, and would see her later at home in Broad Street, Rhodes.

A few hours later, June and Jack Clark were woken by police and informed that Robert had died in a road accident about 500 yards from Broad Street. Robert had been one of five people in a Vauxhall Viva Estate travelling in Manchester Old Road towards Middleton in the early hours. The car had toppled over several times and come to rest on its side against a wall near Armitage Close. Firemen spent nearly 30 minutes cutting through the roof to free those trapped inside. The driver, Mary Boutell, age 44, and passenger, Alan Swanton, 35, suffered serious head injuries, while two other passengers, June Lancaster, 44, and James Seger, 26, received head injuries but were not detained at North Manchester General Hospital. The group was described by police as 'five friends returning from a night out in Manchester'. Robert was thought to have been sitting between two others on the back seat; he died on impact. Dr Rhada Menon, consultant pathologist, said death was caused by brain damage as a result of a fractured skull.

Herbert lived close to the accident site and might have heard the crash, had he been awake. Robert, when growing up in Australia, was the only grandson with whom Herbert had regular contact. Rae McGrady called at Herbert's flat a few days after the accident. 'I said I was so sorry to hear the news and asked him if he was okay,' she said. 'He nodded his head and said, "Yes". I could tell he was very upset but I wasn't surprised that he barely spoke. I also knew instinctively that he'd deal with it in his own way.' Robert was laid to rest with his grandmother, Grace, in the graveyard of All Saints Church, Rhodes. Herbert would be buried in the same plot 16 years later.

Chapter Twenty-seven
It finished him off, that Belsen

By the mid-1980s, the decades appeared to have moved Herbert towards a personal reconciliation of his experiences at Belsen. He had written down his war memories, petitioned the *Middleton Guardian* to run the article about him and boarded a train to London for a remarkable reunion. He did not tell his family, so they were unaware of how he had known about the event held in West Hampstead, an area with a sizeable Jewish population. Most likely, it was organised by the Association of Jewish Refugees (AJR). In his notes, he tried to adopt a tone of sanguine reflection, but memories of the atrocity refused to fall still and silent.

At a reunion at West Hampstead in May of this year, 1985, I met two ladies who survived it all. They too will never forget. They looked quite well when I met them again – such a difference to when I saw them as young girls in Belsen. They, of course, would not remember me, but it was so nice to know that they, together with all other survivors, were saved. If I had not found the place when I did, I don't know if they would have been found in time to survive. I have often said in my prayers, 'Thank you, Lord, for guiding me to them.' I feel content that I may have been chosen at that time to come into contact and be there at the right time when I met that Frenchman. The sight of people dying nearly at your feet and you cannot help them or save them at that moment because they are too far gone was very upsetting. One man I saw was shuffling along, barely able to put one foot in front of another. He was obviously a very proud man in his day, tall and of big bone, but now he was very skinny, the same as the others. He was just ahead of me that morning. He went down on his knees and rolled over onto his left side. I ran to him, but he had gone. I was very distressed by this. I had spoken to him a short time before. He had snow-white hair, a good bearing.

Every last one of them was cruelly treated. On my patrol through the camp, I saw men and women together, squatting over a shallow trench, trying to relieve themselves when there was nothing to release themselves of. They didn't care who saw what, no thought of embarrassment. In a way it was subhuman, something you would think done in the early ages when humans hunted for their food and lived in caves. This is what the Nazi regime did to once-proud people. I try not to think or remember what I saw in that terrible camp, but it is no use. I cannot close it from my mind. Forty years have passed, but the picture is still there.

Herbert had not told anyone beforehand about the piece that appeared in the *Middleton Guardian* in May 1985, which meant that some of his family learned details of Belsen at the same time as the readers of the paper. 'I was totally gobsmacked. I knew nothing about it. It had never been mentioned,' said Herbert Jr. 'I'd never even heard of Belsen and knew absolutely nothing about what went on there. Dad might have spoken about it to my older sisters, June and Freda, and probably my mum, but he never did to me. The main thing he said about being in the army was that he had a job to do and he did it. It clicked afterwards why he used to storm off – he wanted to be on his own, basically. You've got to remember that it was more or less one man on his own who found Belsen and he didn't get any proper treatment for what he was going through. As I've got older, I've thought about it quite a lot and it makes me very, very sad. It's almost like something you read about in a book, made up, but this was real and it was my mum and dad's life. It finished him off, that Belsen.'

Most families, on learning of a loved one going through such an extreme ordeal, might have rallied, perhaps organising a formal get-together; by proxy, they too were now embroiled in the story. 'We just didn't talk about it,' said Herbert Jr. June Clark, Herbert's eldest daughter, held to the same outlook. 'I didn't know about the interview until it was printed and was surprised about it,' she wrote in a letter [to the author of this book]. 'But I thought that at last he was coming to terms with it. He still never told us and we didn't ask. We loved him too much to upset him, which we knew it would. My dad was a quiet, unassuming man, gentle and kind. He didn't class himself as a hero, but he will always be my hero, no matter what.' Herbert Jr understood his father much better after reading the article. 'I think my mum and dad had largely gone through it together. I can understand that. He had been a normal man trying to bring up his family and doing his best to forget what had happened, which was impossible really. I must say, though, that he did all he could to take his mind off things and, all considering, I think he got as much enjoyment as he possibly could out of life and lived to a ripe old age.'

A photocopy of the press cutting was sent to Steven Kenny in Australia; he understood his father's conflicted emotions. 'He was a very, nay, *extremely* private person. He hated a fuss being made. I think it literally embarrassed him. I doubt very much that he would have really wanted this exposure [in the form of a book] but he did let the cat out of the bag, so, I really don't know any more. I guess I am also kind of a private person,' he said. 'I hate a fuss being made on my account. I much prefer to just get on with being me. I'm not interested in others, unless I can help them in some way – as long as they never take advantage of that. And I don't want them prying into who or what I am, for the most part. I only ever really let down my guard to people I consider actual friends. I guess my dad will live on in me, in that sense, until it's my time to reap what I sow, for better or worse. And I won't "go gentle into that good night". I'll be kicking and screaming the whole way. As far as I'm concerned, he was the best, kindest, most loving dad – and husband to my mum – that anyone could ever have wanted. And I still miss him a lot. Always will, of course.'

Linda Kernaghan, Herbert and Grace's youngest daughter, became ill and died of cancer in May 1989, aged 44. She was survived by four children: Paul, Steven, Jacqueline and Julie-Ann. Jacqueline married Gary Walker and gave birth to a daughter, Lauren Elizabeth, in June 1992. Lauren died in September 1992, aged three months old; she was laid to rest in the same plot as her grandmother, Linda. Herbert had experienced the unusual circumstance of being pre-deceased by a great-grandchild.

Herbert remained a keen ballroom dancer and one of his partners, Stella Hatton, became what he termed 'a lady friend' for several years. They were a good match. Stella, nine years the younger, was known for her energy and zeal. She suffered from chronic hay fever but was otherwise healthy and lived without walking aids or medication until she was almost 99 years old; she died in September 2020. She had sung in choirs for many years. 'She kept up the dancing until the end. She loved to eat out. Our regular outing was to the Royal Toby in Castleton, Rochdale, where she'd have a ginger beer and a good tuck-in,' said Gaynor Lord, who cared for Stella in her later years and became a close friend. 'She had a very healthy appetite for food, as she had for life. She also loved going to garden centres. She was someone who knew a lot about a lot.'

Stella, a seamstress, had married at the age of 19, but it was an ill-fated union. At their wedding reception, her husband was reprimanded by guests for trying to kiss a bridesmaid. Stella miscarried early in the marriage and did not have children. She told friends that her husband was a heavy drinker and miserly; he died of lung cancer in 1970, aged 50. Stella's unhappy marriage was said to have influenced her perspective on life. 'I think it made her more determined to enjoy herself. She had quite a few male friends afterwards. She'll be laughing up in heaven at me saying this, but it's true. Even so, I could tell by the look in her eyes that Herbert was considered special,' said Gaynor.

When Herbert met Stella she was living in Schwabe Street, Rhodes. She had moved back to the area to care for her mother, Alice McDonagh, after living for many years in Prestwich. 'She used to talk about Herbert, but she never said whether he'd spoken to her about what happened to him in the war,' said Gaynor. Herbert's relationship with Stella led him into a small friendship circle based at Rhodes Autumn Club, a group for 'senior citizens', of which Stella was secretary; she wrote a report of its weekly gatherings for the *Middleton Guardian*. 'She was a nice woman,' said Herbert Jr. 'I thought she was all right but a few others said she had her nose in the air and was after his money. I think she was good for my dad.'

Len Foulkes was a neighbour of Herbert's in Croft Gates Road and he too had befriended Stella and her sister, Win, after the death of his wife, Annie; he did odd jobs for the pair. The four of them attended the club to play bingo or enjoy the turns. 'Herbert and my dad would walk together to the club,' said Elaine Foulkes, Len's daughter. 'As my dad got older and a little frail, you'd see them linking arms, walking through Rhodes like a pair of old pals.' The two men vied for Stella's affection, which caused unease among the group. Herbert, in particular, was prone to jealousy. He was also frustrated by Stella's reluctance to marry him, according to Gaynor. 'I think he asked her a few times. She thought a lot of him but wanted to keep things as they were. He was annoyed at first but accepted that was how she felt,' said Gaynor. Herbert Jr said the pair had been close, but the relationship hadn't 'blossomed'. 'He once said to me, "I can't get to where I want to be" and I took that to mean that it wasn't a physical relationship,' he said.

While with Stella, Herbert was quiet and reserved at social events. 'I never saw him smile much, not even on photos. He was difficult to weigh up. He only spoke when he had something to say but you could tell he was a genuine and caring man,' said Elaine. Len had been a marine in World War Two, but Elaine doesn't recall their war service ever being a topic of conversation. 'Dad would have definitely told me if Herbert had mentioned anything about the war or Belsen in particular,' she said. 'He was like that, he liked a good chat. He was always up for a singsong and would get out his banjo. He'd pass Bert a pair of castanets and encourage him to join in.'

The last few years of Herbert's life were spent at Little Heaton Residential Home in Walker Street, Rhodes, formerly a primary school attended by many of the Kenny children. Chris Hoyle, Herbert's granddaughter, visited him a couple of times with her mother, Freda. 'He seemed happy enough there. He had his own little room. There was only one real issue – he told us he wasn't being given a cooked meal for his tea. It turns out they were serving up corned beef sandwiches. My mum complained and it was sorted out afterwards,' she said. Rae McGrady would see Herbert occasionally, walking in Rhodes. 'In my mind's eye, I never see

Mr Kenny growing old,' she said. 'He was always so smart and – I'm not sure what the word is – a *thinker*, I suppose.'

Herbert died on Tuesday, 1 May 2001, aged 88, after a heart attack. He was survived by 5 children and 23 grandchildren. On his death certificate he was listed as a security guard, relating to his role working for Mars at Baytree Mill. A funeral service was held at All Saints Church on Wednesday, 9 May 2001, at 10.30am. Three hymns were sung: 'Jerusalem', *Psalm 23* ('The Lord's My Shepherd') and 'Abide with Me'. Herbert was laid to rest alongside Grace and their grandson, Robert. The vicar did not mention Herbert's time at Belsen; he had not been told about it.

Chapter Twenty-eight
If all good people unite and speak out

———

Don Sheppard, aged 103, is thought to be the last surviving soldier to have played a part in the liberation of Belsen. He keeps fit with regular strolls around the garden of his home in Methersgate, near Basildon, Essex. He has three children, six grandchildren and four great-grandchildren. During army service he was a sapper with the Royal Engineers attached to the 51st (Highland) Division and combined this with a role as a dispatch rider. His war began badly when a shell exploded as he dived for cover soon after landing on the beach at Normandy on D-Day; 63 years later, an X-ray showed that a piece of shrapnel had lodged in his lungs. He told the hospital staff: 'It doesn't hurt at all, so there's no point in removing it – not at my age!' At Belsen, he had ridden his motorcycle ahead of a convoy of military digger trucks and tractors used in the mass burials. 'What I saw there changed me for ever; it altered my personality,' he said. 'I have never stopped pondering why human beings can do things like that to each other. If it happened now, we would all have been treated for post-traumatic stress disorder but back then we just carried on.'

Within a few years, the liberators of the concentration camps will all be dead. The only people able to bear witness to the Holocaust will be survivors who were children at the time. Many will have been too young to have detailed memories, although they will clearly be aware of the impact it had on them and their families. Florence Schulmann was born three weeks before Herbert pushed open the gates at Belsen. Her parents had been transported from Poland; her three-year-old brother was gassed at another camp. Heavily pregnant while at Belsen, her mother's waters broke and she asked a female SS guard for a blanket, expecting to be shot. 'But this woman calmly opened her bag and handed over a packet of cigarettes. She said that she could trade it to get whatever she wanted in the camp,' Florence told the *Times of Israel* in May 2020. The guards, aware that liberation was imminent and they would soon be accountable for their crimes, had begun falsifying compassion. Florence was born next to a pile of corpses. 'All my life, day and night, I have lived with the Shoah [Hebrew term for the genocide perpetrated by Nazi Germany during World War Two],' she said. She described her childhood as 'dour'. 'The mood was very sombre at home. My parents would brood,' she said. 'They kept me in a cocoon. As soon as I had a cough, they would take me to the doctor. My parents came out of that darkness completely traumatised, they never talked about the war.' Florence was a shopkeeper for many years but, now aged 79, she has retired and lives in Popincourt in the centre of Paris. Along with other 'babies of the camps', she has committed her experience to film 'so that my story won't be disputed by historians'.

The last first-hand association with Belsen will be lost with the death of the youngest survivor of the camp, probably around the centenary of its liberation, in 2045. Fears have been expressed that this warning from history may then fall from a shout to a whisper, to silence. Bernhard Mühleder, a guide and researcher at Mauthausen Memorial, a 'place of remembrance' based at the former site of the Mauthausen concentration camp in Austria, said: 'An audience perceives events more strongly if the narrator has lived through them.' On the same theme, at a speech made in January 2020, the former president of Israel, Reuven Rivlin, said the world needed to deliberate on 'how to pass on Holocaust remembrance to generations who will live in a world without survivors'.

In Britain, formal provision has been made to ensure the Holocaust is not forgotten. The National Curriculum for England stipulates that, as part of Key Stage 3 (for ages 11 to 14), it is compulsory that it is taught to all pupils 'to extend and deepen their chronologically secure knowledge and understanding of British, local and world history, so that it provides a well-informed context for wider learning.' The National Holocaust Centre and Museum in Nottingham educates primary school children about the Holocaust. The Imperial War Museum has a permanent exhibition on the Holocaust, attracting approximately one million visitors each year. The Wiener Holocaust Library in Russell Square, London, has more than a million items on the Holocaust, the Nazi era and genocide, including published and unpublished works, press cuttings, photographs and eyewitness testimonies. The

Holocaust Educational Trust (HET) was founded in 1988 to 'educate young people of every background about the Holocaust and the important lessons to be learned for today'. A major initiative has been the national Holocaust Memorial Day, held each year on 27 January, the date of the liberation of Auschwitz in 1945, the largest concentration and extermination camp.

An impromptu conversation at a weekly meeting of the Leeds Jewish Welfare Board (LJWB) in 1995 led to the setting up of Holocaust Centre North, based on the campus of the University of Huddersfield. A few people at the meeting recognised a common bond: they were all Holocaust survivors. 'It was a big moment,' said Barbara Cline, who had worked for more than 40 years for the LJWB. 'They had been in Britain for 50 years and had never spoken about their experiences. This burden had been bottled up for so long and it was incredibly liberating to finally talk about it with people who could relate and understand.'

Eugene Black was at the meeting and helped form the Holocaust Survivors' Friendship Association (HSFA). Eugene, born Jeno Schwarcz in a town now known as Mukachevo in western Ukraine, had been one of 3,000 Jews taken on a week-long journey to Belsen in March 1945 crammed into cattle trucks without food or water – only 500 survived the trip. When he arrived, he was so hungry that he rummaged through the pockets of the dead in search of crumbs to eat. He weighed under six stones when the camp was liberated; he was 18 at the time. He became an interpreter for the British Army and in 1948 met his future wife, Annie, an Englishwoman working for the army. They moved to England and raised four children, later settling in Pool-in-Wharfedale, West Yorkshire. Eugene worked for Marks & Spencer for 35 years. He spoke at schools and in one of his last speeches, he said: 'I hope that we can all learn to live together in peace, and that all forms of discrimination and persecution are challenged and that the past does not repeat itself. I believe that this is the hope for the future and that together we can make this happen if all good people unite and speak out.' He died in September 2016.

★

The unmitigated shock of the Holocaust and its psychological aftermath was imposed arbitrarily upon Herbert, his fellow soldiers and the relief teams, much the same as it was for prisoners such as Eugene Black. These days, the task of preserving, interpreting and sharing the story of the Holocaust has passed on to those who have selected the role as a calling or job of work, sometimes both. Hannah Randall is 29 and has been at Holocaust Centre North for five years, firstly as a volunteer and now, Head of Learning. She spends her working days among grainy pictures of the suffering and the dead; display cabinets containing blue-striped concentration camp uniforms and the clothes of dead children; artefacts of the dead – letters, postcards, documents, trinkets. If, for a few seconds, she should close her eyes, perhaps for respite, the audio recordings of survivors' testimonies appear to reverberate even louder through the centre. For Hannah and others who work in similar museums and centres, it is a perpetual Day of the Dead. 'It gets to me most, I suppose, hearing the voices of people who were in the camps. I have to pass through that part of the centre to get to the toilets, so you're doing something really normal against such a profound backdrop. After a while, though, you largely switch off from the environment and it starts to have less impact,' she said.

Hannah became interested in the Holocaust after two concentration camp survivors, Val and Iby Ginsburg, visited her school to talk about their experiences. Iby, a Hungarian, told pupils that after liberation she had been working as an administrator at a hospital in St Ottilien, near Munich, when she met Val, a Lithuanian who was recuperating after his ordeal. They married and moved to Brighouse, West Yorkshire, to work in the textile mills. Hannah learned more about being forcibly displaced when her mother married Ahmad, a refugee from Iraq; Hannah was ten at the time. 'I'm not sure why I got particularly interested in the Holocaust and I accept that some people find it weird and would rather not talk about it,' she said. 'I've learned to compartmentalise my life because otherwise you can end up with psychological and mental exhaustion.'

Students on placement schemes at the centre are advised to visit a café or call on a friend on their way home from work, to avoid returning to an empty house; it was important that they 'decompressed'. The prevalence of home-working since the Covid pandemic has made it more difficult for Hannah to 'switch off'. She and her partner, Lee, an engineer, have a seven-year-old son. 'It's tricky because I have to get work done, but I have to be careful to keep it away from my son. It means I'm sometimes working on my Ph.D, which is about Holocaust denial, when I'm surrounded by Pokémon stuff and plastic dinosaurs.'

A principal aim of the centre is to combat ideology that might foster antisemitism. In the month following the outbreak of the Israel–Gaza war in October 2023, police in West Yorkshire recorded 43 incidents of antisemitic hate crimes, seven times above the monthly average; there were no actual physical attacks, but verbal and online abuse. Graffiti was daubed on a wall close to the centre. These episodes have understandably caused additional stress for staff. 'We're a good, close team and believe we are helping towards positive change,' said Hannah. 'It is especially rewarding to work with children. I hate the word *resilience* but I think that is what I have learned most about myself in the five years that I've worked at the centre.'

★

The entry to Rhodes is marked by tokens of commemoration to both world wars. On one side of Manchester Old Road is a small metal sculpture, etched with 'Lest We Forget', and on the other is the garden of remembrance. The land was donated to the borough of Middleton in 1927 to establish a memorial to the 647 men from the town who died in World War One. The names of a further 286 were added to the low curved walls after World War Two, positioned either side of a stone inscribed: 'To all those who died in service to their country.' A further stone has been added to mark Holocaust Memorial Day. Herbert missed the setting of this memorial stone in August 2013; he had died 12 years earlier.

Much has changed in Rhodes. The huge chimney, 'the Colossus of Rhodes', that stood tall over the district (or *village* – it's still a moot point) has long gone. Ben Lancaster, a local demolition man, and his team took nearly four years between 1979 and 1982 to dismantle it brick by brick; council officials refused to let him use explosives because it was too close to the main road. The huge CPA plant has closed down; houses have been built on the site. The Waggon and Horses pub has been converted into flats, despite a petition drawn up claiming it would become a 'drugs den for social misfits'. The Little Heaton Social Club closed in 1993. It struggled to pick up after the police sting and was demolished. Flats now stand on the site. Albert Burton's scrapyard became a wood yard, before the land was given over to a small housing estate. The Barbers Arms has been converted into offices; it closed as a pub after a landlady was found guilty of making off with the takings.

The *Middleton Guardian* has amalgamated with another paper and become the *Heywood and Middleton Guardian*, with a circulation of about 500 copies per week; in the mid-1980s it sold in excess of 15,000. These days local 'news' is gleaned mainly from social media.

Herbert may no longer flit through the streets of Rhodes but the advancement to Everyplace UK that began when he was alive, is complete. Rhodes is now a mixed racial area with mainly Pakistanis and Africans augmenting the indigenous white population. A 'refugee support hub' for approximately a hundred asylum seekers has been established at the Comfort Inn, behind the Wilton Arms Hotel, where Herbert used to hold his weight-training sessions in an outbuilding. Police were called in September 2023 after a knife was wielded in a fight between asylum seekers. Soon afterwards, Britain First, 'the UK's only patriotic political party', staged a protest march calling for refugees to be repatriated to their countries of birth. Footage was uploaded to TikTok shot outside the Comfort Inn and more than 2,500 people posted comments. Among the first few were: 'They all need setting on fire' and 'they need blowing out of the water before they reach are [sic] shores'. Locals expressed their feelings on social media: 'I feel unsafe in Rhodes past sunset. They walk about in big groups or sit there getting pissed, shouting abuse at you. We don't want it in our village. Rhodes used to be such a nice place to live and now it's horrible.' The majority appealed for equanimity: 'Seriously, the amount of hatred and racism in this post is shocking!! No one knows what is really happening with these people and is blindly speculating. I honestly thought this town was better than this, but clearly not!'

Afterword

Herbert Jr lives in Boarshaw, Middleton, two miles from Rhodes, with his wife Beryl, in an immaculate semi-detached house. The back garden is long with neat borders, dotted by trees, shrubs and sheds. He is 82, long retired and happy with his lot. His marriage has been, in his words, 'wonderful'. As he has grown older, he has thought more often of his father. 'What happened affected the whole family, really, but maybe not so much me as it did my elder sisters [June and Freda] and my mum,' he said. 'I don't really know what they went through.' He is beginning to understand that the role played by his father might be of interest to future generations. 'I'd rather he hadn't been the one who discovered Belsen, but in all honesty he was the right man for the job. A lot of others wouldn't have been able to cope with it. He was very level-headed and afterwards did all he could to deal with it and get over it, if that was possible.'

During my three years at the *Middleton Guardian* I was seldom sent to cover stories in Rhodes. The news emanating from there was generally anodyne: golden wedding couples, a new vicar installed at All Saints Church, or a huge perch landed at the lodges. Herbert Kenny and what had happened to him was the exception.

Endnotes

1. 'I went to play with my friend . . . ', Jean Faulkner, *Middleton Memories*, a nostalgia-based community magazine.

2. 'The things I saw completely defy description . . . ', Ben Barnett, Liddell Hart Centre for Military Archives, King's College, London.

3. 'We reached a high wooden gate with criss-cross wiring . . . ', Captain Derrick Sington, from *Distance from the Belsen Heap* by Mark Celinscak, University of Toronto Press, 2015.

4. 'There were faeces all over the floor . . . ', Brigadier Hugh Llewellyn Glyn Hughes quoted in obituary of Simon Wiesenthal (Nazi hunter) in *The Economist*, September 2005.

5. 'We have not died, but we are dead . . . ', Hanna Lévy-Hass, *Diary of Bergen-Belsen, 1944–1945*, Hanna Lévy-Hass (Haymarket, 2015).

6. 'The food that we'd got, breaking open these compo rations wasn't right . . . ', Major Dick Williams, from audio files held at the Imperial War Museum.

7. 'There was no flesh on the bodies . . . ', General Miles Dempsey, *The Manchester Guardian*, 18 April 1945.

8. 'Jungle law reigned among the prisoners . . . ', Harold Le Druillenec, *Daily Herald*, 21 September 1945.

9. 'At the time of the food distribution they behaved more like ravenous wolves . . . ', This account of events, which took place at Belsen Concentration Camp between 13 April and 21 May 1945, has been written in response to general request expressed by members of 113 Light A.A. Regiment, RA, TA., late 2nd/5th Battalion The Durham Light Infantry and also of members of other units of 100 A.A. Brigade. It is written by the Adjutant, Captain Andrew Pares.

10. 'We left pieces of rope around and some hanged themselves . . . ', Sergaent Norman Turgel, *Daily Mail*, 27 January 2021.

11. 'The one thing I saw that pleased me was the SS men being bullied into work . . . ', Emmanuel Fisher. His Belsen diary is now part of an archive at the Imperial War Museum, and Index on Censorship.

12. "I couldn't believe what I was seeing . . . ', Corporal Ian Forsyth, *The Guardian*, April 2020.

13. 'And then, almost as though they had emerged from the ground itself . . . ', Reverend Leslie Hardman, BBC Interview (date unknown).

14. 'We went into a few of many huts of what I shall call the living dead . . . ', James Hardman, *Hereford Times,* 14 November 2015.

15. 'As we came through the entrance to the main building, there were three trucks filled with naked corpses . . . ', Colonel Bernard Bernstein, from the oral history section of the Harry S. Truman Library and Museum based in Independence, Missouri.

16. "We'd heard all these silly stories about the Germans and concentration camps . . . ', Lieutenant-Brigadier George Leonard, *Daily Mail*, 2 April 2011.

17. 'I faced the stark reality of life for the first time . . . ', Andrew Matthews, from a Holocaust Educational Trust Blog called *Remembering Belsen: the Price of Assistance*, 22 April 2015, written by Jenny Carson.

18. 'I have never seen such horror in my life . . . ', Luke Harding, 14 April, 2005, *The Guardian* (used with permission). Available at: https://www.theguardian. com/world/2005/apr/14/secondworldwar.germany (Accessed: 15 June 2024).

19. 'The Liberation of Bergen-Belsen' (n.d.) Imperial War Museums (used with permission). Available at: https://www.iwm.org.uk/history/the-liberation-of-bergen-belsen (Accessed: 15 June 2024).

20. 'It was a rarity to see anyone from another country . . . ', Elinor Wilson, *Middleton Memories*, a nostalgia-based community magazine.

Every effort has been made to trace the copyright holders, and the author and publisher apologize for any errors in this list. We would be grateful to be notified of any corrections and pleased to insert the appropriate credit in future editions.

Bibliography

After Daybreak: The Liberation of Belsen, 1945, Ben Shephard (Pimlico, 2006)

Bombers & Mash: The Domestic Front 1939–45, Raynes Minns (Virago, 1980)

Britain and the Jews of Europe 1939–1945, Bernard Wasserstein (Leicester University Press, 1999)

Commando Despatch Rider, Raymond Mitchell (Leo Cooper, 2001)

Diary of Bergen-Belsen, 1944–1945, Hanna Lévy-Hass (Haymarket, 2015)

Dirk Bogarde: The authorised biography, John Coldstream (Weidenfeld & Nicolson, 2004)

Distance from the Belsen Heap: Allied Forces and the Liberation of a Nazi Concentration Camp, Mark Celinscak (University of Toronto Press, 2015)

Dunkirk to Belsen, The Soldiers' Own Dramatic Stories, John Sadler (JR Books, 2010)

Jews and Other Foreigners: Manchester and the Rescue of the Victims of European Fascism, 1933–1940, Bill Williams (Manchester University Press, 2011)

The Last Gentleman of the SAS, John Randall and M.J. Trow (Mainstream, 2014)

Liberating Belsen Concentration Camp, Leonard Berney (self-published, 2015)

Life after Belsen, Simon Bloomberg (self-published, 2017)

The Long Road to Victory, John Hillier (self-published, 1995)

Necropolis, Boris Pahor (Canongate, 2020)

The Neighbour from Bergen Belsen, Yaakov Barzilai (self-published, 1997)

The Penguin's Progress, Eric Merry (Plato, 2017)

Playing for Time, Fania Fénelon (Atheneum, 1977)

The Reluctant Jester, Michael Bentine, (Bantam, 1972)

Remembering Belsen: Eyewitnesses Record the Liberation, Ben Flanagan and Donald Bloxham (Vallentine Mitchell, 2005)

The Story of Belsen, Captain Andrew Pares (official army booklet, 1945)

To Meet in Hell: Bergen-Belsen, The British Officer who Liberated It, and the Jewish Girl he Saved, Bernice Lerner (Amberley Publishing, 2020)

The War Diaries of Oliver Harvey, 1941–1945, Oliver Harvey (William Collins, 1978)

The Woman with Nine Lives, Iby Knill (Scratching Shed Publishing, 2010)

The Woman Without a Number, Iby Knill (Scratching Shed Publishing, 2016)

Acknowledgements

———

My partner Kellie While gave unwavering support at all times, whether technical, editorial or, quite often, emotional. A million thanks. Kevin Pocklington, my agent, believed wholeheartedly in the project (more a mission, actually) from the start, and we found a staunch ally in Trevor Davies, my editor at Cassell. Martin Purdy, a military historian of distinction, was hugely generous with his time, offering invaluable insight and editorial suggestions. My other two military experts, Phil Tomaselli and Ian Langworthy, guided me through several technical aspects and provided essential archival documents. Richard Lysons was an astute and enthusiastic copy-editor of the first draft. He also undertook some exemplary research on my behalf. Mike Barnett checked the copy for any geographical or ethical sensitivities. Bryan Ledgard did some sterling work improving the quality of photographs kindly donated by the Kenny family. Chris Hoyle and Ray Roberts gave me wonderful support and showed inordinate patience, kindly inviting me into their home on numerous occasions to undertake interviews.

Herbert Kenny Jr showed me similar hospitality, again over many visits. Steve Kenny, after understandable initial reticence, was a conscientious responder to my emails. Though it was a taxing emotional chore, he spent time thinking about and relating his dad with great consideration and dignity, as did all the Kenny family, including Herbert's daughters, June and Freda, albeit through letters and third-party queries. I was assisted by several conscientious folks in Middleton who each have great knowledge of their town, among them Harold Cunliffe, Geoff Wellens and Col Wagstaffe. My two sons, George and Alec, were enthusiastic, interested supporters throughout, similar to my parents, Roy and Jean Hodkinson. I also received unstinting support from other family members: the Kerrs - Karen, Tony, William and James; Kath Bishop; Chris While and Julie Matthews; and Peter and Arabella Duffy. On a project of this magnitude, many more agreed to interviews or provided information or vital sprigs of kindness and encouragement: Dale Hibbert, Bernie Wilcox, Gaynor Lord, Sally Bayley, Margaret Wellens, Norman Wellens, Stuart Bray, Janina Haslam, James Heward, James Wallace, Elaine Foulkes, Rae McGrady, Lynn Etchells, Phil Gaunt, Shaun Moseley, Tom Frattaroli, Emily Wood, Lisa Edgar, Caroline Woolfall, Kimberly Clark, Jacqueline Collins, John Abraham, Terry Eves, Gary Canning, Richard Whitehead, Terry Christian, Jacqueline Smith, Glynis Duffy, Hannah Buckley, Ian Bent, Darran Hurst, Chelsea Sambells, Hannah Randall, Yasmin Gledhills, Miles Moss, Andrew Copeland, Paul Maleary, Duncan Jordan, Tim Rushton, Trevor Hoyle, David Hammond, Jonathon Dillon, Harry Goodwill,

Tom Marshall, Alan Taylor, Yvonne Byrne, Frank Jackson, Shane Kenny, Melanie Keenan Watson, Trevor Hoyle, Graham Williams, Nige Tassell, Austin Colling and Gerard Myers. I was greatly assisted by several organisations, among them the Holocaust Centre North, the Association of Jewish Refugees, the Wiener Holocaust Library, Gedenkstätte Bergen-Belsen, The Liberators of Belsen Concentration Camp website, the Liberation of Bergen-Belsen Concentration Camp and the Army Film and Photographic Unit Living History Group Facebook groups. Thanks, all.

Index